NARENDRA MODI

A POLITICAL BIOGRAPHY

ANDY MARINO, who has a PhD in English Literature, is a British author and TV producer. He lives and works in London but travels extensively. Marino is the acclaimed bestselling author of *A Quiet American* and *Hershel: The Boy Who Started World War Two*. No other author or journalist, Indian or foreign, has so far had the kind of detailed access to Narendra Modi as Andy Marino. He accompanied Modi aboard his helicopter during rallies and spoke to a range of political leaders, family members, friends and opponents of Modi.

Praise for *Narendra Modi: A Political Biography*

'Andy Marino has done the best book on Modi to date. It is the only biography that gives an unbiased view of who Modi is.' –Tavleen Singh

'This political biography analyses the contrasting views on the Gujarat model of governance with detailed statistical inputs to provide a balanced account. Personal details of Modi's early life, his rise through the political ranks, and his personal philosophy on religion and politics are revealed in this fast-paced, revelatory and readable book.' – *The Financial Express*

'Containing exclusive details ... this book strives to present a fair picture of the man behind Gujarat's transformation. [The] biography promises to give readers an insight into the inner workings of Modi's methods of governance.' – *The New Indian Express*, Chennai

'Andy Marino's biography stands out in providing a balanced and factually objective account.' – Deepak Lal, James S. Colman Professor Emeritus of International Development Studies at the University of California, Los Angeles, in *Financial Times*, London

'The uniqueness of Andy Marino's portrayal is that he has got the subject himself to talk about his life and times. [He] throws light on key details most other biographers have either consciously avoided or just glossed over ... [The] most holistic biography of Narendra Modi since 2002.' – Abhiram Ghadyalpatil

CONTENTS

INTRODUCTION

THIS IS THE STORY of an extraordinary life.

The 2014 Lok Sabha poll has set the course for Indian politics and policy well into the next decade. It has arguably been the most dramatic and important election since March 1977, when Indira Gandhi was defeated after revoking the Emergency. The Emergency ended before most Indians alive today were born. Today over 60 per cent of Indians are under thirty-five years of age. This election will belong to young India and that is why, despite rising disenchantment with politics and politicians, voters are energized by the prospect of change.

When I began working on this book, the compelling nature of the subject struck me: Narendra Modi is both a complex and simple man, but within a multilayered persona. He can be decisive, firm, unyielding. And yet he has a calm about him that enables him to surmount crises with dispassionate meticulousness, even detachment.

I travelled with him on his campaign rallies, interviewed him over several weeks and observed him closely as he went about his work.

Though gregarious in private, Modi hasn't granted interviews often. Where he has, they have been short and pointed. Our conversations, however, were open-ended and went back and forth over his life and work. It is possibly the first time he has granted such access to any journalist or author, Indian or foreign.

In the voluminous recorded conversations we had, he revealed for the first time details about his early life and the most controversial period in his political career: the communal riots in Gujarat in 2002.

Modi spoke with candour, without notes. Nothing, in terms of questions, was taboo. We spoke in English in which he is increasingly fluent. The obvious misgivings readers may have though are: one, how well can a British author decode the complexities of India? And two, would this book end up as an attempt to airbrush Modi's faults and play up his strengths?

To answer the first question: sometimes an outsider's perspective can shed clarity on events that those too close to them, out of passion or prejudice, might miss. Having worked in India, I am familiar with Indian politics without being swayed by a particular ideology or point of view.

As for the second misgiving: my account of Modi's life is based on extensive research over almost a year and interviews with a range of people, in politics and outside it, for Modi and against Modi, and this has enabled me to assess his work and life with cold objectivity.

No biography carries credibility if it is mere hagiography. Having written two biographies, published by leading publishers in Britain and the United States, it was important for me to get the tone and balance of this book absolutely right. For this reason too, footnotes and references have been meticulously catalogued for each chapter at the end of this volume.

And yet objectivity does not mean flying in the face of incontrovertible evidence. Modi has been the subject of the longest, most intense – and probably the most vituperative – campaign of vilification since the 2002 communal riots in Gujarat.

In recent months, after he was anointed the BJP's prime ministerial candidate Modi's development record in Gujarat too has come under close scrutiny. Allegations that he is authoritarian, runs a surveillance-based state, is prone to making factual errors in his campaign speeches and has no alternative vision for India have been made by both his political opponents and the media.

I have carefully examined every one of these – and several more – to get at the facts and separate them from the fiction.

As prime minister set to take India a new course of development and governance, Modi deserves a narrative that is balanced, objective and fair – but also unsparingly critical of his foibles. I hope this book meets that high standard.

PROLOGUE

W E DROVE TO THE helipad along closed-off roads. In front went the jammer, with its domed electronics bolted to the roof. The eight silver SUVs, following two or three abreast, were packed with soldiers and black-clad commandos of Narendra Modi's Z-Plus security detail, the highest level the Indian government offers its VIPs.[1]

They were there with good reason. Pakistan's Inter-Services Intelligence (ISI), tireless in its efforts to wage a proxy war on India, had stepped up its attacks since Modi began his nationwide election campaign. The ISI trains terror cells and sends infiltrators into India, usually via Jammu and Kashmir (J&K). It smuggles arms and explosives over the border into Gujarat. The porous, poorly policed Nepal border with Bihar is another conduit.

Narendra Modi, as Gujarat's chief minister, was target number one of the ISI-financed terror network known as the Indian Mujahideen.[2] At rallies across India, Modi has drawn crowds in lakhs and the danger of a suicide bomber is ever present. During his twelve years as chief minister, he was firm in his resistance to incursions and terror plots. Pakistan's civilian leadership has recently said it 'can work' with Modi as prime minister but the threat to his life from a proxy terror attack remains palpable.

As our convoy sped along, soldiers and police were placed every 100 metres on the roadside with their backs towards us, looking for suspicious movements in the undergrowth and down the wide avenues. On arrival at the helipad the commandos leaped from the cars and sprinted towards the chopper while soldiers in khaki fanned out, machine guns at the ready, to provide a wider ring of cover. It was only when we were in the air that the vulnerability would be replaced by the relative safety of the skies. Then there would be only Modi, a couple of senior assistants and me in the passenger compartment, with the pilot and co-pilot up front. No commandos on board.

An aroma of unburned fuel from the helicopter's exhausts leaked into the cabin as the rotors spun faster. I leant across to make myself heard to Modi. The pitch of the rotors had changed to a tighter, more aggressive note and we rose smoothly into the air while rotating to face west. A smile broke across his face: 'You'll love it,' he said, above the engine noise, speaking about the rally he would shortly address and our interaction with the crowd. 'It will be the best.' The chopper's nose dipped and the craft surged forward.

There had been rain overnight. A mist hung below the cloud cover, restricting visibility to around 10 kilometres at our height of 1,500 feet. As we raced over towns and villages, vegetation was everywhere in shades of dark chrome and cobalt green. The rectangular grid of streets and buildings arose straight and cube-cut from entangling foliage, flat grey concrete roofs glistening grimy and rain-streaked, as if they were relics of an ancient civilization.

Modi sat quietly peering over his spectacles as we flew along, a big man in a small cabin. He mulled over a few handwritten notes, facts and figures, for the speech he was going to deliver. After that he skimmed through some articles culled for him from the previous day's newspapers. Outside, the sky brightened slightly as we headed south, the villages below now showing pitched, red-tiled roofs. More temples flashed up at us in the brightening morning light.

The fields were still green but the topsoil shallower, the vegetation lighter and sparser as the ground became rockier and showed more outcrops and escarpments, heading towards the wide littoral of the Arabian Sea.

Modi's critics allege that Gujarat's transformation is nothing but a grand illusion, smoke and mirrors, and that in truth the state is in a terrible mess, a cauldron of poverty and religious bigotry just as it was before Modi took over. Alongside the endless controversies about Modi's personality, his disputed success in Gujarat was one of the dominating themes of the 2014 general election.

For anybody writing the story of Narendra Modi's political career, the chronology is compelling.

Modi was appointed by his national party as chief minister of Gujarat in October 2001. (He was not at first elected.) Astonishingly, it was his first-ever political tenure. Till then he had only held administrative party positions. He was a back-room worker and strategist for the BJP, rising to become its general secretary, but he had never stood for public office.

Only a few months into his new job, Gujarat was plunged into bloody communal riots. The state suffered murderous clashes between Hindus and Muslims in February and March 2002. Ever since, Modi has widely been held responsible. His most virulent opponents claim he planned and orchestrated the riots, which resulted in the deaths of 790 Muslims and 254 Hindus, with 223 people missing. The United States denied him a visa in 2005 on that basis and despite this diplomatic affront to India, owing to Modi's position as an elected state chief minister, the Congress-led UPA government raised only the very mildest of formal objections.

The Gujarat riots of 2002 set in stone the image of Modi. Until very recently that view, largely unchallenged, had not changed significantly. In the meantime, Modi was re-elected as Gujarat's chief minister thrice. The BJP's majority in Gujarat was almost as large as it had been when he was first elected in late 2002. In the December 2012 assembly election, it is believed that over a quarter of the state's Muslims voted for him. But the angst remains.

As our chopper came in to land, crowds surged forward below us and a line of security men spread their arms in an attempt to hold them back. When the cabin door opened, the air outside had turned quite pink and I was briefly startled by it until crackling noises everywhere revealed clouds of gunpowder smoke from firecrackers, almost invisible in the daylight. The cordite smell reminded one of the real danger of gunpowder in the Hindi heartland of Uttar Pradesh and Bihar.

Again there were the commandos and soldiers, a separate detachment sent on ahead to meet us, and again we loaded ourselves into a convoy of cars and SUVs. Now we passed along decorated, celebratory streets full of balloons and bunting, lined, it seemed, with nearly half the population of the town.

At the rally, filled with heaving crowds, Modi spoke without notes and without a teleprompter. I noticed that no word was stumbled over or swallowed, and how first one arm and then the other would be slowly raised to emphasize a point before returning to rest. It gave an impression of both relaxation and strength. At all his campaign rallies, Modi uses his body language to add force to his oratory. His voice rises and falls several pitches as he tears into the Congress and other parties. The cadence and tonality is quite unique

– rarely seen in India or indeed even in the West where politicians can otherwise be robust to the point of evangelical.

During the first four decades of Independence, India followed the economic consensus of the time that existed almost everywhere outside the US and Hong Kong: a mild or not-so-mild socialism of big, state-directed economic planning led, in India's case, by an upper-caste elite. The Nehru-Gandhi family cemented its prerogatives during this time and emerged as a political dynasty.

Even when the hegemony of the Congress began to be challenged in 1977 by the Janata Party (and later the Janata Dal) after Indira Gandhi's period of dictatorship, the left-wing ideology that confined India to its low annual growth rate remained. Always the avowed concern was for the poor, and government policies seemed designed to ensure that there would always be plenty of poor people to be patronized – chiefly with sacks of rice or grain – at election time.

Modi has positioned himself as a living rebuttal to that narrative. Would the country follow him?

On the stage, a well-wisher manages to place a red turban on Modi's head. It perches there, slightly too small for him, as he begins his speech. The audience is larger here and more restive than the day before. Its chants and applause are louder – almost explosive. Modi is in a combative frame of mind as well, attacking the UPA-2 government and linking the prime minister's characteristic silence with the government's many failures – corruption, inflation, security. He accuses the Congress leadership of being 'mute' and failing to speak up for India.

It was a nice conflation, typical of Modi's penchant for a sort of wordplay, conceptual yet not intellectual, that could be immediately understood by all his listeners. It was an aspect of his popular appeal, this common touch with words, and it subtly communicated an essential point about his background as well: Modi was one of them, a working-class man they could identify with, not one of the old status quo political class, the Delhi elite. He breathed change.

As the crowd chants his name, Modi's voice rises:

'At the time of independence, people aspired for self-rule and good governance. More than 60 years have passed but people are still asking – why don't we have good governance in the country?'[3]

In his speeches, Modi consistently focuses on the electoral argument around this essential issue: the reform and strengthening of political institutions, and the relationship between citizen and state. What is at stake for India in the sixteenth Lok Sabha poll, he says, is a basic choice between reform and empowerment on the one hand, and retrenchment and entitlement on the other. Do you want the government doing things for you (badly), or the government helping you to do things for yourself?

More sharply, underlying his question and aimed at the heart of the Congress party, was the ultimate challenge: dynasty or development?

Back in the chopper, at the end of the rally, Modi again settled over some papers, this time a printout of emails sent to him. It is interesting that while he is a calm and self-contained man in private, he clearly appreciates and sometimes perhaps even needs to hear some pleasant messages, which his staff select from voluminous correspondence. He told me that he has suffered twelve years of public 'Modi-bashing' since the time of the riots, and that his decision early on was to 'let the media do its work: there will be no confrontation. I never waste my time in confrontation.' Modi rarely replies to his tormentors, instead practising what he calls 'detachment'.

Saurabh Patel, Gujarat's minister for energy and employment, a successful businessman before he was a politician, joined us in the chopper on the return journey and Modi passed the email printout to him. He read it and handed it back with a little gesture – one of those eloquent, energy-conserving hand movements – that said, 'You see?'

Modi passed the paper to me. A Ukrainian lady had written to him. She was recently married to an Indian and now that she was getting to know the country she congratulated Modi on what he had achieved in Gujarat. But her main point concerned the 2014 election. Back in 2005, she said, they had a chance to change the system in Ukraine – it was the time of the 'Orange Revolution' – but they blew it. If you have the chance to change India, she wrote, don't fail us, because there is nobody else who can do it.

Modi is constantly referred to as divisive. Many increasingly compare him to Margaret Thatcher, whom the British Left called fascist. This animosity is compounded by social factors. Modi is an outsider, an OBC who has spent his political life learning how the system works but who remains apart from it. Modi operates with ruthless efficiency by appealing directly to the people over the heads of other politicians. But he is an outsider who is now on the inside.

Narendra Modi today occupies the prime minister's residence at 7 Race Course Road, at the end of a long and unexpected journey for the poor, backward-class boy from a small Gujarat town called Vadnagar.

PART 1

Beginnings

1

THE EARLY YEARS

NARENDRA MODI WAS BORN on 17 September 1950 in the small town of Vadnagar in Gujarat, about 110 km directly north of the chief minister's bungalow in Gandhinagar where he now resides. The bungalow is not a great distance from his birthplace, but in another sense it is a very long way indeed.

India's first general election took place shortly after Modi's birth. Pandit Jawaharlal Nehru's Indian National Congress won an overwhelming majority – 364 out of what were then 489 seats – in the Lok Sabha. At last, after the upheavals of Independence and Partition, the elected Union government began to function according to the Indian Constitution, enacted on 26 January 1950. As Nehru stood to speak as prime minister of the new government in 1952, little Narendra, to the delight of his parents, was forming his first words.

Vadnagar in 1950 was a quiet, semi-rural backwater, somewhat broken down and without electricity. Its citizens had no aspirations beyond their own parents' position in life. India was not a country of social adventure or opportunity, and life for the vast majority was a routine, self-contained existence. It could be said that like India itself, Vadnagar had a great future behind it: stately ruins to the north of the town hinted at an ancient centre, and gave evidence of what a massive and impressive regional capital it had been in a past millennium.[1]

Modi, when asked about his childhood, describes how the town was once home to 10,000 Buddhist monks. It is true that the richness of its archaeology supports an intriguing and influential history, but that epoch was very long ago. By 1950, after waves of invasion and colonization down the centuries, the Indian people, including those in Narendra's home town, had adjusted their expectations downward. They were, though, beginning to imagine a future at last in their own hands. It might hold only a distant promise of something better – whatever that might mean – but there was at least that sliver of hope.

The railway was already there in Vadnagar, of course, and Narendra's father, Damodardas, earned his living from a tea stall set up on the platform of the town's station. The small stall or shop remains there today just as it was, showing its age: a small shed of blue-grey tin or steel, patched and padlocked, matching in antiquity the architecture of the platform itself, under whose eaves it stands.

Damodardas was descended from a family named Ranchoddas that moved to Vadnagar to open a grocery store late in the nineteenth century. He was thirty-five years old in 1950 and married to Hiraben, a local girl. When Narendra arrived he joined two elder brothers: Som, who was six years old, and Amrit, just four. There would come a sister, Vasanti, two years after Narendra was born, and then two more brothers, Prahlad in 1955, and Pankaj in 1958.

The Modi family was very poor by modern standards, although they would not have felt particularly deprived at that time or within their community. The tea business lifted them above the precarious existence of the day labourer or sharecropper.

All eight – parents, brothers and sister – lived in a three-room house of brick augmented by mud. It was single storey: small, not absolutely tiny, about 40 feet by 12 feet, with the bedroom and the sitting room at the front, facing the unmade lane, the dim kitchen in the middle, and a storage room for fuel at the back. Water had to be fetched from a well and stored in clay vessels. The flooring was mud-covered bamboo. There were no windows cut into the walls, and when the cow-dung cooking fire was lit the air turned thick and smoky.[2]

Except for the kerosene lamp, the dwelling's only other illumination, the scene was indistinguishable from one several centuries earlier. Later on, Damodardas made some improvements, adding an upstairs room and a couple of windows. But both bathing and laundry were done in the lake nearby.

The Modi family were of the Ghanchi[3] caste, traditionally producers of vegetable oil – a 'ghanch' was a local oil press of great antiquity. It was a caste that cut across religious lines and there are also many Muslim Ghanchis in Gujarat. An OBC (Other Backward Caste) is sometimes confused with being low caste. The Modis, as Ghanchis, were of the general ranks of workers, and what may be called lower middle class – poor, but with very many castes of Indians below them.

How significant this social ranking and disadvantage would have felt to young Narendra in a small, rural town is unclear. The likelihood is that as he was growing up, he was hardly aware of it. It certainly left no mark on him in terms of social feelings – either of resentment or inferiority – and he rarely refers to his origins to make a point in political debate, even though it would likely help him to do so.[4]

The Modis, although they lived in a close-knit neighbourhood, were on the side of it that was closest to Vadnagar's Muslim community. Mixing with Muslims was normal and the majority of Narendra's childhood friends were Muslims. One of his best friends was Jasood Khan Pathan. He observed Muslim holy festivals as well as Hindu ones. He felt nothing unusual in this, and neither did anybody else, not his family nor the parents of his playmates. Narendra was given a nickname – 'ND', his paternal initials from 'Narendra Damodardas'.

Anecdotes of Narendra's attitude in school abound. He worked diligently in the classroom. Teachers and students recall an early gift for rhetoric in the school's debating society. There is the much-quoted incident when Narendra stubbornly refused to let a class monitor mark his homework – insisting that the teacher alone was qualified to do so. Yet early appearances can be deceptive: many stellar school debaters turn into bank clerks or store managers, and academically outstanding students sometimes grow up to become office managers and mid-level bureaucrats.

Tales from childhood can provide ready-made outlines that slot neatly into the jigsaw portrait of a leader. Sometimes the stories take on the hue of legend: it is well chronicled, for example, that Narendra liked to swim in nearby Sharmishtha Lake, and that in this lake lurked crocodiles. An early story relating to Narendra and the lake recounts that there was an ancient shrine – in later versions a beautiful temple – on a rocky outcrop not too far from the shore.[5]

On certain holy occasions the small flag atop this shrine would be changed. One such day, after heavy rain had agitated the crocodiles, the flag did need changing. Despite being advised against it, Narendra and two friends, Mahendra and Bachu, swam to the outcrop and back again. In later retellings the outcrop would become a distant island and Narendra would swim alone.

Meanwhile, people on the shoreline beat convenient drums to scare off the reptiles (or more likely draw them away from where the boys swam). Narendra returned safely, having changed the flag, and the crowd, by now grandly swollen, cheered loudly: all present agreed that such actions befitted a future leader, or words to that effect.

Today, at sixty-three, Modi shrugs at these stories of over half a century ago. Eyes twinkling, he simply says that his childhood was normal.

Talking to former schoolmates and teachers, the predominant trait in young Narendra appears to have been quiet stubbornness. When he felt justified in a certain belief or course of action, he could, like all children, be both obstinate and mischievous. Yet beyond everything, and to the relief and joy of his mother and father, Narendra was unremarkably normal: happy, energetic and averagely popular.

But even as a normal child, certain characteristics stood out. Chief among these was Narendra's physicality. He was a wiry and athletic boy. This may be important because physical confidence from an early age can shape self-perception. There are few recollections though, despite many childhood friends, which attest to Narendra's sociability or that he was particularly interested in team sports.

Today Modi says he likes cricket but only as a spectator; and cricket anyway is the thoughtful individual's team sport. Swimming appealed to him as a child, but by nature it is a solitary pursuit. A flavour of solitariness persists in the anecdotes that Modi tells me about himself. In these he is always present, but often on the edge of groupings and proceedings, biding his time before making a decisive contribution to the story or drama.

Religion permeates every pore of India: it is everywhere and it is unremarkable; the culture is saturated in it. Myth and ritual – or their memorials – are blended into almost every social action and meaning. Religion in India is everyday life. What this could mean is that certain tendencies young Narendra displayed were interpreted as culturally rather than religiously inspired.

For instance, when still quite young, a strain of asceticism emerged in Narendra. It was widely noticed among family and friends. First he gave up eating salt. Then he gave up eating chillies and even oil. The savours of life were forsaken, but to what end? Narendra still enjoyed jaggery, he says with a smile today, but as a boy had given it up.[6] Renunciation or asceticism may indicate piety but can also be a sign of ambition, often social ambition to begin with – the equivalent of acquiring gentility as a precursor to other forms of advancements.

It is possible that Narendra embarked on his path of asceticism for sound and secular reasons: he felt inwardly that he was slightly different from other people, and during our long conversations that facet often emerged. It was therefore natural to explore and understand this feeling of being different by subtracting from his life what others commonly took for granted. In that way he would 'normalize' his feeling of separateness and discover something about himself. For example, he might have been reassured that he had willpower and was not greedy. The act is self-revealing; the self-denial helps you to comprehend your individuality. In other words it builds character.

As he sits in his large office, a terrace to his left, sofas to his right, a sense of calm pervades him when he talks of his childhood and early years. And yet he is quick to chuckle at old memories. At his home he is even more relaxed, and says simply: 'There are times when, before I became chief minister, I did not eat a meal in the same house for months and years.'

Narendra was a ferocious reader, although his stubbornness led to him refusing to persist with Sanskrit.[7] Modi's early devotion to Swami Vivekananda is well-attested, but it was an intellectual admiration of an 'ecumenical' figure who made over Hinduism for modern purposes, revealing its kinship to other faiths through his 'enlightened liberalism'.[8]

Young Narendra's apparent religiosity may be the result of attempts to categorize a type of behaviour (and a kind of personality) which, at the time, and among his social class and environment, was relatively unusual. In India misfits and seekers typically find their way to gurus and ashrams; the more extreme become sadhus or monks. Religion traditionally soaks up disruptive spiritual energy. But Narendra simply went his own way, and this was a course of action difficult to interpret outside of a religious frame of reference. It may have been an unusual trait but then Modi was already an unusual young man.

That he was often keen to cooperate and help out, to be involved, is clear and allusive. After school, Narendra would race to his father's tea stall as if working there was the excitement he had been looking forward to all day long and nothing in the world was more fulfilling than serving tea to railway passengers: 'I was in the train compartment, the small boy who used to serve tea, and take the money.'

Children were expected to help out in the family business, however small it was, and they accepted the duty. But young Narendra wanted more than most others: to be involved in a larger, more grown-up world beyond the classroom. Was childhood important to him, or was he slightly bored by it and indifferent to play, wanting instead to know and do more than was expected of a child? When asked about it, Modi is non-committal. 'By and large, everyone likes their childhood and I was also like that,' he says.

Did his strength – of both body and mind – make Narendra feel older than he was? And did this idea of the self, held back a little by childhood, instil an interest in history, politics, a sense of the world – and so also patriotism, a respect for the past and by implication his elders whom he wished to join? In conjunction with his thoughtfulness and wide reading, such an evolving identity may easily awaken a feeling of duty and belonging in the widest sense. Thus Narendra was only eight years old when he began to attend the local shakha of the Rashtriya Swayamsewak Sangh (RSS). It was a decision that laid down the direction for the rest of his life.

What did it mean for Narendra to be born in Gujarat instead of elsewhere in India? What sort of cards had he been dealt by fate? India is vast and varied. How might he have grown up and flourished had he been a Bihari or a Bengali, for example? How much did Gujarat, its culture, tradition and sensibility, mould Modi?

The state comprises one-third of the total coastline of the country – after tracing the inlets, folds and bays of its littoral. The state leans to the political Right because Gujaratis, thanks to their long coastline, have since time immemorial been traders and businessmen.

Across the Arabian Sea lie the emirates, caliphates and kingdoms which have been commercial partners and competitors long before Muslims arrived in India as conquerors and settlers. A two-way traffic in goods also meant a two-way traffic in traders and workers. Arabs and Muslims, mostly Sunnis, have long settled in Gujarat. The maritime nature of trade inspired and bred an adventurous, explorative, business-minded Gujarati ethos of many faiths which put down commercial roots all over the world. Today the British corner shop is a Gujarati institution; and in the United States motels have become almost generic for Gujaratis.

As testimony to its mercantile heritage, Gujarat has something of an Arabic flavour to it aesthetically in its colours and designs and costumes, especially in Saurashtra and the south. Looking further back, and at the lineaments of some of the tribals' decorations and features, there is even a hint of Africa. And the first Indians to trade with and settle in, especially, East Africa were Gujaratis. This has required an adaptive cultural nous. Gujaratis, unlike those from landlocked states, are outward-looking. And they are receptive too: Parsis, for example, fled today's Iran nearly 1,400 years ago to find a safe haven in Gujarat.

Not only trade and contacts with foreigners but commerce among its towns and villages has affected the state's politics. More than elsewhere in India, what happened in the towns of Gujarat was always quickly felt in its villages, and vice versa, precisely because over the centuries a vigorous business culture had bred an unusual degree of communication between town and countryside.[9]

This was expressed in an abundance of roads and therefore an abundance of mobility and engagement. This interconnectedness and market-friendliness gave Gujarat a culture of individuality and entrepreneurship – but also a feeling of shared identity. Over time it proved both a blessing and a curse. It convulsed the state whenever communal conflict occurred, and then afterwards swiftly repaired the damage to get back to the business of life.

Bengal stands out in sharp contrast to Gujarat. Bengal may be emblematically and temperamentally to the Left.[10] It has a different kind of individuality – one that favours political principle over profit that is somehow rooted in geography and history. Kolkata (then Calcutta) was the imperial capital of the British Raj until 1911. A colonial officiousness of bureaucratic rigour might have seeped into the Bengali temper and emerged, bereft and angry at the loss of its authority-by-association, at just about the time that the Russians were discovering their revolutionary fervour.

V.S. Naipaul said in 1964 that 'Calcutta was dead,' and that the break with the Raj had done it: 'Here the Indian renaissance had begun; so many of the great names of Indian reform are Bengali. But it was here, too, that the encounter had ended in mutual recoil. The cross-fertilisation had not occurred, and Indian energy had turned sour.'[11] This, Naipaul implied, led to a turning away from – and a rejection of – the future, a retreat into a glorious past, into a homeland of memory and identity.

Kolkata is in many ways reminiscent of Paris – another city of the Left, with its combative energy and romantic self-absorption – Howrah Bridge its Eiffel Tower, riparian Hooghly its dense Marais. It is home to India's intellectuals and theorists, its poets and high-art film-makers, as Paris's left bank of the Seine billets France's artistic revolutionaries. Like Paris, Kolkata is haughty and proud and inward-looking; and after its own fashion, stylish. And, like the French, too, self-sabotaging.

What if Narendra Modi had been born in Kolkata? With his feeling of difference, his solitariness and his interest in reading, perhaps he would not have felt himself so different to the spirit of the city. He might therefore have fitted in better. Might Narendra early on have transfused the cinema of Satyajit Ray into his bloodstream and become a radical film-maker, or a photographer like Sunil Janah (Modi is also a wanderer, and he does like cameras)? Is it improbable, given his rugged individuality, that he would have sought the orthodoxies of the Communist Party of India? Could he have fallen for Tagore instead of Vivekananda and even now be a disciple living simply at Shantiniketan? Or would he more likely have resembled Mamata Banerjee, emerging – given the opportunities available to him in Bengali culture – as a populist politician and a hammer of the poor, rather than a technocrat and modernizer whose Gujarati upbringing allowed him to believe implicitly in commerce and free markets?

Would Modi now be challenging for the prime ministership had he not been suffused by the same environment that created Mahatma Gandhi, Sardar Vallabhbhai Patel and – yes – Muhammad Ali Jinnah? It is unlikely his appeal, had it developed elsewhere, would have crossed so many state borders. Everybody is shaped and limited by their environment.

There is a danger in over-interpreting these imponderables. But for a man who could soon govern the destinies of over a billion people, it is important to understand the psychological influences of his cultural environment: they carry clues to future conduct.

2

ON THE ROAD

THE RUSSIAN AUTHOR ANTON Chekhov said that all stories must 'turn'. Narendra's early life reveals a bright, vigorous and sociable boy. He was poor but serious in his duties, chanting every day in the temple of Giripur Mahadev. Narendra was keen to be helpful but he could also take offence and brood sullenly.

There was an energy, an emotional churning in him, but his moods were not the keynotes of contradiction: they are found whenever an unusual personality is emerging. A complex character has different parts, and moodiness can be a sign of trying to reconcile them. Times were hard. There was no electricity. What Modi remembers is that as a child he always had ideas about how to do things – chores, tasks, games, lessons – differently, more efficiently, and that from his earliest years this provoked comment and sometimes opposition.

'Even when I was in school,' Modi says, eyes gazing at the far distance as he searches for memories of his childhood, 'I used to question my teachers. Not about the teaching but sometimes about the methodology of the teaching. I sometimes said, "Sir, why do you do it like that? You could do it so. It is easy – you could do it. Why don't you do this?" And sometimes my teacher would say: "You are an urchin. You are annoying me, you small kid."'

Modi has rarely spoken about his early life but in our conversations he opened up to reveal a boy who constantly searched for answers outside conventional frameworks.

By his own account, Modi did not rate himself an outstanding scholar. Rather, he followed his own interests, and would not be diverted from them. 'That was my temperament. Even in the family system, sometimes when my mother was doing her work I would say, "Why, Ma, are you doing it like that? Can you not do it like this?" And I wanted to help her, I wanted to do it differently. Even how to wash clothes – I was always using new techniques. People used to watch me. In my childhood I used to wash my clothes and my family members' clothes in the public lake. They used to come to see how I was doing this.'

Narendra's mother never mistook her son's keen interest in chores as a sign of love for domesticity. On the contrary, the perceptive Hiraben saw the inventiveness and intellectual hunger, and became afraid that 'one day Narendra would run away, leaving behind this home, town and *sansar* [world]'. She could see what others did not, that he 'seemed to be disinterested in family life'.[1] Paradoxically, it was the attempt to draw Narendra back towards the family and settled domestic life that finally led to his permanent departure.

Narendra's enthusiasm for changing and improving things, his need to align the world to the way he saw things, gives additional weight to the idea that childhood was somewhat constricting for him. He clearly wanted more than Vadnagar could offer.

Modi today nods in agreement at this conclusion. 'Innovation, new ideas, that was basically my temperament.' He smiles. A restlessness pervaded him.

The attraction to the RSS was, at the age of eight, obviously not political in the sense of hewing to a particular ideological position. Narendra came to the RSS by way of contact, at the age of six, with a Congressman named Rasikbhai Dave, whose office was close to his father's tea stall at the railway station. It was a time of agitation for a separate Gujarat state, then part of the Bombay State. Gujarat would earn statehood in May 1960, a few months before Narendra's tenth birthday.

He collected pro-Gujarat lapel badges from Dave and then acted as his 'agent', distributing them to his school friends. Politics may look distant and hazy to a six-year-old boy – this was 1956 – but helping to create your own state would be something he could grasp. 'I got a sense of participation,' recalls Modi. 'But there was no deep political understanding.'[2]

It was in the evenings, after he finished helping his father at the tea stall, that Narendra, a couple of years later, began to attend the local youth meetings of the Rashtriya Swayamsevak Sangh. That part of the RSS that caters for an eight-year-old is best described as a sort of Boy Scouts group. Yet it is part of a larger organization that is right-wing, nationalistic and ideological. The name literally means 'National Volunteer Organization'.

The RSS was banned in 1948 in the aftermath of Mahatma Gandhi's assassination by one of its former members, Nathuram Godse, yet it was also commended for averting a coup against Nehru. Acquitted by the Supreme Court of involvement in Gandhi's murder, the ban on the RSS was revoked by the government in return for formalizing itself with a constitution. Sardar Vallabhbhai Patel, then home minister, advised the RSS to stay out of politics and remain a sociocultural organization.

By the time Narendra began to attend its local shakha most evenings, where he would have been one of the youngest participants, the RSS was acquiring quiet respectability as a disciplined force. It was the kind of environment, of ideas and debate at RSS meetings, rather than the rote learning of school, that stimulated him. There he could learn more about worldly matters, and perhaps congregate with the adults who fascinated him.

It was then that he first met the man who would become his guide and mentor in the RSS, Laxmanrao Inamdar, or 'Vakil Saheb' as he was known because of his lawyer's qualification. Inamdar inducted young Narendra as a 'balswayamsevak', a junior cadet, and began to teach him what it meant to be a volunteer,[3] initiating Narendra in what he would later describe as the 'silent revolution of making men' in an organization built around 'renunciation, dedication and hard work'.[4]

Together with Swami Vivekananda, his idol from earliest childhood, Vakil Saheb would prove the enduring influence on Narendra's political outlook and his ideas of human potential: 'He used to teach us always to try to discover the other person's virtues and qualities, and try work on them,' says Modi today. 'Don't focus on the deficiencies. Each and every person has so many deficiencies, but you have to focus on his (positive) qualities.'

Worldly matters were soon to intrude on Narendra's innocence and the routine rounds he made between school, tea shop and shakha. One of the great shocks for post-Independence India, and possibly still its greatest humiliation, was the Chinese aggression of 1962. The Sino-Indian war took place, not coincidentally, at the same time as the Cuban Missile Crisis, when India (supporting the Soviet Union in its stand-off with the United States) was distracted. Chinese logistical as well as tactical superiority swept aside Indian defence forces, despite there having been indications of trouble on the border for the longest time.

Communist troops poured into several areas administered by the North-East Frontier Agency (NEFA). In the Battle of Namka Chu at high altitude near Bomdila in Arunachal Pradesh,[5] the 7th Indian Infantry Brigade of the highly decorated 4th Division – the 'Red Eagles' who had served in so many theatres in World War II – found itself surrounded and 'cut to pieces'.[6] Unthinkably, its commander was captured and tortured. The brigade was subsequently disbanded in official disgrace to save the government blushes, although it had fought bravely almost to 'the last bullet and the last man'.[7]

The administration of Assam, flabby, corrupt and spavined with bureaucracy, collapsed and ran. Delhi, and India as a whole, seemed to be psychologically paralysed by the attack, and its humiliation was complete when China unilaterally declared a ceasefire after demarcating a line of actual control and showing India in no uncertain terms who was the dominant regional Asian power. V.S. Naipaul's brutal conclusion about India's propensity to surrender to invaders – 'Any conqueror will do' – was, ironically, uttered in the silence surrounding the fallen Indian soldiers, with their antique rifles and inadequate summer uniforms, abandoned by Nehru's government at icy Namka Chu.

After the initial shock of defeat wore off the Indian public grew furious and fiercely patriotic. This bellicosity undoubtedly filtered down to Narendra, then twelve years old, during his nightly RSS meetings.

Nehru was roundly blamed for his pacifist foreign policy and the deluded Congress attitude of 'brotherhood' towards the aggressive and double-dealing Chinese communists. The invasion proved to be a wake-up call for both government and military. Narendra's own response to the crisis was to inform his father he wished to attend one of the Sainik schools. These formed a new network of military-style youth academies which had been established the year before by the (now-disgraced) minister of defence, Krishna Menon.[8]

Aged thirteen, Narendra was about to leave Vadnagar Primary School No. 1 for the local high school, and at such a juncture the idea of applying instead to a junior officers' academy was not entirely outlandish. It was exactly the sort of idea that would have been inspired in Narendra by attendance at RSS shakha evenings. But his father, Damodardas, forbade the move. The Sainik school was quite a distance away, in the Jamnagar district on the Gulf of Kutch, which meant Narendra moving away to board there. The cost – there was not a spare rupee in the Modi household – or perhaps the awareness of the social divide, also gave Damodardas pause.[9]

If so it was ironic, because the founding idea of the Sainik schools was to address the problem of class in the Indian army's overwhelmingly upper-caste officer cadre and give poor boys a chance to make their way into it. But Damodardas would naturally have been worried about young Narendra's treatment there, or indeed afterwards. Perhaps he simply disapproved of military life, or the influence of a presence outside the family exercising itself on his son.

His father's refusal, for whatever reason, perceived by Narendra as an attempt to keep him in Vadnagar, meant only that the boy inched a little further away from the vision of a future in Vadnagar. Clearly he had already thought about it and sensed that much lay and beckoned beyond the confines of his small town.

There may well have been a rewarding career awaiting Narendra in the army. After its humiliation by the Chinese in the north-east there were signs that change was afoot in the Indian military. Very quickly, over the next two years, a massive reorganization and expansion began. Training, planning and logistics were all given the highest priority for improvement. This proved timely, because the easy Chinese victory had the effect of emboldening Pakistan, its close ally.

In a short but furious war that began in August 1965, India swiftly and successfully retaliated against Pakistani infiltration into Kashmir. India regained some of its honour while Pakistan lost ground and failed in its plan to capture the state. That conflict marked the beginning of the political gyrations and economic collapse that turned Pakistan into the country it is today.

Before the 1965 war its growth outstripped India's by some measure. Afterwards, a chastened but increasingly fanatical leadership attempted to shore up military power at the expense of civil society. By the time of the next India–Pakistan war in 1971, it was spending a suicidal 55 per cent of government revenues on its military, up from an already burdensome 10 per cent in 1966. Today Pakistan still spends a disproportionate amount, including debt servicing, on defence, while education receives only 2 per cent of GDP.[10]

The teenaged Narendra watched the 1965 conflict unfold after the pre-emptive bombing and strafing attacks on Indian Air Force bases. He was stirred. He personally witnessed aspects of the conflict at close quarters because Vadnagar was on a supply line to the battle front, meaning soldiers would arrive at the station moving up to combat or, sometimes wounded, returning from it. He served them complimentary cups of tea.

'Narendra was charged up and voluble on how all Pakistanis should be decimated,' recalled a resident of Vadnagar who knew him back then.[11] Narendra would also daily be reminded, as the bandaged heroes sipped his chai at the stall he still helped out at, that he had been forbidden by his parents to seek an active role in India's defence – a frustration which at the time must have felt extremely pointed. They had other plans for their son, and one particular part of these plans was the spur for Narendra's departure from the family home, never to live there again.

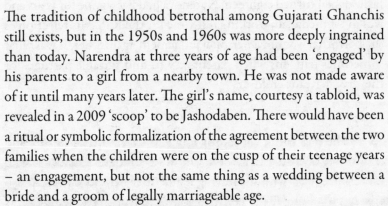

The tradition of childhood betrothal among Gujarati Ghanchis still exists, but in the 1950s and 1960s was more deeply ingrained than today. Narendra at three years of age had been 'engaged' by his parents to a girl from a nearby town. He was not made aware of it until many years later. The girl's name, courtesy a tabloid, was revealed in a 2009 'scoop' to be Jashodaben. There would have been a ritual or symbolic formalization of the agreement between the two families when the children were on the cusp of their teenage years – an engagement, but not the same thing as a wedding between a bride and a groom of legally marriageable age.

This was exactly when Narendra was told the Sainik military school was out of bounds to him. Some years later would come a meeting, with many family members present, during which he could have the opportunity to observe his betrothed but not necessarily speak to her. The final stage, signalled by Jashodaben turning eighteen, would be the commencement of an initial period of cohabitation. Whatever actually happened, the chronology of events suggests that as soon as Narendra fully understood the situation he decided, literally, to make his move.

He abruptly left Vadnagar and his family home when he was seventeen and Jashodaben only fifteen years old. As one observer put it: 'It was a child marriage, and neither was it consummated nor was there cohabitation. Modi refused and went away as he was never interested in marrying. A case of null and void.' The tradition of leaving home at an early age to seek spiritual knowledge is part of both Hindu and Buddhist faiths – as the examples of Lord Ram and the Buddha attest.

Jashodaben was not eighteen years old but only fifteen when Narendra left Vadnagar. The first meeting between the couple took place well before the cohabitation stage could arrive. After the introductory meeting – the first time Narendra had ever seen his 'bride' – he quickly decided it would also be the last. By the time Jashodaben turned eighteen, Narendra had been gone for years and was in Ahmedabad, working full-time for the RSS. His rejection of the betrothal was not a personal judgement against her; it was what sometimes happens when parents try to find suitable partners for their recalcitrant children.

As a politician Modi constantly looks to his country's culture and traditions, believing that India can draw strength from them and modernize itself without leaving its identity behind. But he is also enfranchised under the constitution of a democratic republic. As such, he observes a sharp distinction between individual rights and coercion from whatever quarter.

He felt that way when he was seventeen, perhaps not as lucidly as later, yet his emotional suffrage was already robust. Narendra refused to do something he did not want to, no matter what the cultural or family pressure. It was, he believed then and continues to believe now, his constitutional and human right to withdraw from an arrangement made without his consent – and he duly exercised that right. Jashodaben, likewise, was not compelled under Indian law to remain contracted to Narendra, and could have asked her parents to find another suitor, or found one herself.[12]

Modi's 'marriage', which he never speaks about, has been used by the media in an attempt to discredit him both as a politician and a man. Jashodaben, who never 'remarried' and is now retired after a long career as a schoolteacher, is presented as the unhappy, lonely, but still loving and faithful wife whose only hope is that one night Modi will come home for dinner. The section of the media that paints this tear-jerking picture is the same media that rails against the injustice and backwardness of child marriage – except where Modi is concerned.

The tension of falling out with his parents over the childhood betrothal coincided with Narendra's graduation from B.N. High School in Vadnagar and attendance at the local college, which he soon abandoned.[13] He had not especially enjoyed school except for its extracurricular aspects of debating and dramatics. Inquisitive but restless, Narendra may have been equally unimpressed by the prospect of several more years of conventional education and formal study. He would later acquire, though correspondence, a master's degree in political science from Gujarat University.

Some sort of emotional pressure was meanwhile building within him, and this led to a sudden decision to leave home. His family was naturally shocked at Narendra quitting his education and setting off with no clear objective except, as he told them, to see the Himalayas. They raised objections, yet they were met with an ultimatum: he was leaving no matter what, but at the same time he demanded their blessing. There was no other visible source of conflict except for Narendra's headstrong attitude, not unusual in a seventeen-year-old, and evident in him since early childhood.

His own enduring affection for his parents was implicit in his request for their blessings, but it was still an emotional tactic and he got what he wanted. Damodardas and Hiraben 'decided that if he wanted to go, he must be allowed. His mother cooked *kansar* (a sweet dish traditionally cooked on auspicious occasions); *tilak* was applied on Narendra's forehead which signifies the opening of the third or spiritual eye.'[14]

The incident is notable because it displays, just as did his refusal of marriage, a characteristic that Modi the politician would later come to embody. This was his reverence for tradition but also his selective rejection of it. He respected and desired cultural authority, such as his parents' ritualized blessing, before he disobeyed their wishes and set off on his own path.

This sort of tension is implicit in the kind of politics Narendra would eventually cast himself into – with the RSS and later the BJP – which idealized Hindu culture and wished to preserve it, against the atheistic socialism of the Congress party and the Left. Would there be a way of making that tension creative and fruitful, of finding a path through politics that could both draw on India's traditional culture and make use of it for innovation and progress? Or would modernity and tradition prove to be so much at odds that one of them would have to be sacrificed?

Narendra's initial two-year odyssey away from home marked the beginning of what was to become a more than thirty-year period of nomadic wandering, by the end of which Modi could claim that there was literally nowhere in India he had not set foot on. Some of this nomadism, namely the adventure embarked on by the seventeen-year-old in 1967, was characterized by constant, restless movement. Even when Modi was based somewhere specific, he was forever in motion between different states, or between towns and villages. He never had a settled habitation, and seldom ate twice in succession in any one place. He looks back at his days as a wandering ascetic with some fondness.

> There was no comfort in my life. I had a small bag and my whole life was in that bag. I was not keeping anything else with me. For 30 years I was like this and every day I was eating with different families. I have never taken one type of food; I have never taken the food of my choice. This morning I will go to this family and I will say, 'Yes, I will come, please give me some food.' Second day another residence, third day, third residence. Every month I am taking my food in a different home.

The memories are still fresh and Modi tells me that the life he led all these years is what made him who he is. Modi says that he always accepted whatever meal was on offer from whoever he was visiting on a particular evening. This was how he developed a habit of indifference to food: all was equally welcome and tasty as far as he was concerned, so long as it was vegetarian.

Exactly what Narendra did between the ages of seventeen and nineteen, where he went and why, remains obscure. Scraps of information from his walkabout, however, can help assemble a rough itinerary and give a theme to his meanderings. Sitting at home today, he smiles and waves away questions about those years of wandering. But some hints emerge. More than anything else, it was a pilgrimage in the footsteps of Swami Vivekananda. By the time he left home, Narendra had devoured most of the Swami's literary works, lent to him by a Vadnagar local, Dr Vasantbhai Parikh.[15] Vivekananda had made a deep and, it would turn out, a permanent impression on the young man.

Narendra set out from home, carrying very little. He owned few clothes anyway, and what money he had put away from what he had earned – not only from his father's tea stall but also from lugging containers of cooking oil for a few paise a time for a local businessman – would be barely enough to sustain him for two weeks, never mind two years. But it is good to be poor when young because it offers the priceless opportunity to learn not to be dependent on money. This would prove to be one of the most valuable lessons Narendra learned during his period of uncertainty. It would pay dividends later on, hardening or inoculating Modi against temptations presented by a career in the chaotic world of Indian politics.

Young Narendra initially made his way to West Bengal and to the Belur Math, on the west bank of the Hooghly river near Calcutta (as it then was), some time in the early summer of 1968. The Math is the principal temple-monastery and headquarters of Vivekananda's Ramakrishna Mission, established at the end of the nineteenth century, although the present building was built only in 1935. At the time Narendra visited, Swami Madhabanandaji Maharaj was its president.[16] Unfortunately for Narendra, he discovered the Math was strictly a postgraduate institution and the Swami told him if he wanted to study there, he would first have to complete his college education.

After a short stay of about a week at the Math, and an exploratory sojourn in Calcutta and its hinterland, Narendra headed north. Whether he paid his way by working or was dependent on alms is lost in the mist of time, but at one point he found himself, travelling via Siliguri, as far north-east as Guwahati or even further, and deep in a 'remote jungle'. There, miles from civilization, he stumbled across a hermit or mendicant with whom he struck up a friendship. The man was 'very thin, it seemed that he had transparent skin'.[17] There was little sense of urgency in Narendra's journeying, and he spent about a month helping in the ascetic's garden plot, spending time discussing 'spiritual matters', before he decided to move on.

Eventually, Narendra arrived at the other monastery Swami Vivekananda had set up, the pleasant bungalow of the Advaita Ashram near Almora, in the foothills of the Himalayas. It makes sense that he would have made his way north after Calcutta before heading west again on a fresh path, picking his way across Bihar and Uttar Pradesh into what is now Uttarakhand, because he had already crossed India once, from the west, after leaving Gujarat.

Narendra's adventure was an exploration. But was he seriously seeking to become a monk at this point, or was he simply a little lost and unsure of what direction his life should take? At Almora he could at least absorb some more of Vivekananda's influence, although the answer he received from the monks was the same as in Calcutta: graduate from college and then try again.

Eventually, after at least another year of wandering, Narendra returned to Gujarat and the final location associated with Swami

Vivekananda, the Ramakrishna Mission in Rajkot.[18] His route there took him via Delhi and then south through Rajasthan. He wished to see new places and not retrace his steps. He skirted the Himalayas as far north-west as Himachal Pradesh, then a Union Territory, a place Modi still adores and whose electoral charge he would get over twenty years later as BJP general secretary. Not quite nineteen, Narendra was still on his own discovery of India. Many ideas formed in those impressionable years. They have stayed with him, he admits. But he prefers today to talk of the future, of his vision for India, governance, development and economic reforms.

At the Rajkot Mission, as if playing his role in a mystic parable, Narendra was turned away from the monkish life for a third time. Swami Atmasthanandaji Maharaj, who arrived in 1966 and incidentally still remains there, was the one who finally told Narendra that he should forget about becoming a Ramakrishna monk, that he was fundamentally unsuited to it. This is certain, because Modi himself admitted it when he returned to the Belur Math in Kolkata in 2013 and met the Swami there. In fact Modi thanked him for his wise guidance of many years before.[19]

The monks were astute in 1969, and identified in young Narendra what he could not yet see in himself: that whichever quest he was on, it was not one that would be best answered in the life of an ascetic monk. Swami Atmasthanandaji told him that his destiny lay elsewhere, and elsewhere he should seek it. From that point onwards Narendra changed course. The making of Modi was about to begin.

It had been an invigorating and comfortless, lonely and gregarious two years for Narendra – emotionally exposed, and welcoming of the sorts of hardship one seeks out in youth and avoids when older. But it was two years well spent because it decided him on his course at a deep psychological level. He had rewired his brain and gained an understanding of himself that removed any doubts about his future.

Narendra's devotion to Vivekananda was sincere. It was a good fit with his own personality. Swerving away from a monkish existence by no means implied that he should leave the Swami's teachings behind. The Swami himself was a jolly, worldly man, comfortable in American high society, besides being a spiritual philosopher. Modi maintains that the core of his own character was always 'innovation, new ideas', and in a way that is an echo of what Vivekananda had brought to Indian culture and also to the West.

The late nineteenth century was a period in which, having been released from orthodoxy and empty ritual, religion was finding new ways in which it could be applied to society. 'No good will come of sitting idle and having princely dishes, and saying "Ramakrishna, O Lord!" unless you can do some good to the poor,' said Vivekananda. It was action that counted.

One day in late 1969 or early 1970, unannounced and without warning, Narendra reappeared at the threshold of his family home in Vadnagar. He had been absent and silent for two years – a period of torment for his mother, who pined for him and worried incessantly. She says she nearly lost her mind. Now her son looked physically changed: hard, lean, weather-beaten, bearded. He had returned as a man. Narendra stood self-contained and calm in the doorway, in counterpoint to the hysterical shouts from his sister, which brought Hiraben hurrying from the gloomy inner kitchen to the front room opening onto the lane. She broke down and, almost inarticulate, asked the sort of question a parent whose teenage son had stayed out too late would ask: 'Where have you been?'

'The Himalayas,' replied Narendra laconically. That was where he said he was going when he left in 1967, and technically he was not lying. Narendra resisted his mother's impulse to conjure a homecoming feast and insisted on a plain lunch of roti and vegetables. Then, like any other teenager, he went out. His father Damodardas was not home; he was out working. But it was not his father whom Narendra had gone to seek. He headed directly to the RSS shakha to try and contact Vakil Saheb, his original mentor, and the man who now would take him under the wing again, but as a man not a boy.

As soon as he had disappeared into town, Hiraben did what any mother would do and began rifling through the small bag of Narendra's belongings. It contained almost nothing: a change of clothes, a pair of shorts and a shawl (for the cold mountain nights). There was also – she had no clue where he got it – a photograph of her that Narendra carried with him all the time he was away.[20]

Narendra stayed overnight with his family, then set off again the next day. After two years away he rested with them for barely twenty-four hours. Should anything be made of this? He was not to return again to Vadnagar for over twenty years, and even today he maintains very little contact with his brothers. One of them took a job in a lathe-turning factory and disappeared from view; one now works in the information department of the Gujarat government, which means Modi is his boss; but they rarely meet, and never professionally. Another is the leader of a local merchants' association in Ahmedabad, one which has crossed swords with Modi's administration in the past.

Hiraben, ninety-four, now lives with her daughter, and it is only his mother that Modi seems diligently to attend, showing true devotion. As for the rest of the family, while relations are mostly cordial and memories mostly benign, there is little evidence of closeness. When Modi jokes with the media that he can be trusted not to be corrupt because he has no family dynasty to promote, he is telling the truth.

A mother will naturally defend her son against an impression of familial discord: 'For him *desh prem* [love of the nation] is more important than anything else in life,' she claimed in 2002, when a reporter quizzed her on why Gujarat's new chief minister did not support her financially. 'Once, he found a one-rupee coin on the road. I told him to spend it on himself. But instead he gave that coin to a poor man's daughter in our village, who needed money to buy books and pencils.' She remembered a single coin from forty years ago in the search for something intimate to confide about her son. And to underline Narendra's good character she added a non sequitur: 'No matter what the temperature is, he always takes bath in cold water.'[21]

Much has been made of Modi's emotional coldness. Having spent more time interviewing him than almost any other contemporary journalist or author, I can say with some certainty that Modi is clinical but not cold. He has a calm about him that is at odds with the fierce persona he exhibits at public rallies. 'Actually, of course, people used to say that I was a loner,' he admits, using the past tense. But when asked whether there is a close friend he could call on if he had a personal problem, Modi's reply is curiously, almost mechanically, unemotional. 'In my life that situation has not come. But when I was working with the RSS, there was one gentleman who was my mentor – Laxmanrao Inamdar. Whenever I was facing any problem at that time, I used to talk to him. Now I have an autopilot system in my thinking process.'

There is a sense of enormous energy, pent up, but in private also stoicism. It is this stoicism that has enabled him to survive the blows that have come his way, virtually non-stop, since 2002.

The 'mission' on which Narendra embarked without delay after his wandering ceased was to consume him. Whatever inner restlessness had sent him across India in search of Vivekananda and a home in the Ramakrishna Mission now compelled him to find another abode. Returning to Vadnagar and his family had proved only that he could never go home again. Narendra, at nearly twenty, was now a different person, one his family barely recognized, and in an important sense he was lost to them.

Chronology is the first element of deduction, and careful consideration suggests the abandoned betrothal, within the tightly knit and traditional Ganchi society in mid-twentieth century Vadnagar, was likely the breaking point. Exactly how healthy relations between father and son were even before that, however, is uncertain. Was there some lingering resentment on Narendra's part over the decision to deny him entrance to the Sainik school? Did that disappointment compound with the disagreement over Jashodaben? More importantly was Narendra's increasing focus on the RSS, and his developing friendship with Vakil Saheb, an additional source of friction?

Significantly or even emblematically, Modi still remembers how very disappointed his parents were when he missed Diwali celebrations one year. It was the very day that Vakil Saheb was inducting Narendra into the RSS and repeating the vows with him.[22] Damodardas might have felt his son's choice only as a small betrayal or disobedience, but as Narendra spent increasing amounts of time at the RSS shakha before he took off on his two-year sojourn, a sense of rejection on his father's part could have been reinforced to the point where the relationship was severely strained.

Inevitably fathers see their sons growing up and slipping away, escaping their influence, and sometimes a fierce love causes them to resent it. When it also happens that a replacement father figure is involved, especially one so locally glamorous as Vakil Saheb, the hurt can be significant and the paternal feelings of redundancy and emotional loss powerful. Yet the fulfilment of the son's new direction can often lead to great things. The tragedy, however, lies only in long-term alienation, especially when death intervenes.

Narendra's childhood, and his extended immersion in the diverse landscape of the country when he left home, formed an important part of the adult Modi's vision of India, his idea of the vastness of the country and the vastness of its history, intertwined and enabling its future. By 1970, after more than two long and tortuous years wrestling with and then settling the issue in his mind, he took the decision to dedicate his spiritual interests to a practical cause.

Yet, in a way that would inform his political philosophy in the future, he always dipped into the sea of India's tradition and wisdom before setting any new course. 'To move forward, to overcome hurdles it is important to take a step back' is today a part of his mantra of governance. It was at that time, when Narendra the seeker was repeatedly being turned away at monastery doors, that he developed this inclination to look in two directions at once.

He stepped off the path of the mystic and ascetic and instead began his career of political service. Narendra bade farewell to his family once again and travelled to Ahmedabad to live and work with an uncle who had a business in the city. There, he began a much deeper involvement with the RSS.

3

POLITICAL AWAKENING

NARENDRA ARRIVED IN AHMEDABAD as a penniless and jobless nineteen-year-old just as Gandhinagar was about to take the title of Gujarat's capital away from it. He was certain only about what he wanted to do: work in the RSS and commit himself to some sort of political service.

It is notable that Narendra's arrival also coincided with the aftermath and recovery from the terrible 1969 communal riots in the city under Congress administration. The riots led to the deaths of anywhere between 600 and 2,000 people.[1] The slow-burning fuse had initially been lit, incongruously, by damage done to al-Aksa mosque in distant Jerusalem. Muslims blamed Israelis and vice versa, although it later became known that an Australian tourist, a Christian fundamentalist, had set the fire.

There had already been unrest in Gujarat's Muslim population owing to this, and tensions remained high in Ahmedabad, partly because of an incident earlier in the year when a Hindu policeman had insulted the Koran. A Muslim crowd surrounded the police station and he had been forced to issue an apology over a loud hailer.[2] The proximate cause of the riots was a flashpoint at the Jagannath Temple in Ahmedabad during a Muslim celebration on 18 September, abetted by a negligent media that failed to publish hasty Muslim apologies for some initial, and trivial, skirmishes.

An important point is that the Reddy Commission's report into the unrest exonerated both the RSS and the Bharatiya Jana Sangh (BJS – forerunner of the BJP) of involvement, and even commended the RSS for its later relief efforts on behalf of 50,000 displaced people of all communities.[3]

India in the 1970s was about to enter a tumultuous period of upheaval and change. It began with the war against Pakistan over Bangladesh, and was followed by civil unrest and a descent into political dictatorship and repression under Indira Gandhi's Emergency. The country would be imprisoned by the very party that freed it from the yoke of the British. By the time the decade ended, the Congress was in power again after having been briefly rejected by the electorate, its thirty-year stranglehold on Indian government broken after Morarji Desai's Janata Party won the 1977 general elections. By then Narendra had undergone another transformation, this time into a seasoned political operator, albeit from, as he puts it, 'behind the curtain'.

In 1970 his uncle, Babubhai, held the franchise for a rudimentary canteen next to the State Transport Office and gave Narendra a job there so he could earn his keep while he lodged with him. Much more serving of tea ensued over the next year or so, but it was a means to an end. Narendra had re-established contact with Vakil Saheb at the nearby RSS headquarters, Hedgewar Bhavan. Gradually Narendra made himself more and more useful to the everyday running of the place where he increasingly spent his spare time. He also impressed his teacher so much that Vakil Saheb, who had been at the heart of the Gujarat RSS for two decades and was the father of its development, began to see a protégé in the young man from Vadnagar.

This process took place over a period of about eighteen months, at the end of which Narendra was rewarded with an official position of 'pracharak' in the RSS. It was the lowest rung on the ladder but he was in. Before that, though, there was the Bangladesh war with Pakistan, during which an incident occurred that may well have contributed to Vakil Saheb's decision to 'adopt' Narendra.

The Pakistani generals' hubristic and misguided offensive, named 'Operation Chengiz Khan', began with surprise attacks on 3 December 1971. Thirteen days later – one of the shortest wars on record – the aggressor had not only been defeated, but had also lost East Pakistan, soon to become the independent country of Bangladesh. India's victory was not all celebrations, however. Pakistan had launched a horrific campaign of pogroms the previous March, amounting to genocide. It was designed to defeat the Bangladeshi independence movement and wipe out the Hindu professional and intellectual classes of the independent country, leaving it with no way to function effectively. It was a scorched earth policy: there were over half a million murders of doctors, teachers, journalists and politicians, at least 200,000 rapes and eventually nearly ten million refugees, many of whom ended up in Indian refugee camps or sleeping on the streets of Calcutta.[4]

It is a clue to where Narendra's political thoughts were at the time that he managed to get himself thrown into jail during the traumatic period leading up to the short, sharp war. The problem was the Indian government was jumpy. There was in prospect a soon-to-be-declared external Emergency, the second in its history since Independence. The first was declared when China attacked in 1962, encompassed the 1965 war with Pakistan, and was called off in 1968. When Pakistan launched its 1971 aggression, the second wartime Emergency was immediately instituted, and it was in the febrile atmosphere of the period that Narendra ran afoul of the law.

The RSS was holding sit-down demonstrations in sympathy with the Bangladesh solidarity movement and practising 'satyagraha', Mahatma Gandhi's method of non-violent protest.[5] Narendra at this time was only informally tied to the RSS but says that he travelled up to Delhi to take part in one such protest.[6] In a country on the brink of war, where the security of India was 'threatened by external aggression', to demonstrate against the government was tantamount to sedition.

The protesters were demanding the right for RSS workers to join the army, which was yet forbidden. 'But instead of sending us to the warfront the government arrested us and sent us to Tihar jail,' recalled Modi.[7] His imprisonment was brief and Narendra was soon released, indicating that the episode was simply the authorities sweeping clean the streets. It was in early 1972, just after the war ended, that Vakil Saheb stepped in and took Narendra formally into the RSS fold.

His new home was quite basic, but it was the grandest residence Narendra had lived in, and he shared it with another dozen young RSS recruits. Thus began the long apprenticeship that would lay the deep foundations of Modi's organizational expertise. He began at the very bottom.

'My daily routine was as follows,' said Modi: 'Waking up at 5.00 a.m., fetching milk, waking everybody up, participating in morning prayers, making tea and serving everyone. It was followed by cleaning utensils, going to the shakha, returning and making snacks for everyone. Then I served breakfast from 8.30 to 9.00 a.m., after which I had to clean up the entire building, consisting of eight to nine rooms. I swept and mopped the whole place, and washed both Vakil Saheb's and my clothes ... For lunch, I used to go to some swayamsevak's house by rotation. After returning to Hedgewar Bhavan I again got to work and made tea for everyone. This was my routine for at least a year, and this was the time when I met many people.'[8]

Vakil Saheb was a canny man. Not only did he ensure that Narendra understood the fine grain of the RSS from a worm's-eye view, but he also ordered him to resume his neglected education, and sent him off to study history and even the extra Sanskrit that Narendra had refused to learn at school. In the rare moments Narendra could spare from his washing and cooking duties, he actually managed to complete an extramural course from Delhi University, and gained a degree in political science.[9]

He had failed to gain entrance to a Ramakrishna monastery, but in its routines, demands and disciplines, life as a humble novitiate in the RSS rivalled that austere existence. Later he would chafe at the restrictions, but for the moment he was happy to be on the inside and possessed an enterprising attitude:

He recalls: 'If I was the person that cleans the car, I made sure to clean the car very nicely, so that even my boss thought: "That is a good boy, teach him to drive, he will be useful for our driving." Then I become a driver. So basically, whichever assignment is given to me, at that point of time, I am totally involved in it. I never think about my past, I never think about my future.'

Little by little his duties and responsibilities increased. 'Then, slowly, I started looking at the mail that came in and then writing the replies. My work kept on increasing slowly.'[10]

In the fifth Lok Sabha elections held in March 1971, Indira Gandhi campaigned as leader of the split Congress(R) – 'R' standing for 'Requisition'. It was originally a breakaway group from the more conservative 'Old' Congress – Congress (O), 'O' standing for 'Organization' – under K. Kamaraj, which was soon eclipsed and eventually absorbed into the Janata Party.

She won a landslide victory with 352 out of 518 seats. In the state assembly elections in Gujarat the next year the party replicated its performance, but the post-war euphoria over Bangladesh quickly dissipated. 'Garibi hatao' had been Indira's populist slogan in the general election, but the grand promises she made to the poor were soon unravelling. In the era of central government planning and the 'licence raj', which treated businessmen with suspicion, rational economic choices and free markets were endangered species. The monsoon failed in 1972 and this, alongside Indira's adherence to the Soviet centrally planned economic model, led in the summer of 1973 to an agricultural crisis. Food prices were rising quickly as scarcity hit hard, provoking in Gujarat the first of two uprisings that would precipitate the internal Emergency of 1975.

A student-led, statewide bandh in January 1974 turned into a two-day riot in Ahmedabad, forcing the resignation of Chief Minister Chimanbhai Patel the next month. Thus commenced what became known as the Nav Nirman Andolan, or 'reconstruction movement', which hoped to turf the Congress out of Gujarat.

Months of protests and agitation against government corruption and high-handedness followed, leading to 8,000 arrests and more than 100 deaths, mostly at the hands of the police. Nav Nirman was a genuinely popular movement and at the beginning had little to do with the RSS: it was supported by housewives, academics, doctors, lawyers and workers.

Everybody spontaneously spilled on to the streets. Throughout 1974 the call for fresh assembly elections grew louder, and increasing numbers of members of the state legislative assembly (MLAs) began to resign in sympathy.

Meanwhile, to the east in Bihar, a second agitation began. It was led by Jayaprakash Narayan (JP). He emerged as the hope of protesting students and called for a 'Sampoorna Kraanti', or (peaceful) 'Total Revolution'. After what occurred in Gujarat, Indira Gandhi now began to grow seriously worried. Before long, the movement for radical change – arising out of anger against privilege and corruption as well as disastrous socialist policies –

was beginning to break state borders and threatening to become a national phenomenon. The government reacted violently against citizens who were complaining about its failed economic policies. When JP visited Bengal he was attacked by a Congress crowd in Calcutta who danced on the roof of his car.[11]

A third element that brought about the Emergency, and possibly the crucial one, was meanwhile percolating through the judicial system. The loser in Indira Gandhi's Rae Bareli constituency in the 1971 Lok Sabha elections, Raj Narain, had lodged a formal complaint against her, alleging electoral irregularities. Indira had used one of her civil servants from Delhi to run her campaign, which was strictly forbidden. On 12 June 1975, a new state assembly elections in Gujarat voted out the Congress and installed a coalition of Opposition parties. That day, the Allahabad High Court declared Indira's 1971 election to Parliament null and void and banned her from holding any public office for six years.

After protesting the decision for a few days, Indira Gandhi declared an internal Emergency on the night of 25 June 1975. Massive, nationwide detentions of thousands of her political opponents, and even of dissenters within the Congress party, took place overnight. These arrests were carried out under the alibi of 'Presidential ordinances', which later became law under dictatorial fiat, along with amendments to the Constitution – including declaring India a socialist and secular state – a provision the founding fathers, led by Dr Babasaheb Ambedkar, had considered unnecessary in 1950.

Lal Krishna Advani and Atal Bihari Vajpayee were prominent at that time in the BJS, the political arm of the RSS. On 26 June they were in Bangalore attending a meeting, and were promptly arrested and transported to the city's central jail. Like very many other fresh internees, they could hardly believe what was happening. India was a democracy after all, with a Constitution that guaranteed civil rights and freedom of speech and representation. How could it possibly be abrogated at the whim of a single person merely because she decided that the state was threatened by 'hostile' elements, namely its own people? A coup, like the conceit in Indira's implicit royal claim of *l'état, c'est moi*, was at first incredible. By the time it sank in, those who were previously in a position to counter her politically were in prison or hiding.

Censorship of the press came into operation on the night of 25 June. Power supply to Delhi newspaper presses was turned off. But because a couple of newspaper offices were not on Bahadur Shah Zafar Marg, the road where most of the newspaper buildings stood, they avoided the black-out and managed to go to press the next morning.[12] Like the other newspapers, they too were soon subject to direct censorship, and were allowed mainly to print articles featuring filmstar appearances and speeches by Sanjay Gandhi. Almost all foreign journalists were banned – though not the Russians. India had been swiftly turned into quasi-police state. Worst of all, many in Delhi's chattering classes were attempting to justify it, if only to save their own skins.[13] In his book, *India: a Portrait*, Patrick French writes that 'It looked as if India might be moving towards a new form of government – dictatorship.'[14]

By now the RSS in Gujarat had interlocked with the Nav Nirman movement and established a large network of pracharaks, supporters and activists who were still operating in top gear owing to the recent state election. Gujarat's new Janata Morcha government, headed by Babubhai Patel, meant that, along with Tamil Nadu, it was one of only two big states in India where the Emergency diktat of Indira Gandhi had any slight chance of being resisted. As such, Gujarat became a magnet for Indian democrats fleeing to safety from other parts of the country, and began to

transactional
aptitude

resemble a wartime Resistance stronghold in Vichy France. One of the first acts of the RSS under the Emergency was to establish a coordinating committee of this resistance, the Gujarat Lok Sangharsh Samiti (GLSS).

It had been over three years since Modi had moved into Hedgewar Bhavan, learning by heart every system of the organization from the very smallest cog to the heaviest lever. Surprisingly quickly, he became the man to go to when something needed doing. Modi chaperoned and assisted visitors, oversaw correspondence and eventually organized offices, transportation and meetings of the party.[15] There seemed no task he did not know how to handle, no formality or process within the RSS he was unfamiliar with or found too mundane to take care of. Some called Modi a workaholic but he was steadily making himself indispensable.

How well he had accomplished this became clear when the GLSS was initially convened in early July under the chairmanship of Vakil Saheb, who promptly appointed Modi its general secretary.[16] This appointment was to prove the turning point, the crucible of both Modi's career and character. It was because of his clandestine activities during the Emergency that his rise in the RSS began in earnest. Modi, barely twenty-five years old, was chosen by Vakil Saheb because by now he understood how everything worked, knew everybody, was good at handling people, and was trusted. There is often talk of Modi's egotism, roughness and arrogance alienating people; but evidence suggests, even if this was so, countervailing qualities counted for a lot too, or Modi would never have been given so much responsibility so early.

In the days immediately after the enactment of the Emergency, Indira was alerted to how much of a thorn in her foot Gujarat could be, thanks mainly to the activism of the RSS. The organization was again banned as it had been in 1948. The Congress even attempted to discredit it by claiming weapons were found in the RSS offices in Ahmedabad.[17] Most of its official representatives were speedily rounded up by the police and put into prison. Modi, at this point still a junior worker at Hedgewar Bhavan in the eyes of the authorities, was left relatively free to operate, although because of his new secret role he was in a perilous position.

'At that time I was active with this agitation,' he says. 'I was in very close contact with youth leaders, student leaders. I was behind the curtain but I was very close to them.' Straight after the GLSS convened and set out a plan of action, Keshavrao Deshmukh, the RSS figure with whom Modi was supposed to coordinate, was spotted by the police and arrested. He realized that another RSS leader, Nathalal Zagda, was also in imminent danger and so leaped on a scooter and rode to pick him up, ferrying him to a safe house – one of many secret places of refuge Modi would soon organize.

At last his talent for administration was put to the test. 'It was a threat to democracy,' says Modi. 'I was underground and the police were in search of me to arrest me. But I wanted to meet my people, I wanted to convince them that we had to save democracy.'

He set about compiling lists of contacts who could be trusted to carry out clandestine tasks, and then used their knowledge of another wider circle of sympathizers and democrats to arrange accommodation for activists who needed places to hide. He also began raising money to pay living expenses of political refugees and activists, and arranged for disbursement of funds. Modi calculated, in his brisk manner, that 'for every full-time underground worker, one needed the support of at least 10 families who had no fear of the consequences'.[18] Luckily, there were plenty of Gujaratis willing to volunteer. Very quickly, the 'enemies of the state', whom Indira's security forces were searching for on the streets of Ahmedabad and elsewhere, melted away into safe houses.

Just as there exist from his childhood apocryphal stories of Narendra's actions designed to show his character in a flattering light, so there is another crop of stories from the time of the Emergency. Although these too might be less than completely true, even his bitterest critics admit that Modi did much good work at this time, a lot of it at grave personal risk. Two examples of such apocrypha: Chhayank Mehta tells of how, after Deshmukh's arrest, it was discovered that the papers he was carrying were still with him. These contained plans for the future actions of the GLSS, and it was essential somehow to retrieve them. To this end Modi planned a distraction with the help of a female swayamsevak from Maninagar. They went to the police station where Deshmukh was being held. While she posed as a relative and contrived a meeting with the prisoner, Modi somehow took the documents from under the noses of the police.[19]

A similar story has Chandikadas 'Nanaji' Deshmukh arrested while carrying a book of addresses of sympathizers and possibly safe houses. Modi then had to remove every one of them from the underground network and begin the difficult task of finding alternatives.[20]

Another apocryphal tale has Modi 'breaking into jail' in Bhavnagar to meet the journalist Vishnu Pandya and Shankersinh Vaghela (who today, ironically, leads the Congress opposition to Modi in Gujarat and is a sworn enemy). For this reckless excursion he disguised himself and again made use of a female activist, 'a lady who was a regular visitor to the jail', to allay suspicion.[21] The prison outing has never been confirmed by either Modi or Vaghela.[22]

There are other stories which are certainly true – for instance, the manner in which Modi managed to send word of conditions under the Emergency to the outside world by publishing samizdat material that he smuggled aboard Delhi-bound trains in time for a meeting of foreign Commonwealth leaders taking place there. Booklets with titles such as 'Indian Press Gagged', 'Facts versus Indira's Lies' and 'When Disobedience to Law Is a Duty' were distributed to politicians from foreign countries by local RSS members, and the truth of the Emergency started to make its way to the international media. He coordinated the underground print propaganda and was in charge of sending material abroad to Indians who could spread the word about the repression and resistance in India. Such samizdat played a crucial part in eventually forcing Indira to hold new elections.[23]

Modi was also responsible for transportation and travel to Gujarat of those opponents of Indira still at liberty. In this role he met with the socialist and trade union leader George Fernandes, whose brother had recently been imprisoned and tortured by the regime.[24] Modi too, in the course of his duties, was compelled to travel, often with pamphlets that could have got him arrested. To minimize the risk he became a master of disguise, something that came naturally to one who always paid attention to his appearance.

On one outing he would appear as a saffron-robed sanyasi, on another as a turbaned Sikh. One time he was sitting in a railway carriage, hiding behind a thick black beard, when his old schoolteacher sat down next to the grown-up 'urchin'. The disguise worked perfectly, but some years afterwards the teacher attested that as Narendra disembarked, he introduced himself and offered a hearty salutation.[25]

While the Emergency allowed him to prove his mettle, more important to Modi was the change it wrought in him and how it broadened and clarified his political beliefs. 'During this period I had the chance to work with so many other parties,' he told me. 'I was lucky to work with Gandhians. I was lucky to work with socialist leaders. I was lucky to work with Islamic organizations, the Communist Party, with liberal organizations – so many people. That period was a good period to mould me. Because of that and the democratic values that I found, it became a part of my DNA. Yes, that was one of the best experiences that I had. I became aware; I understood the Constitution, I understood the rights, because before that I was living in a different world. The Emergency became a university for me.'

Sympathizers of Indira Gandhi like to explain that she imposed the draconian Emergency and imprisoned her opponents or sent her son to pull poor people off the streets and forcibly sterilize them not because she was dictatorial at heart. Instead, they claim she genuinely cared for the country and this was her unique way of showing affection. It is more likely that in ending the Emergency Indira was thinking of herself, not India. She was aware of her growing international reputation as a tyrant, the daughter of a great democratic leader whose legacy she had damaged. As the journalist Tavleen Singh points out, the pressure to end the Emergency came simply from Indira Gandhi finding it unbearable that 'the Western media had taken to calling her a dictator'.[26]

There was also of course the shrewd calculation that with her opponents imprisoned, demoralized, disorganized and exhausted, they would be ineffective in campaigning and she could win the new general elections. It was to the credit of the voters that they proved her wrong. The delayed sixth Lok Sabha poll, held in March 1977, two months after being announced, saw an informal alliance headed by the Janata Party win 345 seats to the Congress's 189.

For the first time in the history of independent India, the Congress had been defeated. Morarji Desai was elected prime minister and A.B. Vajpayee appointed external affairs minister. But the alliance, comprising ideological opposites, collapsed in less than three years.

One of the most remarkable things about the Emergency is how India appears almost to have forgotten it happened. A large proportion of its population was born after 1977 and the dark period of dictatorship must seem as distant to it as the days of the Raj.

To demonstrate how short memories could be even back then, in January 1980 India re-elected Indira Gandhi with a majority.

There were two important consequences that arose from the Emergency. The first was that the RSS broke out of its constricted space as a fringe and eccentric movement and emerged with credit, its reputation enhanced as a defender of democracy.[27] Thanks to Indira's period of dictatorship, many ordinary people who would never have countenanced the RSS or any of its Sangh Parivar associates discovered that most of its workers were hard-working patriots, not at all the violent fanatics and Gandhi-murderers propaganda had caricaturized them as. For the first time in independent India's socialist-dominated history, an alternative right-of-centre ideological outlook gained at least a toehold in mainstream political debate.

The second, less fortunate consequence of the Emergency was a form of political Stockholm Syndrome, which is the psychological state whereby a hostage comes to sympathize with and even justify his captor. This was seen especially in the media, which – with honourable exceptions – genuflected in front of Indira's regime. One senior journalist, who was present as a young reporter throughout and knew many of the guilty, reached this conclusion: 'India's political culture changed forever during the Emergency. It was on account of the absolute power that the prime minister was seen to wield that an atmosphere of servility and sycophancy came to surround her and her family.'[28]

The Emergency had the effect of installing a pseudo-royal dynasty at the centre of Indian politics and society. Its almost feudal power, abetted by the massively centralized bureaucracy, was set to spread across the country in regional political dynasties. The paradoxical phenomenon of liberals and progressives allying their own interests with a privileged elite was about to begin.

Nearly thirty years old in early 1980, Narendra Modi's political journey would begin only seven years later when he officially joined the BJP. But the BJP itself did not yet exist. It would be formed towards the end of 1980, the first year of Indira Gandhi's last term as prime minister.

PART 2

The Ascent

4

LEARNING THE ROPES

MODI'S LIFE WAS ABOUT to change and expand. He was in a much more visible position after the Emergency. Having impressed his colleagues with unstinting labour during the underground resistance, he would now be rewarded for it. One consequence of his role in coordinating between the GLSS and figures from outside the state had been that Modi was introduced to people involved in politics on a national level. They took away with them favourable impressions of the young and diligent Gujarati pracharak.

Many people important in the RSS and its associated organizations had been traumatized by their imprisonment, through physical mistreatment or solitary confinement. A return to normality in Gujarat – a sort of 'democratic reconstruction' – took time and care, and Modi worked hard to restore regular functioning in the Sangh Parivar. At some time in 1978, he was promoted to the rank of 'sambhaag pracharak', a regional organizer. It was a significant responsibility for someone so young (he was twenty-eight) but an acknowledgement that he was already regarded as a capable and trusted administrator.

Modi was given the RSS brief in the vibhaags (administrative areas) of Surat and Vadodara, 'while his field extended from Central and South Gujarat's Kheda district to Valsad's Umergaon'.[1] The job entailed, once again, near-constant travel, something he was used to and relished. Then out-of-state connections interrupted his duties in early 1979 when he was summoned to Delhi by Dattopant Thangadi, a senior member of the RSS with whom he had already established a friendship in the underground. Modi was commissioned to research and write the official RSS account of the Emergency period.[2] He had already written one book on the subject about Gujarat in which he avoided mention of his own exploits. The new book involved yet more travel, except this time nationwide, speaking to all manner of people involved in the anti-Emergency underground, including those from other parties and movements.[3]

It also meant neglecting his position in Gujarat for a period of time, and perhaps risking the advances he had recently made in the state RSS hierarchy. But this was doubtless balanced out by his first excursion into the national, Delhi-level organization, even as a back-room player – 'behind the curtain', as he always puts it, half-jocularly, in private conversations. Modi saw the opportunity for what it was and, accustomed to travelling light, jumped on a Delhi-bound train with only a suitcase and the promise of a room at a friend's place where he rested on layovers from his trips to all corners of India. Back in Delhi after a fact-finding research journey, Modi collated interviews and documents preparatory to composing the text of the book.[4]

What he also had was a ringside seat from which to wince at the self-defeating quarrels and infighting that would tear the Janata Party alliance to pieces. This made a deep and abiding impression on him, and introduced a vital word to his political lexicon: discipline. Modi understood from what he saw of ideological quibbling, egotism and other unedifying displays of political selfishness that discipline was the only way to achieve anything.

As Morarji Desai's administration squandered a historic opportunity to change the course of Indian history, Modi was privately formulating a practical ethic of political service he would apply to his own career. An important element of it was the stress on 'practical' at the expense of 'ideological'. As an aspiring administrator more than a politician, he gained an essential insight: that it was more important to understand a situation from all angles than to argue over narrow points of theory and miss half of the overall picture.

Vajpayee, as leader of the Jana Sangh since 1967, had worked hard to hold the Janata Party together, but the inevitable collapse, when it came, was devastating. The Janata won only a single Lok Sabha seat in Gujarat in the 1980 general election. India did not at this time have any parties speaking up for the free market. The Swatantra Party had fallen away in 1974. India seemed only to have socialist dogmas inherited by freedom fighters via Cambridge University and the London School of Economics (LSE), which was founded by Fabian socialists.

Nehru's subsequent leadership of India after Independence in effect had bequeathed an all-encompassing socialist outlook that was by now the national ideology. Even today the Representation of the People Act requires all Indian political parties to pledge allegiance not only to the Constitution but also to socialism. The clause, added to the Constitution by Indira Gandhi during the Emergency, was amended and strengthened by Rajiv Gandhi in 1988 and passed without any objections from the Opposition. It means in effect that if you are an Indian, you are legally bound to be a socialist or to vote for one.[5]

What India's putative 'right-of-centre' had – instead of free-market-oriented economic liberalism as in America's Republicans or Britain's Tories – was a nationalistic, traditionalistic, Hindu

movement under the parentage of the Sangh Parivar. It was not
only socially conservative but also economically conservative – in
that it offered no practical or free-market alternatives to Nehruvian
socialism.

Nobody in the Janata Party, for example, had thought of
getting rid of the licence-permit-quota system; it was simply taken
for granted that it was the way things were done. If anything,
Desai's government had been even more damagingly faithful to
the centralist command-and-control system than Indira Gandhi's.
An alternative way of seeing reality would take another decade to
develop, and would ironically be released into the body politic by
the Congress.

The fragmentation of the Janata Party meant that the energy
of the political opposition, having failed in office, required new
channels in which to flow, and new vocabularies to articulate their
ambitions for the country. So it is no coincidence that the 1980
general election 'marked the point from which religious identity
began having a greater impact on Indian politics'.[6]

The reason it did so was partly because of the 'pressure cooker'
effect of the Congress occupying almost the entire politico-
economic space. As a result, Opposition energies went off in
different, more cultural directions to find their identity and gain
voter traction. It seemed the only avenue available. But it was also
in direct response to the strategic machinations of the Congress as
it set about making itself immune to political challenge.

The Bharatiya Jana Sangh (BJS) since 1951 had functioned
as the semi-official political arm of the RSS. After the collapse of
Morarji Desai's administration, and having tried and failed to hold
the alliance in place, the BJS was in an etiolated condition. It was
stuck in a dead end. It had given up on the Janata Party and decided
to reinvent itself, partly at the behest of Vajpayee, who became the
president of a new formation, the Bharatiya Janata Party (BJP) or
Indian People's Party, created in 1980.

The BJS had been a nationalist party for those seeking a nation, and in a way it succeeded only too well in its aims, as M.J. Akbar described: 'It began as the party of refugees from Pakistan. The robust economic and social resettlement of the dispossessed, evident by the '70s, paradoxically, liberated them from the party which helped them. After the high-drama blip of the Emergency and Janata Party phase, the BJP reinvented itself as a champion of a psychological rather than an economic need.'[7]

But a psychological need is as real as any other, and this psychological need was precisely the territory the BJP would occupy – that of a receding Hindu identity, cut adrift by the domination of the political centre stage by the Congress, with its frayed Gandhian ideals of the holiness of poverty; and hidden behind the back of that supposed humble piety, lay the iron fist.

The BJP, it was clear early on in 1980, would need to fill the patriotic vacuum created by the nihilism of post-Independence socialism; one with a 'continental' sense, the sense of belonging to a people specifically of India'.[8] The new BJP's relation to the RSS – which significantly at this point opened its doors to non-Hindus[9] – would be the same as that of the BJS: it would be the political arm of the parent organization, although they would be two different entities, and one could fraternize among both until one formally joined the new party. It articulated five main aims: nationalism and national unity, democratic development, Gandhian socialism (there was it appears simply no imaginable alternative to socialism), principled politics and genuine secularism – still of course a much-disputed term.[10]

The BJP would prove a sturdy and significant presence in Indian politics, and within two decades it would be governing the country. Yet its birth in 1980 was very much an idea awaiting fulfilment.

India in 1980, as in 1970, was about to enter a decade of turmoil and
upheaval, marked by riots, military action at the Golden Temple
in Amritsar, Indira Gandhi's assassination, an anti-Sikh pogrom
– and then the optimism over young Rajiv Gandhi's premiership
that itself turned to ashes in consequence of, among other things,
the Bofors scandal.

Dictatorship had been tried and found wanting by the Congress.
Clearly, another way to secure its uninterrupted governance of
the country was required, and this involved marketing itself (with
special offers) to various sections of the population that would
reliably vote for it. Vote banks were about to be born, and the
laboratory for testing them would be Gujarat where, in the summer
of 1979, Narendra Modi had returned.

Madhav Singh Solanki became the new Congress chief minister
on 7 June 1980, ending nearly four months of President's Rule.
He arrived with a massive majority of 149 seats out of 182 and a
plan that would set Gujarat aflame and lead to years of increasingly
destructive riots that set caste against caste and Muslim against
Hindu.[11] It would, though, secure a decade of Congress rule in the
state by consolidating the votes of various minorities in the party's
favour, splitting the BJP's Hindu constituency by dividing it along
caste and class. It was a masterwork of dark political calculation, and
one from which Modi learned another important lesson.

Solanki, along with other Congress leaders in Gujarat such as
Sanat Mehta and Jinabhai Darji, had the brainwave that political
success, not to mention the moral high ground, could be claimed
by identifying the electorate in terms of their social status rather
than – as had been the case – political loyalty. This could bring
in votes if the Congress pursued a strategy of identifying the very
poorest and most marginalized groups (which comprised 56 per
cent of the population in Gujarat) and offering them incentives. In

other words, paying, in one form or another, the supporters of other parties to vote for the Congress instead.[12]

The vessel of this electoral inducement would come to be known as 'KHAM', which took the initials of the target communities: Kshatriyas, a 'warrior' caste which felt its historical glories were insufficiently supported by its status in modern society; Harijans, the underclass Dalits who remained largely unorganized and thinly spread, and therefore ignored by political parties; Adivasis, exploited forest dwellers and tribal communities often abused and used as bonded labour; and of course Muslims, the most visible, vociferous minority, to whom the most enticing promises would be made to bind them to the Congress.

In one of the many ironic reversals of Indian politics, the Congress in Gujarat had stolen the clothes of the Janata Party, for it had been Prime Minister Morarji Desai who had first proposed formal rights for Other Backward Classes (OBCs) through the Mandal Commission which V.P. Singh put into action a decade later. The aim had been to improve the lives of those groups in society seen to be lagging behind economically and socially. The underprivileged OBCs were to be allotted a portion of public sector jobs and places in educational institutions. The proposal recommended a riot-provoking 27 per cent reservation. The report was hastily put on the shelf in 1980 by Indira Gandhi and forgotten about until Prime Minister V.P. Singh resurrected the recommendations in 1989–90, with predictable results.

As far back as in 1972, in Congress-ruled Gujarat, the Baxi Backward Classes Commission had been set up 'to identify socially and educationally backward communities that would qualify for preferential treatment' – reservations in other words.[13] It reported to the Congress administration in 1976, adding eighty-six groups of OBCs to the list of scheduled tribes and castes that already enjoyed 31 per cent reservations in Gujarat's public sector and in universities.[14] Its findings were adopted by the Janata Morcha government in 1978, after the end of the Emergency.

Another commission for improving the lot of sixty-three minorities and backward classes – who had been excluded in the earlier Baxi report – was formed on 20 April 1982 under retired high court judge C.V. Rane. It reported on 31 October 1983. Fourteen months later Solanki decided to implement its recommendation of an extra 18 per cent reservations, bringing the total quota to 49 per cent. This was enacted immediately prior to the March 1985 Gujarat assembly elections, cynically timed to boost the KHAM vote. Solanki reversed the Rane Commission's stress on the definition of OBCs by income and insisted instead on caste, ignoring its cut-off limit of an income of Rs 10,000, probably to lure the relatively prosperous Kshatriyas. The result again was statewide rioting.[15]

This sort of madness had gone nowhere at the national level, of course, and Indira Gandhi had shelved the Mandal Commission report precisely because she recognized its absurdities and dangers. For example, the minorities and castes identified were not uniformly unrewarded, and many people within various groups were doing well economically.[16] There also existed, quite naturally, vast regional variations in their fortunes. In Gujarat in 1985, however, Solanki saw that there was political and electoral profit to be had in implementing his own version of the Rane Commission recommendations.

In the ensuing riots,[17] which began in February 1985 during the assembly election campaign, the anger of the mobs was underlined by the shock that reservations were cumulative, so that if quotas were not filled in one year, they 'rolled over' to the next, adding to the reservations all the way to a possible 100 per cent. 'The thought that they could be effectively barred from all seats of learning was enough for upper-caste people to go berserk, wrote one author.'[18]

The army was called in, and the prime minister and the Union home minister had to visit Ahmedabad to try and calm the situation. Nevertheless, twenty-three houses were burnt to ashes in the Dabgarwad neighbourhood and 180 people died while 6,000 were made homeless.[19]

But OBCs were becoming persuaded that the Congress was on their side, and the effect was social polarization. As there was a majority of lower-caste voters, this suited the Congress perfectly: 'This strategy was a conscious top-down effort to realign the social basis of the party system in Gujarat,' says one leader today. It was evidence too of how communal tensions in Gujarat were sponsored and nursed, because 'caste conflict can get morphed into communal violence through calculated political strategy'.[20] But it also slowly brought new people – middle-class Patels, Brahmins and Baniyas – who opposed the reservations, to support the BJP, and would prove the first small stimulus for the new party.[21]

During the fraught early 1980s, Modi travelled around Gujarat as an RSS sambhaag pracharak, nurturing the organization in his designated areas. Just as he had had a ringside seat for the death throes of Morarji Desai's Janata government, so also he witnessed first-hand the chaos engendered in his state by the Congress strategy of divide and exploit.

The KHAM programme would later evolve into what became known, paradoxically, as secularism practised by political parties both at the Centre and in the states. They had in common the pious fiction of helping minorities and the poor. This was supposedly in the interest of making society fairer, when in fact political favouritism was aimed at certain sections of the population for electoral gain. In the 1980s, it was OBCs and Adivasis who were offered political benefits in Gujarat; later, on a national scale, it would be overwhelmingly and controversially the Muslim minority, starting with Rajiv Gandhi unilaterally overturning a Supreme Court ruling in a simple divorce case.

What Modi learnt from the riots over reservations and the proto-'secularism' of Solanki's Congress administration was a respect for the Constitution and its definition of secularism. Narrowly defined, secularism was 'understood to mean neutrality of the State towards all religions [and] bereft of positive approach towards all religions. The essence of secularism is non-discrimination of people by the State on the basis of religious differences'. [22] The practical implementation of secularism had to apply beyond faith, because everybody knew religion existed in social space, and its difficulties most often were reduced to conflict between castes or between communities – Hindu and Sikh or Hindu and Muslim.

In its wider sense genuine secularism meant treating all citizens equally under the law. The same laws had to apply equally to everyone for this to work. The riots instigated by reservations demonstrated the danger of resiling from that principle. Such abrogations of constitutional principle introduced inequality of treatment to different communities. That these communities could often be defined by religious belief was secondary. Under the country's constitutional definitions, one was first an Indian, and only after that a Hindu or a Sikh or a Muslim or anything else.

Modi had plenty of opportunity, criss-crossing Gujarat on his motorcycle, to observe the damage caused by such an abridgement. The underclasses were rightly resentful of the way in which social advantages were always claimed by the upper castes; the upper castes in turn were protective of their wealth and position, and sceptical that any good would come of special treatment for those below them. Yet if all were treated the same way, how could anything ever change and progress be made? It was all very well being equal under the law in terms of rights, but then what could end the severe inequality and social injustice of India?

Modi pondered this complex problem and began to formulate his conclusions and remedies for it from around this time. When he became chief minister of Gujarat in October 2001, Modi would immediately begin to put them into practice. That he could do so speedily, and on a very wide front, was because by then he could articulate a political philosophy he has since made his watchword: development.

❧

It was from his habitual wide reading and observations as a sambhaag pracharak that Modi started to understand how nothing would ever change while the 'Hindu rate of growth' of the economy persisted under Nehruvian-style state socialism.[23] Since Independence such growth had averaged barely 3 per cent p.a., not enough to make a significant dent in poverty, given India's growing population.

Under the licence-quota-permit raj the outlook of Indian political parties would never change. Inequality and poverty would persist if there was not enough wealth to go around; all that could be done was to take someone's slice of the pie and give it to somebody else. Why not, thought Modi, bake a bigger pie? The solution obviously was to produce more wealth, which would benefit every citizen. But that would entail an alternative economic model: a free-market economy and, on the part of the government, investment in social and economic infrastructure to grant the poor a chance to prosper as well.

That this sort of thinking put him at odds with the Congress was obvious. But it also placed him in opposition to his own colleagues in the RSS whose outlook was equally conventional. It was an organization, in Modi's view, that provided 'basically human resource management on a national scale. If you have it on a national scale you have human resource management quality.'

Its potential to create change was therefore considerable, and Modi had many new ideas. But still his career would prove to be full of friction over the years as he attempted to persuade his colleagues in the RSS, and later in the BJP, to accept and adopt them. 'Not a single proposal, not a single initiative, was appreciated,' Modi says of his experience at this time. 'Always there was resistance, always there were questions. But if I am convinced, I will prove the results. Then results will make them convinced.'

He speaks softly, as we sit one evening in his office. The voice rises in cadence as he recalls the days when he would argue and cajole his seniors in the RSS to think as economic reformers rather than as mere ideologues. It would be a precursor to his growing rift in Gujarat with the Vishwa Hindu Parishad (VHP) and its leader Pravin Togadia. Development, not deity, would become Modi's leitmotif.

'It is a very democratic system in the RSS,' says Modi. 'They debate for hours together, it's an open debate. The perception is absolutely wrong that they are dictatorial. They are very open to discussion.'

Yet Modi's experience in the parivar, because of his alternative views, his own way of looking at and approaching problems, was that of an outsider. 'I always used to sit on the last bench, I never used to sit in the forefront,' he says. 'And I used to listen to what was going on but I never took part in the debate – that was my nature. Most of the time I found that they could not understand me. That was my first feeling. Then I tried to debate it, but they did not debate me.'

In the end he felt that he had to take the risk of alienating his colleagues in order to change their way of thinking. 'I'll give you one small, very good example,' he says, warming to the theme. 'In 1985 or 1986 we had a drought in the state, a very, very huge drought, and even fodder was not available for cattle. The RSS decided to do some social activity, particularly for cattle and poor people. The idea was to seek money internationally and, in the open-ended democratic system of debate, this was discussed for several hours.

And suddenly the final decision was to be taken. I raised my hand. The person who was in the chair, he was angry with me. He said: "Since the last four hours we are discussing and you kept quiet; and now, when we are concluding, you are raising your hand. What do you want to say, now that there is no more time?"'

Modi recalls the incident with relish:

I said, 'If you don't want to listen to me, I will obey the RSS discipline. But I have a suggestion.' They knew me very well. They said, 'OK, what do you want to say?' So I started: 'Why do we do relief work like this? Why do we appeal to foreign nations? What is the need of it? We are a nation, we have human power. Our whole relief work must be on the basis of our human energy, our nation, our manpower. And for that we could have a different type of strategy.'

And I gave a strategy: we have these many branches, this number of relief workers. I was speaking on my own, giving the figures. If we can collect one sweet called sukri – and there is nutritional value in sukri – we can collect sukri from each and every family for six months. For transportation we can get help from the railways. We should not store water for cattle, but we can move cattle from drought-prone areas to green areas. And the government is providing railway trains free of charge.

Then they thought for a while, and they said, 'OK, now we will have a lunch break, then we will think about Modi's suggestions.' When we came back again, my suggestions were accepted. In the beginning we were thinking of collecting Rs 1 crore to do relief work. Because of this scheme, we did service of more than Rs 30 crore.

It is an interesting anecdote: Modi tells it not as self-praise but to demonstrate several elements. First, that conventional thinking was endemic in India at this time, both in the RSS and the Congress:

everybody's thoughts flowed along the same well-worn channels or grooves. Second, that there was no feeling or confidence that India possessed the resources – or resourcefulness – to solve her difficulties alone or to succeed on her own. Third, that there was a new way forward that required an optimistic reassessment and reorganization of their own resources (they were thinking of 'collecting' for relief instead of, as Modi proposed, 'giving service' by sweating their assets). Fourth, that a fresh way of looking at problems was required to enable this, a sort of lateral thinking: it was, for example, possible to bring cows to the fodder rather than fodder to the cows, but it had not been thought of because the railways ostensibly had nothing to do with drought.

The anecdote also encapsulates neatly where Modi's reputation for egocentricity and arrogance comes from, even though it is a simple and honest story, technocratic rather than heroic and in a sense bereft of ego. It is not because he is acting arrogantly, one suspects, that this consensus on Modi's arrogance has arisen. Rather, beyond the RSS and on the national stage, it is because he is expected, as a political parvenu, not to speak in such a confident manner. Perhaps much of the internal opposition comes from Modi's implicit denial of the relevance of class and caste. To his social 'superiors', he remains a working-class arriviste with ideas above his station.

For the Congress, of course, he is an existential electoral threat. And it spotted the threat early. That partly explains the unprecedented and relentless political onslaught Modi has faced since his three consecutive election victories in Gujarat.

5

THE YATRA TO POWER

Religious or cultural purity is a fundamental fantasy.
                                                    – V.S. Naipaul

NDIRA GANDHI WAS ASSASSINATED by her Sikh bodyguards on 31 October 1984. Her son Rajiv took over as prime minister as the country's worst pogrom in modern history got under way in Delhi. It was led by vengeful Congressmen still unpunished today. In Gujarat intermittent riots over reservations had already been in progress for some time; even the police themselves had started to riot, burning down the offices of a newspaper critical of their conduct and corruption. Law and order seemed to have completely broken down in the state. The army was more or less permanently patrolling the streets of Ahmedabad. For the first time Gujarat's industries and factories were closing in response to the unending violence.[1]

Modi, meanwhile, went on quietly with his organizational work for the RSS, remaining studiously uninvolved in electoral politics. The BJP had slowly been making small gains at the state level, and in the municipal elections the previous May had won control of Rajkot and Junagadh. Subsequently it had taken all in a series of five by-elections to the Lok Sabha.[2]

But after Indira Gandhi's death sympathy for the Congress across India was overwhelming. In the December 1984 general election Rajiv Gandhi received the largest majority in independent India's history. The Congress won 414 Lok Sabha seats; the BJP only two. It seemed at the time there was little hope for the party to break out and acquire a national presence.

Rajiv decided that Solanki, despite consolidating the Congress vote in Gujarat, was a disastrous chief minister. The riots had again flared up, with renewed intensity. Rajiv sacked him in July 1985 in spite of the record victory in the March state election, where the BJP won only eleven seats. Solanki had led Gujarat for five years and turned it into a war zone: 'Looking back to those years of Congress rule in Gujarat, one wonders at the sheer inefficiency and recklessness of the rulers. Casteism was running riot, Hindu society stood divided, and corruption ruled the roost.'[3]

Yet amidst the smoke and death there was an 'intended' consequence: the new chief minister, Amarsinh Chowdhary, was an Adivasi, so at least Solanki limped away safe in the knowledge that his KHAM strategy had produced one positive result for the backward castes. The very same month saw the death of Modi's mentor, Vakil Saheb. It was a body blow to him but soon a new stage of his career would begin.

After Amarsinh Chowdhary commenced his term as chief minister there was a period of peace on the streets of Gujarat, suggesting that Solanki personally had been a provocation for many. But the underlying problems created by KHAM had not gone away. Between 1986 and 1988 there were nearly 100 bomb explosions in Gujarat, signalling that rioting was settling in and becoming intractable, with antagonisms between Muslims and Hindus increasingly resulting in conflict.

Gujarat society was dividing and ghettoizing itself in the wake of the KHAM revolution: 'Religious divisions were underlined by high walls that came up between chawls inhabited by different communities. Earlier, people could wind through the streets and jump over roofs in each other's areas; now brick and concrete walls with iron gates barred access.' This was happening in 1986, halfway through a decade of Congress rule in Gujarat, and 'by 1990 it was widespread. The boundaries between Hindu and Muslim areas were referred to as "border" and Muslim neighbourhoods were called "Pakistan".'[4]

Within the state government itself there were difficulties as well. The Congress was internally divided and Chowdhary, embattled, was not even on speaking terms with several colleagues loyal to Solanki.

The BJP was reeling after the massive Congress victory in the 1984 Lok Sabha poll which confirmed Rajiv Gandhi as prime minister. The near-wipeout of the BJP in the Gujarat assembly elections a year later further added to its disorientation, even though it took some comfort in an almost 19 per cent share of the vote. The Congress, however, remained unassailable at over 53 per cent vote share.

The turnaround began with the Ahmedabad municipal elections in February 1987. Modi, now thirty-six, had been given responsibility for organizing the campaign. A meticulous calculation was made about how many party workers were needed to canvas how many voters, and what percentage of success was likely from so much energy expended per ward. Such methodical planning helped the party win two-thirds of the seats in the Ahmedabad municipality, a complete reversal of fortune.[5]

Now it was the turn of the Congress party in Gujarat to be worried. It knew it was beginning to reap locally the harvest of divisive policies that had led to ethnic and religious segregation in Ahmedabad. And it also knew that the BJP was the beneficiary of Hindu disaffection with the Congress's policy of favouring minorities. Religious polarization was rife. The ordinary citizen felt under siege. The mafia don (and later terrorist) Abdul Latif even won an election for the Ahmedabad Municipal Corporation from his prison cell. The BJP would capitalize on the outrage.[6]

Events now seemed to follow one another in quick succession, leading to a tumult in Indian politics. Narendra Modi was, so to speak, the man in the right place at the right time to witness and benefit from this. The RSS had often deputed some of its pracharaks to work with the Jana Sangh. That had ceased at the time of the dissolution of the party in 1980, when the BJP was born. In 1986 though, Advani succeeded Vajpayee as party president. The year after, as Modi was being feted as the mastermind of the BJP's success in the Ahmedabad municipal elections, the RSS decided once again to place their men in the political arm of the movement as liaisons, this time within the BJP at various levels.

Modi was an obvious candidate for the role with his organizational success still fresh in everyone's mind. Besides, he knew Advani from during the Emergency, and Advani specifically asked for him.[7] In what was a clear sideways career jump and a major promotion, Modi, at thirty-seven, had made the transition from ideologue to politician – though his remit was as yet organizational. He was appointed organizing secretary of the Gujarat unit of the BJP in 1987.[8]

Meanwhile, as prime minister, Rajiv Gandhi was proving that apart from the illusion provided by early euphoria over his youthful charisma, he possessed scant political nous. Great hopes for a renewal and modernization of India had been vested in him.

He talked of computers but little had actually changed in the three years since his election in 1984. And what action there had been was not encouraging. One decision that was to awaken the Hindu nationalist movement and transform it into electoral power in India a decade later was Rajiv's vacillation and then capitulation to Muslim fundamentalist pressure in the infamous Shah Bano case.[9]

Shah Bano was an elderly and destitute Muslim woman from Indore, Madhya Pradesh, divorced by her lawyer husband. The husband subsequently objected to paying alimony of a few hundred rupees a month as he was obliged to under Section 125 of the Criminal Procedure Code. He filed a suit, taken up by Islamic clerics, that accused the Indian state of 'interfering in the personal lives' of Muslims. The case went to the Supreme Court and was dismissed. Shah Bano was an Indian woman and had a right to alimony. The clerics raised an uproar and reminded Rajiv of the votes they brought to the Congress.

Tavleen Singh was the only journalist with the wit to seek out Shah Bano at the time, and when she found her ('a bird-like woman with a heavily lined face and beautiful green eyes'), the divorcee's wretched plight threw into further relief both the cynical nature of the agitation against her and Rajiv's pusillanimity. 'She seemed confused by the fuss she had created,' recalled Tavleen. She added:

(Shah Bano) told me that all she had asked for was an increase of Rs 100 in the Rs 180 monthly maintenance her husband paid her, and could not understand why this was too much to ask for. She said her husband made thousands a month as a lawyer and could well afford to give her more money.[10]

Rajiv, however, decided to pass a law – the Muslim Women (Protection of Rights on Divorce) Act, 1986 – overturning the judgment of the Supreme Court and thus denying Muslim women their rights as Indian citizens. With that one decision Rajiv forever

changed the nature of the debate over the constitutional definition
of secularism. It would in the fullness of time light the fuse for an
explosion of communalism on a national scale. It was now officially
one law for Muslims and another for everybody else. The backlash
would be among the factors that cost him and the Congress the
1989 Lok Sabha election.

The Shah Bano case had a galvanizing effect on the BJP, which
dubbed Rajiv Gandhi's decision to overturn the Supreme Court
verdict as appeasement of the minority community. It constituted
discrimination against non-Muslim men because they were still
liable for maintenance under the law, although Muslim women
surely had a greater right to be outraged.[11]

So far the BJP had received two major fillips courtesy the
Congress's divisive tactics: first locally with KHAM and the
reservations policy, and second nationally with Shah Bano. Rajiv's
next misjudgement was even more damaging to India's social fabric,
and also far more directly helpful to the Opposition. In a doomed
and maladroit attempt to be even-handed, he allowed the doors of
the Babri Masjid in Ayodhya to be unlocked for Hindus to offer
puja to Ram, but in reality he had opened the gates of a religious
firestorm.

The Babri Masjid was built in 1527 by Babur, the first Mughal
emperor of India, in what is now Uttar Pradesh. One of the seven
holy cities of India, Ayodhya was believed to have been founded
nine millennia ago by Manu, lawgiver of Hinduism, and was later
associated with Lord Ram's birthplace. It was previously known as
Ramkot or 'Ram's Fort'. Until the mid-nineteenth century both
Muslims and Hindus worshipped there. After the Mutiny in 1857,
agitations eventually led to Hindus being forbidden to enter the
inner enclosure. Nearly a century of increasingly tense communal
confrontations at Ayodhya culminated in one of the domes of the

Babri Masjid being damaged during riots in 1934. It was rebuilt by the British.

After Partition, nationalists placed Ram idols within the mosque. Nehru, who feared that the statues would set 'a dangerous example', asked for them to be removed. But there was an upcoming by-election in Ayodhya, and the Congress needed the Hindu vote. The idols stayed where they were.[12] After that, the structure remained locked up except for one day each year when a Hindu priest was allowed inside to perform a ceremonial puja. Then, after the Shah Bano misstep, Rajiv Gandhi decreed that Hindus should be once again granted access.

A steady and relatively calm situation at Ayodhya was upset. The aggressively nationalist Vishwa Hindu Parishad (VHP), which had been campaigning to unlock the doors of the mosque, gained increasing popularity for its sectarian philosophy. As soon as the doors were unlocked, Hindu radicals saw their chance and began to demand that the mosque be replaced with a new temple in honour of Ram. The VHP's divisive and somewhat eccentric Ram Janmabhoomi campaign, started in 1984, might have gone nowhere in India's essentially tolerant multi-faith society. But thanks to Rajiv's actions it was suddenly blessed with the power of retort to the Congress's definition of secularism and grew into an angry, nationwide movement as the spear point of Hindutva.

Communal tension in Gujarat and across India had been building up for some years by the time Modi formally entered the BJP. He was far from the battleground, though, as Advani had wanted him for grass-roots work in the state – the patient, nurturing, people-centred job of slowly building the BJP's presence. Within a very short time after his arrival at the BJP, evidence appeared of Modi's independence of mind and inexhaustible supply of ideas.

A rath yatra is literally a chariot festival that involves transporting religious deities on a chariot – the most important being the one associated with Lord Jagannatha. The yatra-as-political-theatre is an integral part of campaigning and party propaganda in India. It is a way of contacting lakhs of people, especially in rural areas and villages, who might otherwise be quite out of contact with the main currents of political and social argument.

The procession of brightly coloured, decorated tractors and trucks containing famous politicians, film stars and loud crews of enthusiastic party workers, the opportunity for speeches to be heard, complaints to be attended and answers given, perhaps even promises made, are suddenly entertainment and hope joined as one. The prospect of change, of having one's voice heard by important people, presents a rare chance. In villages with endless back-breaking routine, it plants a seed of support for the party, to be harvested later.

Almost the first things Modi began to work on and plan was his first yatra, the Nyay Yatra, or 'Journey for Justice'. It was launched only a few months after he formally joined the BJP. The idea was that it should visit as many villages as possible across the state. In the end it went to nearly every corner of Gujarat, raising consciousness of the new path Hindutva was beginning to take. The yatra was deemed a success, and it raised Modi's stock in the BJP.

Under Advani, the BJP's old Gandhian socialism had been jettisoned – it had been merely an attempt to copy the Congress and did not help to differentiate the BJP. The party was now attempting to forge its own identity as a nationalist presence, an alternative to the unimaginative and backward-looking ideology of post-Independence dynastic India.

In 1987, the BJP adopted the programme of 'Integral Humanism', the brainchild of Pandit Deendayal Upadhyaya, which he first developed publicly in 1965. When one learns of what is involved in this theory, the similarities to what Modi speaks about so consistently, especially in private, begin to make sense. Upadhyaya wanted decentralized government with a self-reliant economy organized from the ground up instead of from the top down, shorn of the central control and planning that was strangling India. The people and the villages should be the centre and they should then be used as building blocks for integrated democratic governance: 'When the state acquires all powers, both political and economic, the result is a decline of Dharma,' Upadhyaya said.[13]

As with Modi's development mantra, Upadhyaya's clarion call was 'modernization not westernization', and he thought modern technology should be adapted to suit Indian requirements rather than imported as foreign ideas to be clumsily grafted on. For example, as V.S. Naipaul noted, India used to build cool, shady houses designed to cope elegantly with tropical heat. Now it threw up stuffy concrete boxes, with air conditioners bolted on that spewed noxious vapours into the environment. There had to be a better way, both for houses and the economy.

Importantly, Upadhyaya's sense of inclusive and unbending secularism could be expressed in nationalistic rather than sectarian terms: 'We are pledged to the service not of any particular community or section but of the entire nation. Every countryman is blood of our blood and flesh of our flesh. We shall not rest till we are able to give to every one of them a sense of pride that they are children of Bharatmata.'[14]

This intersected perfectly with Modi's devotion to Vivekananda; it was the political–economic correlative of the spiritual thinking he had been doing. Critics say that Integral Humanism was 'a doctrine that gave the veneer of the middle path to the hard-line RSS position'[15] and that might seem a reasonable opinion bearing in mind the conflicts of the Ayodhya years. But one should be careful to separate – since he is the subject here – how Modi often diverges from the mainstream.

In the end the problem with the BJP's adoption of Integral Humanism was not with its inclusivism, but with its partial adoption of Upadhyaya's economic ideas. Modi, while chief minister in Gujarat, has been the only one to wholeheartedly implement them, although the infrastructural initiatives of the Vajpayee administration are still remembered with fondness by Indians as they watch the national highway network the BJP built during 1998–2004 slowly crumble for want of sufficient further investment.

Modi's next major project for the BJP was to organize, in 1989, the Lok Shakti Rath Yatra. It set off on 31 January from the temple of Shakti at Ambaji. The yatra's title meant 'power of the people' and it travelled through an estimated 10,000 villages in 'a mobilization against the liquor mafia in the old city of Ahmedabad,'[16] although its purpose was also to raise the profile of the party and funds for it.

It was the first yatra to make an impression on the tribal people of eastern Gujarat. They would later become an important pillar of the BJP in the state. It was perhaps around now, alert to the mythical power of the presiding goddess at Ambaji, that Modi began to ponder the usefulness of the idea of Shakti in his own political philosophy.

It was also in 1989 that Modi's father, Damodardas, passed away. It had been years since Modi had seen him, and at last he returned to Vadnagar to bid farewell. The visit was brief, lasting only a few hours. V.S. Naipaul, speaking of Indian tradition – of how its tradition was capable of undermining all Indian efforts to advance – said: 'Obedience: it is all that India requires of men, and it is what men willingly give.'[17] Modi, first by refusing to marry his childhood betrothed, and second by rejecting the future laid out for him in Vadnagar by his caste and class, instead leaving to pursue his own destiny, had set himself aside from the community he belonged to. By refusing to be obedient he had turned himself into an outsider. The tag of 'outsider' would attach itself to him throughout his political career. He was of, for and by the party but in a way beyond it as well.

By 1990, a new future opening to him in the BJP, Modi had at least closed the circle for himself. He was a new man with a new dharma, and from here his future would quicken and develop, although with many turns and even reversals, but no dead ends.

One sign that in his own mind Modi, now forty, felt distinct and wholly separate from his origins was the way he decided not to refer to his background in his political career. 'I decided in my public life that I will never, never, never use this caste system in politics,' he told me. He repeated 'never' thrice and emphatically.

During the several weeks I spent interviewing him, Modi was always calm, phlegmatic, almost monk-like. When he showed emotion, it was on matters of changing systems, innovating methodologies and introducing new technology. His animation over not using caste – ever – is therefore telling.

'I want harmony, I want unanimity,' he says. It implies that his background has caused disharmony in his own life, or in his mind, and that is at least one reason that he will not refer to it, even though doing so might win him votes of sympathy or solidarity.[18] There was also, of course, his experience of the KHAM years in Gujarat.

The next yatra Modi was involved with is seared into the nation's memory, and it would lead to a turning point in the BJP's, and India's history.[19]

It was on 25 September 1990, in the final weeks of V.P. Singh's administration and two months before the ninth Lok Sabha election, when the Somnath–Ayodhya Yatra set off from Somnath Temple in Gujarat. The temple was a symbol for many nationalist Hindus of the resilience and endurance of India itself, having been demolished and rebuilt many times over the previous millennium. It was rebuilt most recently by Sardar Patel in 1950. The idea of the yatra was to finish at the point of the current politico-nationalist flashpoint, the Babri Masjid at Ayodhya.

Once more, Modi with his careful and deliberate thoroughness organized the Gujarat leg of the yatra through 600 villages, and followed it as far as Bombay (as it then was). He travelled no further. His work was in his home state and he was a busy man, although he may also have been thwarted in further participation by rivals in the party. It is useful to wonder whether the atmosphere on board the procession, led by a hard-line L.K. Advani working to make a name for himself as a national leader, gave Modi slight pause.

No matter how symbolic the journey was, the intention of the VHP to build a new temple devoted to Ram on the site of the existing mosque was in deadly earnest. It put the movement on a communal collision course with India's Muslims regardless of the justice of the VHP's demands. Ayodhya, even without the archaeological data to support its claim (recently established but not settled back then), had been important to Hindus for many centuries.

Historically it meant little to Muslims except that it was a mosque, although thanks to the VHP, the Babri Masjid had now become a point of principle for them too. In New Delhi in March 1987 the largest organized Muslim rally since Independence took place, when over 300,000 people demonstrated to demand the mosque be once again closed to Hindus.

As Advani's Rath Yatra raucously entered Bihar it was brought to a halt by Lalu Prasad Yadav. As always, mindful of his Muslim vote block, Lalu had Advani arrested at Dumka. Advani was subsequently confined at a guest house of the state irrigation department on the Mayurakshi river near the Massanjore Dam, and was greatly humiliated by the incident.[20]

The yatra briefly ground to a halt, but on 30 October, when the procession finally arrived at Ayodhya, young men of the Sangh Parivar, wielding bows and arrows, stormed the mosque and planted a flag. This was accompanied by violence in the surrounding crowds and fifty people died from police bullets.[21] Riots erupted across the country. In Gujarat, where the VHP called its supporters onto the streets for a bandh, communal rioting left 200 dead.

As the decade drew to a close, Gujarat was beginning to reap the harvest that KHAM had planted – the rise of an aggressive and assertive Hindutva movement. Meanwhile, the Congress had been rejected by the Gujarat electorate after a brief return by Solanki in 1989. In the 1990 state elections a Janata Dal–BJP coalition under Chimanbhai Patel took over. The phoenix was beginning to rise.

Modi's performance as a party organizer was again rewarded when in 1990 he was named as one of the seventeen members of the BJP's National Election Committee, a move that formally recognized his success in Gujarat. This promotion was vital in that it took Modi's realm of operations beyond the borders of Gujarat for the first time since he had joined the BJP in 1987.

His final yatra was a year after the Somnath–Ayodhya excursion, and for the first time Modi played a principal role, staying on board for the entire length of the journey. This was the forty-seven–day Ekta Yatra with new BJP national president Murli Manohar Joshi, which began in December 1991 at the southern tip of the country, at Kanyakumari in Tamil Nadu, and finished with Modi and his associates running up the national flag in Srinagar, Kashmir, in the new year.

'What happened is that the separatists used to burn the Indian flag,' he recalls. 'We were not allowed to hoist the flag in Srinagar. And they challenged that whosoever wanted to hoist the flag in

Srinagar, we will kill him. We took on the challenge: yes, we will come there and we will hoist the flag.'

Famously, this was the trip on which Modi refused to put on the body armour he was advised to wear – a successful piece of theatre that raised awareness of the need to stand against terrorism.[22] And yet he had less to fear from them than he did from his own party.

No good deed goes unpunished, and this proved true for Modi soon after his return to Gujarat at the successful conclusion of the Ekta Yatra. He was ambushed by Shankersinh Vaghela, long-term president of BJP, Gujarat, recently also elected an MP. Vaghela 'declined to include Narendra in his team', as one journalist delicately phrased it.[23] It was a deliberate insult to Modi, who had performed well for the party over the last four years, and whose efforts on the ground had helped to lead it into government in Gujarat for the first time.

The question is whether this was because of what is commonly supposed – Modi's reported egotism and self-promotion – or whether it was a more mundane case of envy at a junior doing so well that he outshone his seniors. Moreover, Modi had helped Vaghela's rival Keshubhai Patel on the Lok Shakti Rath Yatra a few years earlier. Whatever the reason, it at least proves true what they say in Westminster, that your opponents sit on the benches opposite, but your enemies are in your own party.

It was at this point that the most consistent element in Modi's personality came to the fore: his patience, along with his shrewdness. In a mode of action that he would repeat several times over in his later career, making it almost a tactical signature, Modi reacted to Vaghela's attempt to sideline him by walking away. He could afford to do this because he knew by now that he would be missed. If Vaghela did not want him, others in the party clearly appreciated his talents.

Modi said nothing publicly but retired from the fray to go on with party work. His stepping back was not a turning away or a sulk, and he soon returned to his back-room duties, organizing the BJP base in five states in preparation for upcoming assembly elections.

During our conversations, Modi repeatedly said he had very fond memories of this period of almost non-stop nomadism as he travelled around Uttar Pradesh, Madhya Pradesh, Rajasthan, Assam and his beloved Himachal Pradesh. To begin with, however, he devoted a lot of his energy to the establishment of a particular secondary school called Sanskardham, in Ahmedabad. It was his homage and duty to Vakil Saheb, and done in his memory.

The school would inculcate in its co-educational students the ethos of a nationalist, Gandhian outlook. There was both yoga and current affairs, with elements taken from the RSS debating forums alongside a government-prescribed curriculum. It was a peaceful, meditative environment designed to produce self-reliant, imaginative citizens. Modi spent a lot of his spare time helping out at Sanskardham, and it appears to have been reminiscent of the duties he performed during his early years at Hedgewar Bhavan. The school opened on 6 June 1992.

> Narendra was available on any matter concerning the functioning of the school. He would give out the minutest of instructions on how to receive and entertain visitors, how to hold exhibitions, and how to see that chauffeurs of VIPs, who were visiting the school, were fed and not left to fend for themselves. No detail was too insignificant for him to attend to.[24]

Modi had responded creatively to political disappointment and setbacks instead of growing angry and plotting revenge. He had several options open to him, but chose to serve at the school in honour of his dead mentor. It almost seems that the school became a substitute family for him. Modi remains involved with the school to this day.

The idea that there was something more to Modi's withdrawal at this precise moment in time lingers in the mind. His new mentor, L.K. Advani, was busy arranging for the events that would lead to the destruction of the Babri Masjid in December 1992. And yet Modi had absolutely nothing to do with what Advani was planning. While the BJP's senior leaders would be at the spot that fateful day, Modi would not. His own trial by fire would come a decade later.

Critics would argue that placing himself in political purdah was mere calculation on Modi's part, and that he did not wish to be associated with the rough edges of Hindutva in order to make himself look better later on. That, though, would require perspicacity verging on the telepathic. Modi also stood to lose traction in the party by not taking part: he would have been absent at a famous 'victory'.

It is argued by those who oppose Modi that he was desperate to add an 'Ayodhya moment' to his political CV, and was frustrated by being uninvolved.[25] Had he wanted to, considering his closeness to Advani, he could have been there.

But the facts are established: Modi withdrew temporarily from active politics in early 1992 as the mood of the country, in the wake of communal violence, insurgency and Rajiv Gandhi's assassination, grew ever more fraught. Modi stayed well away, and in the end it was fortuitous he did so. To their frustration his critics are forced to admit today that he played no part whatsoever in the events surrounding the build-up to, and the actual tearing down of, the Babri Masjid. But no evaluation of Modi's life has so far taken account of the simple truth that he chose to sit out the Ayodhya saga, and instead work with the children of the Sanskardham School. Any objective and balanced assessment of his life and work must note this.

Huge crowds foregathered at Ayodhya in a festival atmosphere. They were restive and excitable by the time Advani and other leaders arrived on 5 December 1992. A stone-laying ceremony the next day would signify the intent to construct a new Ram temple. The ceremony itself on 6 December quickly ran out of control – many commentators believed that was the plan all along – and thousands of kar sevaks managed to reduce the mosque to rubble with their bare hands or simple tools in a matter of hours.

Blame and accusations after the bloody communal riots that followed flew in many directions, with an unapologetic BJP at the centre of the storm. In all, 2,000 lives – mostly Muslim – were lost across the country, with great bloodshed in Delhi, Mumbai and Gujarat, particularly in Ahmedabad and Surat.

The mood of Hindus, especially those on the Right, was angry and aggressive, and yet it had a context, though certainly not an excuse, arising as a reaction to the policies of the Congress during the 1980s, beginning locally with the KHAM programme and the cynical push for higher reservations, alongside Rajiv Gandhi's artless strategy on Shah Bano at the Centre.

The world saw in the demolition of the Babri Masjid the 'threat to the survival of a modern, democratic India'.[26] A new school of secularism was being fashioned and it would imbue the word with a meaning unique to India.

Prime Minister P.V. Narasimha Rao meanwhile was in a terrible position, not least because what happened at Ayodhya was done with the assistance, tacit or otherwise, of some Congress people. He came in for stinging criticism that he did not do enough to halt the demolition of the mosque and metaphorically slept through its most critical hours. In his lonely retirement, Rao revealed to the veteran journalist Shekhar Gupta why he had not taken firm action. 'Why did he not ask the central forces to open fire?' Gupta asked.

What were the mobs attacking the mosque shouting? he asked, 'Ram, Ram.' What would the soldiers opening fire at them have been chanting to themselves while following my orders to kill maybe hundreds? 'Ram, Ram.' Reading the confusion on my face, he said, what if some of the troops turned around and joined the mobs instead? It could have unleashed a fire that would have consumed all of India.

Gupta asked Rao why he had trusted the BJP leaders not to cause trouble when he allowed the gathering at Ayodhya to go ahead. 'It was Advani,' he said, 'and he will be made to pay for it.'[27] Advani did indeed pay for it, when Rao implicated him in the hawala money-laundering scandal, but it was a pyrrhic victory.

In many ways the Babri Masjid demolition marked the nadir of a long period of vexed relations between Hindus and Muslims – and there were very many politicians across parties who were responsible for that. In retrospect, the demolition also marked the culmination of a virulent and chauvinistic Hindu nationalism that made few concessions to India's minority population.

At Ayodhya, and in its aftermath, an intolerant, political point had been made in the name of Hindutva. But after that point the air began very slowly to leak out of the balloon. 'Hard' Hindutva would continue but increasingly become the province of hectoring, marginal ranters such as Pravin Togadia and irrelevant, fringe militant organizations such as the Hindu Jagran Manch. A widening channel gradually opened up in Indian culture, due in part to the benign effects of economic measures instigated by Prime Minister Rao and Manmohan Singh as finance minister. It allowed the draining away of the most intense nationalist frustrations as structural economic reforms at last brought a measure of prosperity to India. A more relaxed Hindu identity began to develop with the country's modern middle class beginning to expand during the 1990s and into the new century.

The energies of religious nationalism, whose original anger and resentment was wrapped up in aggressive Hindutva, started to dissipate. Affluence and economic freedom broadened and softened it until eventually Hindutva began to look like a vessel that could hold something more akin to a confident cultural nationalism among that new middle class enjoying the demise of the licence raj and the pleasures of a global lifestyle.

This transformed the fortunes of the BJP. Advani later gave an interview where he pointed out to a journalist how 'a party based on ideology can at the most come to power in a small area. It cannot win the confidence of the entire country – neither the Communist Party nor the Jana Sangh in its original form.' The journalist objected that the Jana Sangh's appeal had been increasing at the time it disbanded. Advani replied:

> The appeal increased to the extent the ideology got diluted. Wherever the ideology was strong, its appeal diminished.[28]

Perhaps this lesson was learned by the BJP in the rubble of the Babri Masjid, for soon after it ceased to trumpet Hindutva as its core message. Modi, on the sidelines, quietly absorbed all this. He too knew that India could only be governed from the centre, not the extremes. Hindutva, he shrewdly judged, could initially win votes but it was development that offered sustained electoral power.

He would employ that principle as chief minister of Gujarat within a decade – but the outcome at first was fraught with unintended consequences.

6

RISING TO RESPONSIBILITY

I come on walking off-stage backwards.

– Robert Lowell

As EXPECTED, TROUBLE FLARED in Gujarat after the Babri
Masjid was torn down: riots erupted on the streets. The next
ten years would be riven by communal tension. Gujarat was again
a tinderbox.

What had changed by 1992 was that the Congress in the state
had reaped the whirlwind of the divisive and ultimately short-
sighted KHAM revolution. For all but four years since it was
created from the Bombay state in 1960, the Congress had been in
government. There were two brief periods when the state was led by
the Janata Morcha or the Janata Party, both times under Babubhai
Patel. Then, in 1990, Chimanbhai Patel took over at the head of a
Janata Dal alliance which included the BJP. After this point, except
for 1994–95 (and in very particular circumstances) the Congress
was in effect moribund as a governing force in Gujarat. It has not
had a sniff of power in nearly twenty years. That is the source of

considerable angst for local Congress leaders who, off the record, concede that they are even today under tremendous pressure from the central leadership to stop Modi's ascent – using whatever means available.

In 1992–93, battles were about to begin within the BJP itself. It was growing in confidence and looking to take power in Gujarat in the next election. With valuable prizes at stake, manoeuvring for position began in earnest. Patel held together the Janata Dal alliance 'like a bulwark blocking the BJP's avalanche'[1] until he died of a heart attack in February 1994. His finance minister, Chhabildas Mehta, took over as chief minister. Mehta was a Congressman – Patel had 'merged his party into the Congress but with little effect' in 1990[2] – and the accession to power of the Congress in the state assembly under him was a technicality, not a popular mandate. It was now merely biding time until the next state elections due in early 1995.

Three names would figure in the BJP in Gujarat during this period: Shankersinh Vaghela, Keshubhai Patel and Narendra Modi. In 1992, Modi was absent, banished from the state party at Vaghela's insistence after his high-profile success in the Ekta Yatra. Modi is clear about the reasons for his 'punishment', and even today mention of Vaghela animates him. 'I was junior, my age was small, so young, but I was loved by the media – I got huge publicity all over India. My oratory was helping me. But because of that, jealousy arose as a matter of course. It's inbuilt. Vaghela decided that now Modi was here, it could be a problem for him. So in 1992 I was removed from the organization set-up.'

Modi recounted this to me – the first time he has done so on record – without a trace of regret. The calm that characterizes his private personality is diametrically opposed to his robust, even raucous, public persona. It is this meditative inner calm that has enabled him to withstand the most sustained campaign of vilification mounted against any Indian politician since 2002.

Vaghela, as president of the Gujarat BJP, was a very powerful man and even more so, a very ambitious one. Vaghela had been present at Ayodhya despite his subsequent denials, and it clearly annoys Modi to see his old foe on the Opposition benches in the Gujarat Vidhan Sabha. An article published in *Mail Today* on 26 November 2009 underscored Vaghela's role in the razing of the Babri Masjid: 'Shankersinh Vaghela (in the Babri Masjid demolition) is one of 68 people indicted by the Liberhan Commission.'

Above everything, Vaghela coveted the post of chief minister and was prepared to do whatever it took to get there, including abandoning his party, or destroying it if necessary. He saw Modi as Keshubhai's man, which at that time was true. Keshubhai was Vaghela's deadly rival for power in the BJP. This was complicated by Modi's colleague Sanjay Joshi, with whom he had been deputed in 1987 to join the BJP from the RSS, and who was with Vaghela. Joshi and Modi had worked with each other for many years, but sides were now being chosen, turning the two men first into opponents and later bitter enemies.

A last essential element was Advani, who supported Modi and had once again become the national president of the BJP. It was at Advani's insistence that in 1994 Modi was sent back to Gujarat, ahead of the assembly elections scheduled the year after. Advani, who resisted pressure from Vaghela, Suresh Mehta and new BJP state president Kashiram Rana, made Modi general secretary of the Gujarat BJP.[3] He then gave Modi the job of training party workers – 150,000 in all – to help the party win the upcoming state polls using the new model of 'Organization-Centred Elections'. It was exactly the sort of ground-level administration work that was Modi's speciality, and he threw himself into the task.

The result was a success, with the BJP triumphing over a fractured and risible Congress to win a two-thirds majority. It captured 121 seats of the Gujarat Vidhan Sabha's 182 seats with 42.5 per cent vote share, up from 27 per cent in the previous election.[4] In the subsequent district-level panchayat polls, the party sometimes even won 100 per cent of the seats. As a journalist pointed out, 'Never before in history had any party made such sensational progress' in Indian politics.[5] In Gujarat, the phoenix had at last arisen from the Jana Sangh ashes, and a good share of the miracle had been Modi's doing. This of course concentrated the laser-like enmity Vaghela was beaming towards him, which grew more intense when Keshubhai Patel was declared chief minister on 14 March 1995.

Vaghela was seething with rage at what he saw as Delhi's interference in the selection, and he blamed Modi who had just returned from Delhi. He could have been right. Modi certainly saw Vaghela as a dangerous loose cannon who needed to be lashed down. But Vaghela was politically senior to Keshubhai, although a decade younger, and actually commanded a slim majority of support among the party's MLAs.

After the government settled in, which took quite some time with Vaghela engendering resistance, Modi set about undermining his support base, 'weeding out Vaghela's supporters from positions of importance'.[6] A rebellion against Keshubhai began to brew. Secretly Vaghela was already in negotiations with the Congress to gain its support for what he planned to do next.

At the time, Vaghela was a sitting Lok Sabha MP. Modi had used this to thwart his enemy and prevent him standing in the assembly election under a long-standing 'one man, one post' BJP rule. But Vaghela set in motion a coup attempt against Keshubhai in late September 1995. He chartered an aircraft and flew with his forty-seven MLA supporters to a posh hotel in Khajuraho, Madhya Pradesh, to hold a council of war while Keshubhai Patel was on a visit to the United States. There he revealed that the Congress had promised to support him with its forty-five MLAs. This would give Vaghela a majority and meant the chief ministership was tantalizingly close to being his.

'At that time,' recalls Modi, 'Keshubhai and I were very close. Shankersinh Vaghela wanted to be chief minister but I supported Keshubhai Patel. Then there was a revolt, within six months, and Keshubhai had to leave. But then there was a compromise, and in the compromise it was decided that I should leave Gujarat.'

Vaghela's plot spelled the end of Keshubhai's time as chief minister. Keshubhai was made national vice-president as a consolation prize – but it did not mean the position was handed to Vaghela. Instead, Vajpayee negotiated a deal using one of the few remnants of Vaghela's loyalty to the BJP. A compromise candidate for chief minister was chosen: Suresh Mehta. He could be trusted to do Vaghela's bidding while the latter sat in Parliament in Delhi. It suited them both because Mehta was also a Vajpayee favourite.[7]

So Modi was banished once again from Gujarat. It looked to be a more permanent arrangement this time around. Even Keshubhai Patel seemed angry and accused Modi of causing him to lose the leadership. Had Modi been guilty of underestimating Vaghela's support, and of allegedly telling Keshubhai it consisted of no more than a dozen MLAs? This was a calamitous miscalculation if true, but according to one journalist, it was more likely a rumour emanating from Sanjay Joshi, now an avowed opponent of Modi, partly at least because Joshi thought that Modi had tried to claim credit for his work in the recent election campaign.[8]

Modi today contradicts this. He says he was busy during the time after the state assembly polls, working hard for the even greater majorities the BJP would win in the panchayats in September 1995. But it is undeniable that he viewed Vaghela as an unprincipled mercenary out to seek power for himself at the expense of the party, and as a threat to the new BJP electoral hegemony in Gujarat. For that reason Modi worked against him. He was not wrong in his estimation, as history has proved, but at the time a scapegoat was needed and Modi fitted the bill.

With Vaghela holding court in Khajuraho, Modi tendered his resignation on 28 September 1995 in a letter he remains proud of. In it he set out his view of the situation:

> I quoted one incident – in Indian society this story is very familiar. What happened is that there were two mothers, they were fighting for one child, and both were claiming that they were the real mother. And the matter went to court. So the judge says, 'OK, what we will do, we will cut this boy into two pieces. The real mother cried no, no, no, give it to her! And the judge decided, this is the real mother, this is the fake. And I wrote that I cannot cut my party into two pieces. So it is better that I give this party to you and I am leaving.

It is a good story – a 3,000-year-old story – actually a pericope, the 'Judgement of King Solomon', from the Jewish scriptures (1 Kings 3, verses 16–27). Modi's penalty was set to be equally biblical: exile to Assam and Guwahati, there to moulder and perhaps to meet up with his old friend, the hermit.

Instead, Advani stepped in, and on 20 November 1995, Modi was appointed national general secretary of the BJP, suggesting that his efforts in Gujarat had not gone unappreciated where it counted.[9]

Modi was now based in Delhi. He was a protégé of Advani, whose ear and company he had ready access to. But Modi was not enamoured of Delhi. He stayed there only for a little over a month.[10]

'Actually, I am a detached person,' says Modi as we sit in his home one evening, returning to the theme of the ascetic, the monk who could walk away from it all. 'I have no attachment, so wherever

I am, I am fully involved. And I was not in Delhi basically, I was in Chandigarh.'

In 1996, Modi was put in charge of organizing the BJP in Haryana, Himachal Pradesh, Chandigarh, Punjab and Jammu and Kashmir. This was 'a tough assignment'[11] but Modi was successful and significant poll successes followed for the BJP in those states.[12]

According to Modi, the next five years, between 1996 and 2001, represented one of the most fruitful periods of his life, possibly because his new area of responsibility was in the north-west of the country.

> And I was so happy because I was nearer the Himalayas. That was my favourite area [laughs], so I used to go to the Himalayas again and I enjoyed it. But in that period I had a very good opportunity to learn. During that period I visited so many countries; I had the chance to work with so many stalwart leaders. During that time I tried to learn computers and technology, which is useful today for me. So I used those days as an opportunity.

He even had the quiet satisfaction of seeing Vaghela lose his Lok Sabha seat in 1996. 'I always turn adversity into opportunity, always. In my personal life or my political life, I always do that,' Modi insists. 'Defeat: this word is not in my dictionary. I never think of defeat. I never stop.'

Modi's time in the north in charge of various states allowed him to not only travel abroad extensively but get close to several national-level BJP leaders. In addition to learning and mastering yet more minutiae relating to party politics and the internal workings of the BJP, Modi networked with politicians from every other party in north-west India. This was because, in the new age of political coalitions in India, the BJP often needed to govern or campaign in alliance with political partners. 'They were not all yet in alliance with the BJP, but I had a very good chance to work with these people,' he says. He made many friends among the BJP's supposed enemies on a personal as well as political level.

The common perception later in Modi's career that he was a regional leader unfamiliar with Delhi politics was clearly untrue. The other perception that he could not build consensus and was a one-man army too does not stand up to scrutiny given his performance as a conciliator in the northern states under his leadership in the late 1990s when the BJP-led NDA was in power.

No wonder Modi regards this period of 'exile' from Gujarat among the most productive of his life. He was a happy nomad again. It also proved to be good training for what was to come next.

As if to prove that intra-party chaos had not emanated from Modi's machinations, the situation in the Gujarat BJP deteriorated after he left. Vaghela still disliked Modi and remained fixated on power. 'Yes, Vaghela wanted me to pay, and after I left and Suresh Mehta became chief minister, Vaghela again did a revolt,' says Modi. 'I was not in Gujarat at that time. And then he became the chief minister. So that was a time of instability in Gujarat.'

By mid-September 1996, President's Rule had been imposed on the state. Suresh Mehta was indeed gone, having disgraced himself in attempting to rig an assembly vote. The ever-mutinous Vaghela had by now burned all his bridges and left the BJP in August 1997 to form his own outfit, the Rashtriya Janata Party (RJP), from whose ramparts he wooed the Congress. After the lifting of President's Rule, Vaghela's dream came true and he would richly enjoy his 370 days as chief minister of Gujarat, supported by the Congress, which now seemed more Vaghela's sort of party.

At the Centre things were still arguably leaning the BJP's way despite its poor showing in the 1996 Lok Sabha election. The Gujarat by-election victory in the Sarkhej constituency on 8 February 1997 brought into the state assembly a young stockbroker named Amit Shah. Vajpayee had made BJP history by briefly becoming prime minister of India for thirteen days in May 1996, after the departure of P.V. Narasimha Rao, before he had to step down in the absence of a parliamentary majority.

A United Front alliance government led by H.D. Deve Gowda and then I.K. Gujral, and supported from outside by the Congress, would not last long. A BJP government would take office, under Vajpayee, in March 1998. It was India's first National Democratic Alliance (NDA) administration and signalled the beginning of an era of multiparty coalition governments.

By this time economic and administrative reforms, undertaken by Rao as prime minister and Manmohan Singh as finance minister, were beginning to show results. In 1991, a balance of payments crisis had brought the International Monetary Fund to the country's rescue. India was almost bankrupt. The treasury had enough foreign reserves for three more weeks of imports. In return for a bail-out, the minority Congress government was told that it would have to drop the ruinous socialist policies that were bankrupting the country. Chief among the demands was the dismantling of the bureaucratic licence-permit-quota regime which squatted on top of India's business and industry, suffocating them.

As a patient awakening from a decades-long coma after a miracle injection of dopamine, the economy began to respond: growth was now up and a measure of prosperity prevailed, evident in the slow emergence of an aspirational middle class. There was no magic in this: it was scientific, predictable. Rao skilfully guarded Manmohan Singh from reactionaries in the civil service and dynastic interests in the government while he tackled the licence raj and introduced structural economic changes.

The irony is that although the BJP would be the beneficiary of these reforms when it formed the government in 1998, they would also hurt the party in the long term because it was never forced to do enough serious thinking on its own economic philosophy. The BJP had always attempted to differentiate itself from the Congress by proclaiming its swadeshi economic policy, although how it differed from mid-twentieth-century Fabian notions of centrally engineered egalitarianism was unclear.

As Baldev Raj Nayar noted in 2000: 'There is nothing really distinctive about BJP governance in relation to economic policy; that is, there is little to set it apart from the Congress party.'[13] There was one thing though that stood out: the BJP's infrastructure programme, especially of building roads. It was a long-term project whose benefits it was then still too early to discern.

Shankersinh Vaghela had meanwhile ascended to the chief minister's post in Gujarat after alleging corruption in the BJP. Barely a year later, in October 1997, he was himself ejected amidst charges of corruption. He was briefly succeeded as chief minister by his RJP colleague Dilipbhai Ramanbhai Parikh, who survived until fresh assembly elections were held on 4 March 1998.[14] This heralded the death of the RJP, which gained an insignificant four seats, and soon afterwards Vaghela dropped all pretence and joined the Congress party, adding the RJP's seats to its fifty-three.[15] The BJP made a vigorous comeback with an overall majority, winning 117 of 182 assembly seats. Once again Keshubhai Patel was chief minister.

Since his 'banishment' in 1995, Modi had returned to Gujarat a few times, mainly to visit the Sanskardham School. From February 1998 onwards, until the general election campaign ended, he was once more a legitimate visitor. His hard work had paid off. And again Sanjay Joshi – who held Modi's old job as general secretary for organization – was needled by it because he feared Modi would be given credit for his success.[16] Joshi was now as close to Keshubhai as Modi used to be, and although there was antagonism towards him from them both, the sheer scale of the BJP's Lok Sabha victory in 1998 'meant that Modi stopped being a political pariah in Gujarat'.[17]

Back in Delhi on 19 May 1998, Modi formally accepted the post of BJP national general secretary (organization), a significant promotion that probably took account of the election result in Gujarat. He kept his brief of the north-western states but had to spend more time in the capital – once again camping in a room in a friend's house and living, nomadically, out of a single suitcase.[18] Currents were now flowing in the direction of future events, but it would need a storm – or an earthquake – to rearrange that future.

The next two or three years are vital to understanding Modi's subsequent career as chief minister of Gujarat. From this point, Modi's enemies – and he was collecting many – began to introduce a narrative element which depicts him as conspiring to topple Keshubhai Patel and to eliminate other rivals for Gujarat's chief ministership. That seems odd, not only because Keshubhai had recently been returned with a large majority, but also because Modi's accession was still a long way off and would prove critically dependent on a sequence of natural disasters he could not have foreseen, namely the 1998 Kandla cyclone, the Ahmedabad floods of 2000, and then four months later the catastrophic Kutch earthquake of January 2001.

By that time Keshubhai had earned the unfortunate nickname of 'Mr Disaster' for his maladroit handling of all these misfortunes.[19] But it was not until several months after the Kutch earthquake that the national BJP leadership decided he should be replaced. Their decision was also predicated on disastrous election results in early 2000, but the replacement of Keshubhai was a decision long debated and reluctantly taken.

Portraying Modi as an ambitious schemer itching to get his hands on Gujarat from 1998 onwards makes him psychologically plausible as complicit in the riots of 2002. In other words, with hindsight, a narrative about Modi as a ruthless, self-serving politician has been intrinsic to the campaign against him which would gather pace as he rose to prominence in Gujarat, and then across India.

✑

Modi continued to impress the Delhi hierarchy and by 1999 won the full confidence of Vajpayee, who made him party spokesman. He began to travel abroad on missions of international diplomacy on behalf of the party to countries such as Malaysia and Australia. It expanded his horizons.

As he told me: 'I was lucky to visit more than forty countries, and because of that I got very good exposure. I understood how the world is moving, what type of things are developing and where my country stood. I had to think about it: why is my country like this? Why are others improving? Israel doesn't have any rain, but Israel is improving. Why are we not?'

He appeared more frequently in front of television cameras and proved himself adept at handling barbed questions from journalists. Modi was now seen in the Delhi BJP headquarters as an astute tactician and a safe pair of hands. He was present in Kashmir in 1999 when the Kargil war broke out, acquitting himself well.[20] He proved he could hold a firm line in interviews. Modi was unhesitant in criticizing Pakistan president Musharraf's 'breakfast briefings' to journalists without appearing jingoistic.

All this would have made Modi a suitable candidate when a new chief minister was needed in Gujarat in 2001, but at the time he was happy doing his job in Delhi.

Meanwhile, Keshubhai Patel was doing a good job destroying his own leadership status in Gujarat without any help from Modi. It was said that under him corruption was becoming rampant and that nepotism was rife. This was a belief held among many neutral observers both within and outside Gujarat.[21] Swapan Dasgupta gave his diagnosis of Keshubhai's decline:

When he started out, he enjoyed the reputation of a relentless
crusader against corruption. He is [now] known to patronise
bureaucrats whose integrity is suspect. He has wrested all authority
by ensuring that crucial decisions are referred to him. The
Government's achievements can't be transformed into political
capital because Keshubhai's image has taken a nosedive.[22]

In the 2000 municipal elections the BJP lost control in Ahmedabad
and Rajkot cities and was almost wiped out across the panchayats,
losing twenty-one of twenty-three districts. Its vote share fell from
80 per cent to 20 per cent. It lost the precious Sabarmati assembly
seat and the Sabarkantha Lok Sabha seat. In 2000–01, the party
lost every single by-election in the state. Delhi was horrified and
feared the wheels were falling off its bandwagon in Gujarat. Losing
the 2003 assembly elections suddenly looked a possibility. But still
the central leadership did not act.

Then in January 2001 came the calamitous Kutch earthquake.
Voter disgruntlement spiralled: there were also droughts that
affected seventeen districts in 2000 and twenty-two in 2001. Relief
operations were seen to be tardy. The administration seemed at first
paralysed by the natural disaster, and then plain incompetent.

'Official stonewalling and a reluctance to part with information
marked the first five days after the earthquake. When Keshubhai
at last came on TV to warn of possible after-shocks, his clumsy
articulation triggered a panic,' wrote Dasgupta.

In Ahmedabad, 400 km away from the quake's epicentre, nearly
200 tall buildings, shoddily constructed in return for kickbacks,
collapsed, causing 750 deaths. An incipient mood of anti-
incumbency began to be detected. 'Stories were doing the rounds
about how some ruling party netas who used to go around on cycles
and two-wheelers had now become owners of big cars.'[23]

While Keshubhai was sinking, Modi was riding the crest of a
wave. A critical moment was on 28 June 2000, when he made one

of his brief visits to Gujarat. He was still unwelcome, at least by party leaders, but this trip proved that there was a groundswell of enthusiasm building for Modi. The occasion was a reunion of those who had been detained during the Emergency twenty-five years ago under Indira Gandhi's notorious Maintenance of Internal Security Act (MISA).

It was an official function, so Modi's presence was tolerated. He was seated at the very far end of the parade of dignitaries on the stage and his chair, although technically on the dais, was perilously close to the edge. When Modi was unexpectedly called forward by the BJP national president and presented with a shawl and a citation for his underground work during the Emergency, he was given a full five-minute standing ovation by the crowd. *The Times of India* noted that 'Chief Minister Keshubhai Patel, state chief Rajendrasinh Rana, and others were taken aback'.[24]

What the incident showed was that Modi was popular and well remembered in Gujarat, from the time of his work during the Emergency to his hard and effective campaigning in recent elections. People also now knew him from television. That he had been absent for the debacle at the polls a few months earlier served to rub salt into the wounds of the startled chief minister.

'Even Modi was surprised by the overwhelming attention he received,' *The Times of India* wrote, which suggests he was not conspiring to take Keshubhai's job. It is revealing how Modi's critics never include this incident in their accounts of his rise to power. No wonder it would lacerate the accepted narrative that Modi was widely disliked in Gujarat and forced to outwit everybody in order to become chief minister.

A confluence of circumstances led to Modi being appointed what in effect was interim chief minister. One – by no means favourable

– newspaper report from the time says that only after the poor municipal election results and the lost by-elections, 'Fearing a similar disaster in the assembly elections, the national command decided to send Advani's man to Gujarat.'[25] Another report says that Modi 'might have remained a general secretary in Delhi had not the Bhuj earthquake of 2001 forced Keshubhai's exit. He went to Gandhinagar as a "caretaker" while the leadership decided between the then front-ranking state leaders.'[26]

Modi was unhappy in Delhi and dreamed of Gujarat, but clearly had not devised a road map for return. Interestingly, he argues that the BJP leaders eventually sent him back for their own 'political' reasons. The party needed someone with experience, organizational ability and discipline to have a hope of rescuing the situation in Gujarat. But they also needed somebody without influence. Because Modi as a 'back-room boy' was without his own power base, and had never been elected to anything before, they thought that once he was chief minister they could control him.[27] This sounds plausible. Being himself an ambitious man and well aware of the disasters unfolding in Gujarat, Modi must – at least subconsciously – have positioned himself, so that he would appear 'amenable' to an offer.

Modi has given his own account of the events that immediately preceded his appointment as chief minister of Gujarat.[28] At the behest of national BJP leaders he had often been to Gujarat after the earthquake, helping to coordinate the aid programme. But on 1 October 2001 he was in Delhi attending the funeral rites of a journalist friend who had died in an air accident. While there, he received a call on his mobile phone from Prime Minister Atal Bihari Vajpayee.

Vajpayee asked, 'Where are you?' They arranged to meet in the evening, and when they did, Vajpayee made a joke about Modi being overweight; and that it was because he had been in Delhi too long, 'eating all that Punjabi food'.[29]

Vajpayee told Modi he must go and work in Gujarat. Modi's initial assumption was that he was to oversee the state in his role of all-India organization secretary. Modi asked whether it meant losing the other states he looked after, indicating he misunderstood what Vajpayee was saying. When told he would be taking over from Keshubhai as chief minister and should therefore have to submit himself to an assembly by-election, Modi immediately said no.

Instead, he offered to spend ten days a month in Gujarat doing his usual work. Vajpayee kept on persuading Modi to accept the position – it was in the nature of an order – but Modi still refused. Afterwards, Advani telephoned Modi to ask how it went, although he almost certainly knew already. Advani was abrupt with him: 'Look, everybody has decided about you,' he said.

Is this account plausible? The aircraft carrying Modi's friend, former Doordarshan cameraman Gopal Bisht, TV journalist Ranjan Jha and six other passengers including Rajiv Gandhi's old friend Madhavrao Scindia, crashed on its way to Kanpur on the morning of Sunday, 30 September.[30]

A cremation date in Delhi of 1 October fits into the chronology. Modi says he held out for a few days before accepting his duty to the party. On Thursday, 4 October, Modi was in Gujarat, accompanied by BJP national president Jana Krishnamurthi, and was formally elected as the new leader of the BJP legislative party.

Advani's terse message had been accepted by Modi on Monday evening; he had agreed on Tuesday morning, gathered his few possessions and settled his affairs in Delhi. He then flew to Gujarat early on Wednesday, 3 October, to prepare for the next day's business by handing Keshubhai the silken rope and his condolences.

While hesitating over Vajpayee's offer, Modi said he was out of touch with affairs in Gujarat after being away for six years, and did not know anybody there. That was disingenuous. He knew everybody; he clearly enjoyed popular support among party workers if not friendship from party leaders; and he had been in the state for election campaigns – and more recently for post-earthquake rehabilitation work.

What Modi certainly did not have – and he may well have been pointing towards this in his initial hesitation to Vajpayee on accepting the chief ministership – was any governmental or administrative experience. Politically speaking, to go from a party organizer to chief minister in a single step must have felt daunting even to somebody as self-assured as Modi. He was clearly sensitive about the lack of an electoral mandate as well.

Modi was sworn in as chief minister on Sunday, 7 October 2001, during a forty-minute ceremony, six days after Vajpayee's cellphone call. At least 50,000 party workers attended although Congress politicians stayed away, claiming they resented the expenditure (but perhaps betraying anxiety). Further to the clamour that welcomed Modi, *The Hindu* reported the next morning: 'At the end of the function, as party workers threatened to climb on to the dais to greet the new Chief Minister, Mr. Modi appealed for calm.'[31]

Modi was safe for the present from local enemies within the BJP because of his heavyweight backers in Delhi. But he knew he had to act quickly to tidy up the shambles enveloping the party in Gujarat. Assembly elections were due in March 2003; little more than a year remained in which to do it. He likened himself to a batsman in a one-day Test match,[32] implying both that he was short on time and that beyond the assembly elections he did not imagine he would stay on. This suggests that he viewed his appointment as a duty to his leaders in Delhi and that after he had finished he could return to Himachal Pradesh and the Himalayas. Almost the first thing he did was to go and visit his aged mother. Her message to him was simple: do not take any bribes.

Possibly for the first time in his adult life, Modi took her advice.

PART 3
The Return

7

THE RIOTS

*For without a cement of blood (it must be human, it must
be innocent) no secular wall will safely stand.*
— W.H. Auden

THE MORNING OF WEDNESDAY, 27 February 2002, dawned clear
and dry in the Gujarati township of Godhra, administrative
headquarters of the Panchmahal district, near the border with
Madhya Pradesh. There was not a breath of wind and the
temperature was already climbing fast. At 7:42 a.m. a train, nearly
five hours behind schedule, pulled into the platform with the sun
rising behind it. It was carrying 2,300 passengers.

Most of the passengers were kar sevaks or Ramsevaks, Gujaratis
on their way back from Ayodhya in Uttar Pradesh, where nearly a
decade before the Babri Masjid had been demolished by devotees
such as themselves. Some of them might even have taken part,
although many of the children in the train had not even been born
then. Returning from their pilgrimage these men, women and
children had covered over 1,200 kilometres in restless confinement

and fitful sleep. Now they were hungry, thirsty and tired but almost home again and in high spirits. Some of them were even singing and chanting slogans.

They were travelling aboard 9166 Up, known as the Sabarmati Express – the Sabarmati being the river that flows through Ahmedabad, where the train was to terminate its journey. 'Sabarmati' has a second reference for Indians as the name of the ashram established on its banks by Mohandas Gandhi in 1917. It was from there that he set out on his 'Salt Satyagraha' thirteen years later.

The train and its journey were rich in symbolism. At the far end of the journey to Ayodhya it had halted at a spot regarded by many as the place of origin of the Hindu faith which was also a place of recent religious and political controversy. The Sabarmati Express would now return the Ramsevaks to a site associated with the latest phase of Indian history – the struggle against the British, Partition, Independence and a renewed national destiny.

Nearly a full decade after the Babri Masjid was brought down in Ayodhya, the Sabarmati Express stopped for approximately five minutes at Godhra Junction. Then, as it pulled away from the platform heading west, stones began to be pelted at the coaches, and after only 700 metres of travel the train halted again a little way down the line at Signal Falia. This was allegedly because somebody pulled the emergency chain, thus releasing vacuum pressure and automatically applying the brakes.

It was 8 a.m. By now a crowd of up to 2,000 local Muslims, who lived in large numbers in the areas abutting the tracks, had materialized and surrounded the train.[1] They were hurling rocks and repeating cries of 'Maro, kapo, badhane jalavi do' ('Burn them all'), 'Hinduoko maar dalo aur jala do', 'Beat the Hindus. Hindus should be cut and burnt. Islam is in danger.'[2] The voice of the cheerleader of these chants and slogans was loudly relayed over a public address system from the nearby mosque and widely heard.

The train driver could not move forward because the guard, when he attempted to go and reset the emergency chain, was pelted with rocks and forced to retreat into his van.

The pilgrims under siege closed the windows and doors but burning rags and electric light bulbs filled with acid were thrown in after rocks had shattered the glass. The pilgrims pressed suitcases against the open windows, but Coach S6 was soon well alight and those who attempted to escape the flames were assaulted with swords and iron rods as they emerged. One account alleges that a man climbing out was decapitated, and his head tossed back in.[3] A few passengers managed to shelter beneath the carriage but those trapped in the compartments were quickly burned to death. In a matter of minutes fifty-nine people, including twenty-six women and twelve children, perished.

The fire brigade eventually arrived, having suffered several impediments along the way. First the firefighters discovered that neither of their tenders was functional. The clutch plate of one had been removed a few days before, so it couldn't be driven at all, and the other's hose had been put out of action by the removal of one of the nuts connecting it to the on-board water reservoir. The duty crew discovered this when they came on shift at 8 a.m. and they were repairing it when the alarm rang.

They set off for the train station but were confronted by a large, angry crowd, headed by Haji Bilal, a Congress member of the Godhra Nagarpalika and also chairman of the Vehicle Committee, who was sitting astride a motorcycle.[4] He had been an unusual visitor to the fire station the past few evenings – remaining late to watch television, he claimed. This second Muslim mob pelted the tender with stones, smashing the windscreen and windows. Standing in the road, a 'tall, well-built young man' dared the firefighters to move forward and run him over.

The firemen were blocked in from all sides, but judging their own lives to be in danger eventually forced their way through. They

arrived at Godhra station twenty minutes later than they would
otherwise have done and found almost all the victims already dead.
Fireman Vijay Singh saw one desperate woman at a carriage window.
He twice attempted to reach her but the heat was too intense. It
took half an hour to douse the flames in the carriages.[5] Some forty-
three survivors were taken to hospital.

The police on the scene were outnumbered and apparently timid
or terrified. They did almost nothing. Later they fired a few shots in
the air to little effect after an escaped passenger pleaded with them
for help and offered up her jewellery as an inducement.[6]

By this point the mob had fallen back somewhat but continued
to emit both slogans and missiles before launching another attack at
11:30 a.m. that was repelled with rifle rounds and tear gas by the
newly arrived Railway Protection Force (RPF) reinforcements. By
this time the news of what had happened was starting to spread.

The carnage at Godhra Junction was only the beginning.

Wednesday, 27 February 2002 was strictly speaking only Modi's
second day on the job after being elected as an MLA. He had in
effect been chief minister since the previous October, when he
had taken over from Keshubhai Patel. He was not yet a member
of the Gujarat assembly. Four months later, on 24 February, he
stood for and won a by-election from the Rajkot II constituency,
where his majority was 14,000, half what the previous BJP MLA
had enjoyed. This was partly because of the unpopularity of the
Keshubhai administration. Mostly though, it was down to the
reluctance of the Vishwa Hindu Parishad and the Bajrang Dal to
campaign for Modi.

The VHP and the Bajrang Dal were apparently displeased
with the BJP's 'not-so-definite stand on building a Ram temple at
Ayodhya'.[7] Modi himself had had nothing to do with it a decade
earlier, and was no more enthusiastic about the Ram temple cause

in 2002. So before the riots he was at odds with the VHP. Modi had been sworn in as chief minister by the governor on 7 October 2001. He took oath as an MLA on 25 February 2002, barely two days before the riots began. This is not necessarily relevant to how he handled the horrific events in subsequent days but a balanced assessment must note this fact which few previous narratives of the period have done.

Modi customarily arises at 5 a.m. to perform his yoga exercises. After that he surfs news on the Internet before hard copies of the daily newspapers are delivered to the chief minister's bungalow. All was peaceful on the newswires as he ate his breakfast on that fateful morning.

By mid-morning, Modi began to receive garbled reports about a fatal railway incident taking place in Godhra between 9 a.m. and 10 a.m.[8] He acted quickly. He wanted to suspend the session of the day's state assembly as soon as he heard the news but the finance minister was scheduled to introduce the budget, a statutory requirement.

'We completed our budget speech – that was compulsory,' he told me. 'At that time we didn't have any details of what type of incident it was. We had just got the information that there had been an attack and that people had died. But we were not aware of how many people had died. We got that information at about 2 p.m. or 3 p.m.'

Having no clear idea of the situation, he decided immediately after the budget speech in the assembly to set out for Godhra to see for himself. Before he departed, all he knew was that there were a certain number of unidentified deaths. It was still unknown who had launched the attack. Modi convened an emergency cabinet meeting before leaving for Godhra. He issued a statewide alert to law enforcement agencies, cancelling leave and calling to duty all reserves available.

Modi was ready to leave by between 1 p.m. and 2 p.m. Godhra was 115 km from Gandhinagar. He says: 'I wanted to go to Godhra directly but we did not have a helicopter at our disposal. So I flew to Vadodara by aircraft. I requested ONGC [Oil and Natural Gas Corporation] for their helicopter. They agreed but said, "This is a single-engine helicopter. We cannot allow VIPs to travel in this helicopter." And my answer was that I would travel by this helicopter at my risk.'

Modi reached the scene at Signal Falia at around 4 p.m. The sight was worse than he had imagined. 'I had already sent my minister of state (Home) and senior officers in the morning,' Modi recounts. 'They were already there. They told me there was very huge damage.'

Before leaving for Godhra, Modi had issued a statewide alert to law enforcement agencies and cancelled all leave to tackle the storm everyone feared lay ahead. Gujarat was the most riot-prone state of the Indian republic, where ingrained communalism was a running sore in civil society.

Having inspected the burned-out carriages, Modi's thoughts were expressed in his first statement to the press: 'This inhuman terrorist crime of collective/mass violence is not an incident of communal violence.'

Clearly the combination of the targets, certain signs of planning and organization, and the identity of the victims all rang alarm bells. Modi felt from the evidence before his eyes that this was a terrorist act, a conspiracy, not an act of communal hatred. It was an important difference. His instincts would prove correct.

The press release, issued from ground zero at Godhra added: 'The Government will not be lacking in discharging (its) duty ... No efforts will be spared in ensuring law and order.'[9] To this end certain measures were instantly effected. A curfew was imposed in Godhra and in twenty-eight other towns and cities the next day.

A day later, on 1 March, the curfew would be extended to cover almost all urban areas in the state. The police had meanwhile begun rounding up troublemakers from both Hindu and Muslim communities who could be depended upon to take the law into their own hands whenever the opportunity arose. On 27 February itself 217 preventive arrests were made: 137 Hindus and eighty Muslims.

While still in Godhra, Modi directed police commissioners, district magistrates and superintendents of police to return to their respective headquarters in order to monitor the developing situation. The Home Department issued an alert to impose prohibitory orders and provide security for both temples and mosques.[10]

Then Modi learned to his dismay that the VHP had called for a state bandh for the next day, 28 February. Such a call had nothing to do with the executive and he could do little to stop it. But it meant there would be a mob of angry Hindus milling around Ahmedabad in the morning. Modi immediately sent a request to the Government of India to release four companies of the dedicated anti-riot service, the Rapid Action Force (RAF), along with ten companies of Central paramilitary forces (CPMF).[11]

All these orders were given before 8 p.m. on 27 February in Godhra, before Modi set off back to Gandhinagar, where he arrived at 10.30 p.m. 'Coming back, it was late night,' he explained to me. 'So it was not possible to come by helicopter. I came by road to Vadodara. Again, from Vadodara, I came in an aircraft to Ahmedabad. From Ahmedabad I came by road to Gandhinagar.'

It had been a long day, but it was not over yet.

At this time no deaths, apart from those on the Sabarmati Express, had been reported anywhere in Gujarat – the first would not be confirmed until almost noon the next day, 28 February. Meanwhile, Ahmedabad's entire regular police force of 6,000 had already been deployed.

In addition, fifty-eight companies of Gujarat's State Reserve Police Force (SRPF) and four CPMF companies were brought in. The RAF – which had one of its two women's battalions permanently stationed at Gandhinagar – was soon on its way to Ahmedabad, Vadodara and Godhra in an attempt to quell trouble before it had a chance to begin.

As for the regular army, Modi had already asked for its assistance. According to *The Hindu* of 1 March, Modi had 'frantically called the army units to Ahmedabad', which suggests he was deeply worried by developments.

I was talking to Modi, carefully going over the events as they unfolded hour by hour, when he said, 'There's another thing which I have never told anyone.'

Indeed, Modi has never before revealed the details of those fateful days as he was now doing:

> On the 27th, when the incident happened in Godhra, I came back to Gandhinagar late at night, I informally asked my officers to alert the army. *On the 27th itself* I was told that the army was at the border because of the attack on Parliament that had happened a few months ago. There was tension between Pakistan and India so the whole of our armed forces were on the border. And that was the answer I got. The army is on the border, no one can be spared. Then I told them, 'Yes, I can understand that the army is not available at this moment, but they must have some juniors. Just as long as they have uniforms. That too will help us.'

Unfortunately, Operation Parakram ensured that not a single soldier could be spared.

Modi then appealed to Delhi for troops, which was done formally by fax at 2:30 p.m. on 28 February. On the night of 27 February, when he arrived home from Godhra, Modi had telephoned L.K. Advani, then home minister in Vajpayee's NDA-2 government, and made a personal request for troops. The fax now made the request official.

While at Godhra, Modi had consulted with the district magistrate, Jayanti Ravi. On her advice, as she testified before the Special Investigation team (SIT) appointed by the Supreme Court, Modi decided to allow the dead bodies to be carried onward in the middle of the night to Ahmedabad, where their families, or in many cases what was left of their families, awaited them. A hospital in Sola, on the western outskirts of the city just inside the Sardar Patel Ring Road, was chosen as their final destination.[12] The hope was this would ensure Godhra did not become a magnet for Hindu rioters seeking vengeance. Moreover, depositing the bodies away from the centre of Ahmedabad for the funerals meant a media circus would be avoided. It worked, and journalists were absent when the bodies were handed over before dawn.

In the wake of the riots, accusations began to be made that Modi had transported the corpses back to Ahmedabad in daylight and paraded them through the streets in order to stir up anger and aggression among Hindus against Muslims. The original scope of the Nanavati Commission inquiry into the riots was widened in the light of this serious charge against him. Yet that inquiry, and subsequent ones, found the charge untrue. If anything the opposite was underscored. The civil surgeon at Sola certified that fifty-four of the fifty-seven bodies arrived there at 3.30 a.m. on 28 February. There was only a small local crowd and government officials in attendance, and no commotion of any sort. Most of the bodies were immediately collected by their families and loved ones. The remaining nineteen unclaimed dead Ramsevaks were handed to the VHP and a mass cremation was conducted to the rear of the hospital in the presence of medical officials and Jagdish

Patel, a municipal councillor.[13] This is what Justice Ganatra of the Metropolitan Court in Ahmedabad wrote in his order on 26 December 2013:

> SIT has said in its report that because of the gruesome incident and death of fifty-eight innocent men, women and children and more than forty injured persons, the situation at Godhra was tense. Relatives of the victims were trying to reach Godhra. Most of the deceased persons were from Ahmedabad or nearby places. In the meeting at Godhra Collector's office, it was unanimously decided to shift the dead bodies to Ahmedabad so that relatives could claim the dead bodies without travelling up to Godhra. Thus, the dead bodies were sent by the local administration to Civil Hospital at Sola, Ahmedabad, which was located on the outskirts at a less populated area. The dead bodies were transported with police escort at midnight and reached Sola Hospital early morning. The local administration was there to receive the dead bodies. The court has observed that the decision taken by the authorities, considering the prevailing situation, was just and proper and court agrees with the findings of the SIT.

Nevertheless, the narrative of the bodies of slain Hindu martyrs being paraded through the angry streets of Ahmedabad to inflame mobs has been wrongly repeated so often that it has acquired the patina of unquestioned historical fact.[14]

After arriving back from Godhra at the chief minister's bungalow in Gandhinagar at 10.30 p.m. on 27 February, Modi held a high-level meeting half an hour later. In attendance were seven senior administrative and police officers.[15] This meeting, according to several political NGOs and activists, was where Modi issued his 'kill' order against the Muslims of Gujarat – a charge later dismissed by the Supreme Court–appointed SIT.

Modi slept little the night of 27 February. By 8:30 a.m. the next day, he was addressing the state assembly again, updating it about the measures he was taking. He appealed to Congress MLAs not to raise partisan objections.

By 10 a.m. on 28 February, news began coming in of trouble at Naroda Patiya in the north-east corner of Ahmedabad.[16] A mob of Hindus – the SIT Final Closure Report states 'a huge mob numbering 20,000'[17] – many of them VHP thugs intent on burning the area to the ground, had converged on an area where migrant Muslims worked. They were armed and had begun to pursue the terrified Muslims – mainly impoverished out-of-state workers who spoke no Gujarati – through the narrow lanes between the chawls, setting fire to workshops, businesses and people as they went.

As the first sketchy reports of deaths came in, the awful truth of the situation began to dawn on Modi. Where were the police? The fact was he had inherited a state thoroughly marinated in decades of bitter communalism and was left with the consequences of this hate-filled history – a bigotry that had infiltrated the political, bureaucratic and police structure at every level. By no means was it endemic[18] but there is little doubt that communal feelings ran deep. It was wishful thinking that Hindu mobs would be successfully contained by purposeful state action in the face of such communal rage as had been sparked off by the Godhra train arson. This became obvious as the day wore on.

At Naroda Patiya in east Ahmedabad, Babubhai Patel, more widely known as Babu Bajrangi, the extremist leader of the Bajrang Dal, according to the court that convicted him, was personally hacking to death helpless Muslim workers. In this he was aided by a surprising figure, a lady doctor and the proprietor of a maternity clinic who was handing out swords to Hindu rioters and firing a handgun at Muslims. Her name was Maya Kodnani and incredibly she was the

BJP MLA for Naroda, having first been elected to the Ahmedabad municipal corporation in 1995. 'She got down from the car,' recalled one traumatized witness. 'Mayaben said, "kill them", then the mob attacked us. Because of this attack we all stepped back towards our Muslim chawls.'[19]

Kodnani was awarded life imprisonment by the Sessions Court. Bajrangi would also be convicted and jailed for life. But on 28 February 2002, Modi had yet to hear of or even guess at the activities of some of these people. The Congress would later use Kodnani's conviction to call for Modi's resignation, although her position in the BJP predated Modi's tenure. Indeed, as a supporter of Keshubhai Patel she belonged firmly to the anti-Modi faction.

The police, in addition to local politicians from all parties, were often deeply polarized that day, and their immediate local investigation into the Naroda Patiya massacre was a travesty later corrected by the SIT. But it must be said that many policemen and women performed heroically during the riots.[20] *India Today* recorded that the police saved 2,500 Muslims in Sanjeli, 5,000 in Bodeli and at least 10,000 in Viramgam. The out-of-state forces, when they arrived, were also consummately professional.[21]

Former DGP P.C. Pande, who was at the meeting the previous evening at Modi's bungalow, was accused by the activist Teesta Setalvad of helping the rioters. This was a vital element in the narrative of the 'kill' strategy allegedly devised by Modi. But it was subsequently proved by the SIT that Pande was assisting wounded victims in getting them to hospital at the time.[22] Examples of negligence on the part of the Ahmedabad Police were rife until the arrival of the army. But on 28 February, the army had not yet arrived. Many innocent men, women and children, mostly Muslim, but Hindus as well, died before it did.

During the same early hours of 28 February, less than 5 km south-west of Naroda, in Chamanpura, a gated upper-class Muslim residential development known as the Gulbarg Society was being assailed by another baying mob of Hindu rioters. Behind its walls stood Ehsan Jafri, a retired seventy-three-year-old Congress party MP, who was preparing to defend himself with a handgun.

The rumour spread that he made several fruitless calls to the police before the mob grabbed, burned and then mutilated him in death.[23] 'An important aspect of this riot was that it was not as simple as BJP vs. Muslims or just VHP vs. Muslims,' says Zafar Sareshwala, a leading Bohra businessman from Ahmedabad who originally led a campaign against Modi after the riots before changing his views to become a Modi acolyte. 'Lots of Congress workers were equally involved. I personally know of so many Congress people who took an active part in the riots. Even outside Ehsan Jafri's house there were a lot of Congressmen in the murderous mob. Some of them are facing trial for murder in Gulbarg society.'[24] Several Congressmen have already been convicted in the Godhra train burning case.

At Gulbarg society, however, 150 people were saved by the police. What is certain is that Ehsan Jafri made numerous calls pleading with his colleagues in the local Congress party to come to his aid. They did not help him because, as Zafar attests, plenty of them – such as local Congressman Mehrsinh Chaudhry – were among the very mob attacking his house.[25] Sixty-eight Muslims died alongside Jafri at Gulbarg Society, which today remains uninhabited except once a year on 28 February, when family members of the dead congregate there to offer prayers.

The narratives of 2002 rarely take into account the fact that many Congress workers took part in the 2002 riots, just as they did in the Godhra Junction atrocity. At Godhra, among the guilty were Mehmud Hussain Kalota (the convener of the Congress's Panchmahal district minority cell and president of the Godhra Municipal Corporation), Salim Abdul Ghaffar Sheikh (president of the Youth Congress, Panchmahal district), Farroukh Bhana (secretary of the Congress's Panchmahal district committee), Abdul Rehman Abdul Majid Ghantia (a Congress worker) and of course Haji Bilal.

In the post-Godhra riots, both Muslim and Hindu Congressmen participated in the murders. Ahmedabad Mayor Himmatsinh Patel was a Congressman as were Mehrsinh Chaudhry and Vadodara deputy mayor Nissar Bapu (who was eventually acquitted, although his son and son-in-law were convicted and sentenced to life imprisonment).[26]

To claim, as some still do, that the reason no Congressmen opposed the riots was because 'it was obvious that the Congress lacked the strength of ideological conviction to counter Modi' flies in the face of documented facts.[27] Part of the anti-Modi propaganda in the decade since the riots rests upon the slander that the guilty have been protected. But the opposite is true and for once, as Sareshwala emphasizes, the guilty irrespective of party or connections were relentlessly pursued: 'In fact, the reason the VHP/Bajrang Dal and a section of his own party have turned against Modi is that he is refusing to help them escape justice or prison terms. Why do you think they made common cause with the Congress party in recent elections?'[28]

It is notable that when former Congress state minister and Fisheries Board chairman Mohammad Surti was imprisoned in 2008 for his leading role in the 1993 bombings in Surat, the Congress was also silent about it. While very few of the guilty ever face judicial penalties after communal riots in India, the 2002 Gujarat riots, on the BJP's watch, have been an exception. As Sareshwala said in 2013: 'Over 200 persons have been convicted and 152 have been awarded life imprisonment. Many more are in the pipeline. An important aspect of these convictions is that they have been on the basis of the testimony of eyewitnesses. Tell me, do eyewitnesses normally live to give their testimony in India's legal and political system? ... They came and gave evidence against Babu Bajrangi – it is not easy to live in Naroda Patiya and give evidence against people like Babu Bajrangi.'[29]

In a fractured argument, balance is essential. In the rest of this chapter we shall examine the causes and consequences of one of the worst communal riots since Independence in which over 1,000 people, 754 of them Muslim and 274 Hindu, died. The year 2002 was a turning point for Gujarat and Modi in more ways than one.

Here is author Patrick French describing the 2002 riots in Gujarat. His book, *India: A Portrait*, is a model of even-handedness when it comes to history and politics, and his description is exemplary of how the events are still seen in the world beyond India. It is fair to say that French even plays down the brutality and horror of what occurred four months into Modi's leadership of Gujarat.

> In early-2002, a train of Hindu pilgrims was stopped at Godhra station reportedly by a Muslim mob and set on fire, killing fifty-nine people. In response, organized Hindu gangs took revenge on Muslims across central Gujarat; families were dragged out of their homes, cut to death and burned; mosques and Muslim dargahs, or shrines, were destroyed. Through all this, the police stood by in many places and did nothing, following orders from above. Around 2,000 people were murdered, and little effort was made to prosecute the killers or the organizers of the slaughter. Narendra Modi made no expression of regret, and focused on the victims of the attacks on the train, implying that the Muslims deserved what had come to them.[30]

French gets much wrong in just one paragraph, as events have shown, but it is a narrative many unquestioningly accept. Indeed, so horrific was the situation at the time that a mordant humour was afoot, and the grim story in March 2002 was that there was only one bearded man left in Gujarat who was safe.

Since then Modi has had twelve peaceful riot-free, curfew-free years in which to repudiate his reputation as a 'mass murderer', as one journalist dubbed him. Despite this long period of calm, every day brings forth a deluge of media stories painting Modi as the Gauleiter of Gujarat.

And yet, over the past twelve months or so, a pattern of change has begun to emerge in the endless reiteration of Modi's role in the bloodshed of 2002. Voices increasingly question the accepted version of events. An element of a reasonable debate has emerged in public discourse where Modi's reputation is ritually trampled each day ahead of a landmark Lok Sabha election where he is the BJP's prime ministerial candidate. Such new discussions are fraught with tension and difficulty. Anybody who attempts to ameliorate the descriptions of Modi's malice is instantly accused of being on the wrong side of history and sought to be ostracized.

Beneath the surface there are more calculating reasons for Modi's continuous demonization. One is the wide and potent electoral appeal of the BJP's softer and more inclusive reworking of the Hindutva ideal. Another is that Modi is an uncomfortable example for the Congress and other 'secular' parties like the SP, BSP, JD(U) and the Left. His programme of empowerment is a challenge to their own model of entitlement and an alternative development path for India.

But what is most striking – regardless of Modi's role in 2002 – is the narrow-sightedness of the conventional critical position. Modi is hectored daily for a riot that occurred over a decade ago, despite the many investigations which have failed to result in legal convictions or even charges against him.

The record of riots in India as a whole is appalling. Since Partition, two major fault lines, acting as cues for social violence, have been caste and religion. Yet the Congress, during its long time in office, has done very little to close them. It could be argued – and is – that vote-bank politics by the Congress and its allies has contributed to widening the fissures in the country's social fabric.

Of the last six major communal riots in Gujarat before 2002, the Congress was in charge of the state for five. Since 2002 in Gujarat, there have been none, but there have been several in states governed by a slew of other parties, including the Congress. Gujarat is an industrious and mercantile state. It is also historically one of the most prone to communal violence. There have been 440 riots in Gujarat since 1970,[31] and over 30,000 nationwide since Independence, many far worse and sparked by weaker provocation than Gujarat suffered in 2002.

Soon after Partition in Bengal, for example, 5,000 people were killed. In August 1967, in Ranchi, 200 people died and in 1969 in Ahmedabad over 512 were killed. In 1970, in neighbouring Maharashtra, around eighty were murdered at Bhiwandi, near Bombay. In April 1979, in Jamshedpur, Jharkhand (then part of Bihar), 125 died; in August 1980, the Moradabad communal riots saw around 2,000 deaths. Over 2,000 people were slaughtered in Nellie, Assam, in 1983 and another 146 died in May 1984, again in Bhiwandi. In Gujarat, riots over reservations in Ahmedabad in April 1985 and then again in 1986 witnessed 300 and fifty-nine deaths respectively, and Uttar Pradesh in April–May 1987 saw another eighty-one killed. More recently, there have been over 100 small and big communal riots in Uttar Pradesh, including especially in Muzaffarnagar.

There were 'pogroms' too, and some of them accurately match the dictionary definition of the word, most notably the massacre of at least 3,000 Sikhs in Delhi in 1984 and the deaths of many more Sikhs across the nation at the same time. Almost every one of the riots listed above (notably excepting the Jamshedpur massacre, presided over by the Communist Party) took place under Congress rule. At one in Bhagalpur in Bihar in 1989, for instance, over 1,000 died. The subsequently deposed chief minister, Satyendra Narayan Sinha, claimed his Congress colleagues encouraged the violence in order to destroy him politically. That is sadly believable. Tavleen Singh says that most officials, being upper-caste Hindus, grew so emboldened by toothless inquiries into murder that they were uninterested in halting violence against minorities, and that Rajiv Gandhi, for example, was powerless to act against violence after his own inexcusable inaction during the 1984 anti-Sikh pogrom.

All this, though, does not explain why his government in 1987 remained inert after the Congress chief minister of Uttar Pradesh 'allowed his policemen to get away with massacring Muslims as if they were animals'. Singh is speaking of Hashimpura, in Meerut, when police rounded up Muslim men between the ages of thirteen and seventy-five, loaded them into vans, and riddled the vehicles with bullets before throwing the bodies in a canal. One man survived to tell his grisly tale, and after an inquiry the killers lost their jobs only to be reinstated 'as soon as the fuss died down'.[32]

It is of course futile trying to settle a moral argument by saying, 'We killed fewer than you', or attempting to explain Modi's role in the 2002 riots by noting that on other occasions Congress governments acted far less quickly. The media never seems to hold them to an equal accounting. The only real question is: did Modi do everything he could to stop the riots and apprehend and punish the guilty? From everything heard and read in the media, the opposite was the case. That is the narrative which deserves to be examined in the cold light of documented evidence.

On the first full day of rioting after Godhra, Modi tried to secure military aid as fast as possible. He had learned from Advani that because of the Pakistan border situation, troops would have to be airlifted from outside Gujarat. George Fernandes, the veteran socialist politician Modi had first met during the Emergency, was now defence minister in Vajpayee's government. He flew in that night, meeting Modi at 10.30 p.m. on 28 February. The first soldiers touched down at Ahmedabad airport at midnight, and thirteen companies were rapidly deployed around the city the next day, 1 March.

Already, incidents of mob violence that had accounted for the highest single death tolls were over. From this point on the rioting could begin to be fought effectively by the police with lethal force. It is generally unacknowledged, although an incontrovertible fact, that the worst of the massacres took place over the first two or three days, not the next two months. At the beginning the police and paramilitary clampdown was only partially effective but thereafter relative order was quickly imposed with troops on the ground. Before very long, outbreaks of violence were smaller in scale and sporadic.

Soldiers were deployed against rioters less than forty-eight hours after Godhra and only twenty hours after the first death in the ensuing communal violence. It was not ideal, but it was faster than in any other riot, and far sooner than any Congress administration had previously managed. The riots in Bhagalpur in 1989, Hashimpura in 1987, Surat in 1993 and Bombay in 1992 all went on for longer and suffered higher death tolls than they should have as a result of the Congress's dilatory attitude towards restoring order. In Delhi, in 1984, no soldier was seen on the streets until the killings were completely finished – four days after they began.

By the evening of the second day of the 2002 riots, not a word had been uttered by any Congress leader in Gujarat against the violence. 'The Ahmedabad Municipal Corporation had a Congress majority; but did any Congressman come out into the streets to protest against the killings and protect those who were getting killed and whose shops were being looted?' asked journalist and author

M.V. Kamath. 'To the best of one's knowledge, not one dared.'[33] Of course many Congressmen were out on the streets, but as they were encouraging or even committing violence themselves they probably had little time to spare for protests.

Meanwhile, Modi, sworn in as chief minister just a few months ago, went on Doordarshan's 7 p.m. news bulletin on 28 February:

> I pray with folded hands that this is the time for maintaining peace, the need is to control the nerves ... It is necessary to maintain self-control. We are determined to punish those who are guilty and they will not be spared. Will you not help to save Gujarat? Come and help the government. The government is requesting for help. The government is seeking your help to punish the guilty through law. Amidst your anger I pray you to display the unique characteristic of Gujarat – of showing restraint and maintaining peace during adversities. Come, let us serve Gujarat through peace and self-control, let us strengthen the arms of law ... Hatred is never won over by hatred.[34]

Thus the 'Gujarat Hitler' spoke – of self-control and restraint, imploring the people of Gujarat to help the government by remaining calm, maintaining peace and allowing the law to punish the guilty. All this would come true, not necessarily in the next few days but absolutely for the next decade and more. Even at this early and perilous stage, most of Gujarat was indeed restrained.

To follow the narrative of the 2002 riots from the perspective of sections of the media, NGOs and activists, it sounds as if the entire state was aflame. This was simply not so.

Pockets of violence did flare up, smoulder and in certain cases reignite before they were finally damped down, but overall the clashes were confined to very few areas of Gujarat: forty locations out of a total of 248 towns and 18,000 villages.[35] In all, seven out of twenty-five districts were affected by violence. Throughout most of Gujarat that February and March all religious festivals, including Holi on 28 February and Mahashivratri on 12 March, passed off peacefully.

In the midst of the chaos, 6,000 Haj pilgrims were currently, or soon to be, in transit to Gujarat on their way back from Mecca. Modi told the police to escort every Muslim pilgrim safely back to his town or village of residence despite the communal tension on in the streets outside. All 6,000 made it home safely under police escort by 20 March.

Most crucially, Modi appealed to the chief ministers of Gujarat's three neighbouring states – Ashok Gehlot in Rajasthan, the late Vilasrao Deshmukh in Maharashtra and Digvijay Singh in Madhya Pradesh – to send aid in the form of law enforcement and paramilitary personnel. He made the modest request of ten companies of armed police from each state.

Modi confirmed to me that letters were composed on Thursday, 28 February, and faxed to their recipients, then again couriered the next morning, Friday, 1 March. The message for Digvijay Singh dated 1 March was similar to the others:[36]

GOVERNMENT OF GUJARAT

No. SB.V/ISS/102002/173
Home Department (Spl.)
Sachivalaya, Gandhinagar

Date:- 1/3/2002

To:

The Chief Secretary to the Govt. of Madhya Pradesh,

Bhopal. (Madhya Pradesh).

Sir,

As you are aware the ghastly incident of burning down of 58 passengers in the Sabarmati Express on 27th Feb., 2002 has had serious fall out [sic] on the law and order situation in Gujarat. Widespread incidents of arsoning, looting, murder and other violence have been reported from most part [sic] of the State since yesterday.

The State Government has been trying its best to utilise all its available resources and has also requested Government of India to spare additional manpower for maintaining of law and order. However, Government of India was not in a position to spare more paramilitary forces in view of its commitment elsewhere. As the situation is spreading to villages and major highways are also being blocked, our resources are stretched to the maximum. We feel that the services of additional forces from neighbouring States like yours would help the State Government in handling this precious law and order situation. We would therefore request you to favourably consider our request for sparing 10 companies of your Armed Police to help the Government in handling the law and order situation.

Thanking you,
Yours faithfully,

(K. NITYANANDAM), Secretary to the Government of Gujarat, Home Department.

Copy forwarded with compliments to The Director General of Police, Bhopal. (Madhya Pradesh).

All three states Modi wrote to were under Congress rule. Maharashtra eventually sent a very limited number of personnel to help, but the others flatly refused. Astonishingly, there was no response from Digvijay Singh in Madhya Pradesh for nearly two weeks, by which time help was no longer required. When a reply at last arrived, it was the merest brush-off:

No. 1523-1557/2002/C-I

GOVERNMENT OF MADHYA PRADESH
HOME DEPARTMENT ('C' SECTION)

Bhopal, dated 13 MAR 2002

From
R.C. Arora,
Secretary to Government.
To
The Secretary,

Government of Gujarat, Home Department,
GANDHINAGAR.
Sub:- Provision of 10 Coys. Of MPSAF to Gujarat

Sir,
Please refer to your letter No. SB.V/MMM/102002/769, dated 1st March, 2002 regarding the subject cited matter. It is regretted that due to heavy commitments of MPSAF [Madhya Pradesh Special Armed Force] within the State, it is not possible to spare the force at this moment.

Yours faithfully,
(R.C. Arora)
Secretary to Government

Not only was the response from the Madhya Pradesh government curt and lacking in any kind of sympathy for the violence Gujarat was witnessing, the reply was also marked 'secret' even though the original request was not. Perhaps, characteristically, Modi could have remained silent on such an example of treachery, except that later on Digvijay Singh transformed himself into one of Modi's most trenchant critics.

Digvijay Singh's indifference during the riots materially contributed to Gujarat's suffering and Muslim deaths. This was something Modi was careful to point out to him in person at a press conference after a meeting of the National Security Council in 2011.[37]

Although Modi was reassured by the presence of the army on the streets of Gujarat, he was nevertheless a shaken man. In his Doordarshan statement he had spoken of folding hands in prayer and of 'holding the nerve'. These were raw emotions and he felt them keenly. The journalist Sheela Bhatt claimed at the time that he was devastated, and she was probably right. For the first time in his career he had the unpleasant experience of pulling levers to make things happen only to find that nothing, or even the opposite of what he intended, happened.

This was no roadblock caused by back-room politicking. It was real life in which hundreds of people were dying. In the end it would be his responsibility because he was in charge. There was also treachery among his own ranks and opportunistic duplicity from the Congress – the latter to be expected, perhaps, but unedifying.

All this fails to alter the inescapable fact that he was being tested within a few months of taking office as chief minister and within two days of being elected an MLA. He had never held elective office before and had taken oath as an MLA for the first time on 25 February. But that is no excuse. The riots took place on his watch and they were to haunt him for the next decade and more.

Part of this was a campaign of vilification, unprecedented in scale and viciousness, that was launched against him by his political opponents, activists and NGOs. Some of the allegations were important because they sought justice for the victims of the carnage. Others were designed to malign and end the BJP's rule in Gujarat – and Modi's political career that threatened the established order.

The report by Justice Tewatia, former chief justice of the Calcutta and the Punjab and Haryana High Courts, was incandescent about the destructive and inflammatory role of the media during the riots. He described its sensationalism, muckraking and sheer misinformation as contributing to the death toll. A prime example, and one that is commonly thrown in Modi's face as proof of his complicity, came on the evening of 1 March.

Modi had delivered a press statement, and agreed afterwards to a ten-minute interview with Sudhir Chaudhary, a Zee News correspondent (as he then was) at the Circuit House in Gandhinagar. During the course of the interview the murder of Ehsan Jafri at Gulbarg Society the previous day was discussed. Modi, attempting to describe how the terrible cycle of brutality perpetuated itself, said: 'A chain of action-reaction is going on.'

This was subsequently broadcast amidst much agonized, self-righteous editorializing about how Modi was justifying the violence of Hindus against Muslims. First there was Godhra, then there were riots as a natural 'reaction'.

But what Modi *actually* said had been misleadingly edited, so that, when the interview was broadcast, the crucial sentence at the end of Modi's initial statement – a sentence that would change its meaning entirely – was simply chopped off. What Modi said in full was: 'A chain of action-reaction is going on. We want that there should be neither "action" nor "reaction".' ('Kriya pratikriya ki chain chal rahi hai. Hum chahate hain ki na kriya ho aur na pratikriya.')[38]

This sentence, deliberately rendered incomplete, became the staple for those who condemned Modi for either not doing enough to stop the riots or actually being complicit in encouraging them. The missed sentence was rarely referred to.

The writer Arundhati Roy asserted that a pregnant Muslim woman had been murdered and then her foetus ripped from her womb by rioters. When it became clear that nobody knew of the incident and Roy was asked to come and help the police inquiry to find the unfortunate victim, she replied through her lawyers that there was no power which could compel her to attend. She claimed in addition that Ehsan Jafri's daughters had been murdered alongside him at Gulbarg Society. This prompted Jafri's son to write from the United States that there was only one daughter and she was in the US with him.

Roy's response was, as ever, dismissive:

> This and other genuine errors in recounting the details of the violence in Gujarat in no way alters the substance of what journalists, fact-finding missions or writers like myself are saying.[39]

It was the Chaudhary interview though that began a decade-long saga of inaccuracy and slander that appears to be a source of pride to Modi's opponents.

In the press statement prior to the Chaudhary interview, Modi had announced that now – with firepower at his command – a shoot-at-sight policy was being introduced for lawbreaking and rioters. In sum, 10,500 rounds were fired and 15,000 teargas shells expended. This led to the deaths of more than 100 people, the majority of whom were Hindus.

It is a statistic that tells its own story.

Hours after the first death due to rioting, Modi – with George Fernandes alongside him (and whose car was later set alight by rioters) – had put the authorities in combat mode against the marauding mob, assisting the army with trucks, communications and, most important of all, thirty-two executive magistrates, who alone could authorize firing of live ammunition.

By 11 a.m. on 1 March soldiers were patrolling Ahmedabad in areas such as Paldi, Juhapura, Vejalpur, Shahpur, Bapunagar, Rakhial, Gomtipur, Meghaninagar, Dariapur, Kalupur, Naroda and Danilimda. But by then, a murderous attack on Vadodara's Best Bakery on 1 March had caused more than a dozen fatalities.

Within hours, nine columns were on the streets. Immediately, the tide began to turn against the rioters.[40]

The effect of Modi's swift action is demonstrated by the death toll: the vast majority of the killings – 741 out of 1,044 – occurred during the first week of several months of increasingly intermittent clashes. Of those first 741 deaths, 611 took place in the very first three days and included the most notorious massacres at Naroda Patiya, Best Bakery and Gulbarg Society.

Soldiers, meanwhile, continued to pour into Gujarat. The first of fourteen military transports landed at Rajkot in the early hours of 2 March. Troops were also in Godhra by early afternoon and in Vadodara by dusk. That Saturday, 2 March, the shoot-at-sight order had already been executed twelve times, with eight Hindus and four Muslim casualties. This had an immediate effect on quelling mob behaviour. Preventative arrests – over 700 people on that day alone – were also removing rogue elements off the streets. Records show that 482 Hindus and 229 Muslims were arrested for lawbreaking on Saturday, 2 March 2002. By the end of the riots, 66,268 Hindus and 10,861 Muslims had been detained[41] – reflecting the composition of Gujarat's population and indicating an absence of bias on the part of the authorities.

There was an outpouring of rage from Hindus immediately after the Godhra Junction atrocity. But the pattern of conflict soon modified. Muslims began fighting back in pitched battles and attacking Hindu areas such as Bapunagar, in Ahmedabad, as early as 28 February. Later, from mid-March, well-organized rioting by Muslims was seen in towns such as Bharuch. In Modasa, a centre of jihadi fundamentalism where 123 activists of the Students Islamic Movement of India (SIMI) had been arrested only a month earlier, a mob of 1,000 Muslims went on the rampage.[42]

In 2002, a narrow but corrosive seam of extremist Wahabbi fundamentalism, supported and funded by Pakistan, existed across Gujarat. Its adherents were determined to advance what Godhra had started but as the weeks went by their influence shrank. It grew more and more localized, brought to heel by law enforcement. Yet such was the tone of reporting in the media that one could easily remain ignorant about the 254 Hindus who died in the rioting and the 40,000 left homeless after Muslim mobs attacked their dwellings and businesses with petrol bombs.

After the rioting had been quelled, attention turned to rehabilitation. The relief centres, though unpleasant for those who were forced to dwell in them, had free sanitary and health services including regular health check-ups. And yet the makeshift ghettos Muslims were forced into evoked sharp criticism.

A report in April 2002 from the World Health Organization (WHO), however, commended the specialist services in the Gujarat camps including their psychological support, the chlorination and hygiene measures that had successfully kept infectious and waterborne diseases at bay, and the effective immunization programme.[43]

Many NGOs, meanwhile, incensed by the brutality of the riots and the condition of some Muslim colonies, petitioned the courts to prosecute Modi. However, every single petition was rejected. The Gujarat High Court, instead, issued a commendation which stated: 'The efforts put in by the State Government in this behalf, as indicated above, are required to be appreciated.'[44]

The administration, meanwhile, set about ensuring that students would be able to take their annual board examinations even if they had to be transported to the exam rooms from relief camps.[45] A huge operation was set up to allow this to happen, during the first phase of exams in March 2002 while some violence was still ongoing.

That month 900,000 students sat in 1,000 exam centres, with fresh exams for students from the worst affected areas of Ahmedabad and Vadodara rescheduled for mid-April. These arrangements were also used by Muslim students: they clearly wanted to take their exams because they braved bullying by extremist Islamists and even broke a fatwa to further their education and prospects, as was reported in *India Today*:

> Last week, in a move that provoked widespread derision, a group of Muslim leaders, dominated by the Congress and under the influence of the radical Tableeghi Jamaat, called for a boycott of the rescheduled high school examinations. The boycott failed but ended up reinforcing Modi's insinuation that a 'conspiracy' stands between Gujarat and normalcy.[46]

In the end, despite intimidation from within their own communities, 9,000 out of 14,000 Muslim students sat for their exams. These determined and hard-working young Muslims would prove to be very much part of Gujarat's future over the next decade.

Why had the Sabarmati Express been attacked in such a frenzied and lethal manner and – always the essential question – why then? Chronology again being the first element of deduction, the order of events preceding the 27 February atrocity at Godhra Junction needs to be outlined.

There was a historical and geopolitical context in late 2001 and early 2002. Only a matter of months had elapsed since al-Qaeda terrorists hijacked two jetliners in September 2001 and flew them into the twin towers of the World Trade Center in New York, killing over 1,500 people.

In Delhi, meanwhile, in December 2001, terrorists stormed Parliament, killing several security guards before they were gunned down. 'Pakistani nationals' were identified as responsible from documents found on their corpses – documents clearly intended to be discovered. Ten weeks later the slaughter at Godhra occurred, on the very day that the United States began a major bombing blitz on Kabul.

The spike in Islamic fundamentalist terror in India after 9/11 coincided with the United States' rapid military mobilization against the Taliban government sheltering Osama Bin Laden in Afghanistan – a development that raised the level of paranoia in the Pakistani government and in its Inter-Services Intelligence (ISI).

Pakistan, as a narrow strip of territory running roughly north–south, regards the deep expanse of Afghanistan as its fallback position ('strategic depth') in the event of open conflict on its eastern border with India. To have its 'back door' slammed shut by the US/NATO military's presence in Afghanistan provoked a feeling of claustrophobia, and it lashed out at India through its terror proxies.

All its wars with India had been both started and lost by Pakistan. In terms of men and material it was outnumbered nine to one, and had learned by this time that infiltration was more effective than war at keeping its neighbour off balance. This was the thinking behind the ISI's terror attack on Indian Parliament and other atrocities.

By February over half a million Indian troops were deployed along the border in a tense eyeball-to-eyeball confrontation with their Pakistani counterparts. It looked bad, but neither army was likely to receive political assent to launch an attack. Terrorism, though, for Pakistan remained an option.[47] The ISI needed to engineer a further act to neutralize India's ability to threaten Pakistan at that delicate point in time.[48] Godhra would succeed in this beyond all expectations, reaping dividends even today, more than a decade later.

Evidence soon began to appear that indicated deliberate preparation for carnage far beyond mere sabotage of fire tenders.

It was lucky, for example, that the Sabarmati Express was nearly five hours late. The previous night a mob had foregathered in anticipation of its arrival at the station but dispersed after the delay was discovered. Under cover of the night far more damage could have been inflicted, and this led Justice Tewatia to conclude that the planned attack was in the nature of a terrorist operation in its clinical planning and execution. 'The intention of the mob was to put to death *all* the pilgrims travelling by the Sabarmati Express.'[49]

The mob dutifully reassembled at exactly the time of the Sabarmati Express's revised arrival. This required coordination. The report of Justice Tewatia and his colleagues, not long after the event, noted strange movements in the town immediately before the atrocity. The Nanavati Inquiry later supplied exhaustive detail. For example, there had been a sudden increase in the number of firearms licences issued. A number of unemployed Muslims in the area appeared to have recently acquired mobile telephones. Outsiders, lacking ration cards, seemed to have flooded into town in the days prior to the train arson. There was a noticeable growth in the size of the local population in the period leading up to the attack. This coincided with several religious gatherings attended by foreigners.

The local conspirators are now well-known and have been punished. But who set them in motion in liaison with terrorist agents? These contacts, the Nanavati Inquiry concluded, had travelled south to Godhra from Jammu and Kashmir. While the Kashmiri contacts (Ghulam Nabi Dingoo and Ali Mohammad) allowed triangulation with Karachi, they would at the same time be used as 'cut-outs' from the ISI end of the operation, providing it deniability.[50]

This view was shared by Modi's own security advisor, K.P.S. Gill, appointed at the beginning of May 2002. He was Punjab's director general of police who had tamed the terrorism unleashed by the Khalistani secessionist movement in the 1980s. The ISI had been an active abettor of terrorism in the border state of Punjab. Gill was a leading expert on security and intelligence. Modi specifically asked for him, according to then Union home minister I.D. Swamy. Gill examined the evidence and made up his own mind fairly quickly about who had been the prime mover behind the carnage – the ISI, he said, using Kashmiri infiltrators.[51]

Godhra presented a cheap, good-value operation from Pakistan's point of view. Gujarat was fertile ground for unrest. Its Muslims had grown increasingly disenchanted during the 1980s as the textile sector in the state, where many were employed, shrank from sixty-four to only twelve operating mills.[52] The industrial contraction threw large numbers of shift workers into desperate unemployment. The economic depredation among the state's Muslims had hardly improved over the subsequent decade and there was a reservoir of resentment and fear among the Muslims of Godhra that could readily be tapped.

Next was the timing of the operation. It has been pointed out that trainloads of kar sevaks had been commuting to and from Ayodhya for over a month by late February 2002. Many more excursions were planned. But why choose this particular train? Indeed, this was one of the arguments that had been raised against a conspiracy (and in favour of an accident because of a cooking fire on board) before overwhelming physical evidence disproved it.

The Sabarmati Express still runs three times a week. But the train passing through Godhra Junction, scheduled for the early hours of 27 February 2002, was the one closest to the date of the appointment of the new BJP chief minister – supposed apostle of Hindutva, alleged enemy of Muslims and architect of Advani's Ram Rath Yatra in 1990.

Modi had delivered an anti-terrorism statement in the wake of the 9/11 attacks in New York not long before he departed Delhi to return to Gujarat. In the speech he had called for the banning of SIMI because it supported al-Qaeda and had been involved in engineering communal riots in several Indian states.[53] It was banned shortly thereafter.

Given that only a month before, as has been mentioned, 123 SIMI activists had been arrested in nearby Modasa, what better moment for giving Modi, sworn in recently as chief minister, a taste of what he was up against? And what more symbolic insult than setting fire to the Sabarmati Express carrying kar sevaks from Ayodhya where the Babri Masjid had been brought down by kar sevaks a decade ago?

The aim of the militants was not only to spill Hindu blood but Muslim blood as well. Godhra was merely 'a sprat to catch a mackerel', a goading of the Hindus to set off an entirely predictable and much wider conflagration. Thus the operation against the Sabarmati Express was launched in cynical disregard for the well-being of the state's Muslims. Never mind that most of the victims were poor and illiterate migrants working in Gujarat to support their families back home.

As a dispassionate observer, and after a year of detailed research, it is clear to me at least that, from the beginning, the narrative of 2002 has lacked balance and objectivity. Facts were the first victim. The initial bulletins almost all declined to describe the mob as Muslim (even in 2011 Patrick French would use the modifier 'reportedly', despite the conspirators and many of their accomplices already being convicted). It was well known that Godhra was a densely Muslim area, and a pretty volatile one at that. Nonetheless, reports of the Godhra atrocity mostly failed to detail the bare but indisputable facts. *The Asian Age* wrote of a mob 'reportedly belonging to a minority community' attacking the train, with the result that 'several' – rather than fifty-nine – passengers died. *The Times of India* also mentioned a strangely anonymous mob, but in *The Hindu* it was only 'a group of people' and on NDTV the reportage described the attackers as 'unidentified persons'.[54]

Even though the attackers were a mystery the reporters still seemed to know accurately the identity of the passengers aboard the train. Justice Tewatia's report concluded: 'Most of the national newspapers and news channels played down the intensity of the Godhra carnage and projected it as a result of provocation by pilgrims.'[55]

One counterpoint was that kar sevaks in the train had attacked Muslim vendors on the station platform. Another version said there had been an attempt to kidnap a young Muslim girl and drag her aboard the train full of families. The Nanavati report not only disproved the claims of assault on vendors, but went into minute detail concerning the accusation made about molestation of the young girl.

Her name was Sofiabanu.

While the Sabarmati Express paused at Godhra station a cry had gone up that a Ghanchi Muslim girl, Sofiabanu, had been abducted by Ramsevaks. It came from Salim Panwala, who ran up and down the platform repeating the claim and inciting the crowd to attack the train. But it was proved Sofiabanu was not even at the station that day; the first time she stated that a Hindu had attempted to grab her was quite a while later, after she was delivered by 'somebody from her caste' to the Iqbal School, where a relief centre had been set up. As the Nanavati Commission drily put it: 'Under the circumstances, it becomes doubtful and suspicious why somebody had approached her after about five days and taken her to a relief camp and that too at the time when press reporters were present.'[56]

The Commission dismantled her story piece by piece in paragraphs 67 and 68 of its report. For example, the bit of platform where Sofiabanu claimed she was attacked (by 'saffron people' shouting 'Jai Bajrang') was in the middle of where Muslim vendors, railway staff and RPF officers were congregated. Not only did nobody notice at the time, but she never told anyone about the incident – until she was presented to the press five days later.

The man who raised the alarm over the abduction of the girl-who-was-not-there was the same man who the previous evening had bought and stockpiled the 140 litres of gasoline used moments later to incinerate the passengers in coach S-6. The Commission also noted that as Salim Panwala ran along the platform shouting his alarums, his associates Mohammad Latika and Sidik Bakar, making the most of the opportunity afforded by Panwala's diversion, 'had gone running near the open space towards the engine side' from where they could hold on as the train departed and then pull the emergency chain as it approached the awaiting mob. They were all later found guilty.

Like so many false witness statements surrounding the events in February 2002 – including those later coerced, tutored and paid for by egregious human rights activists – Sofiabanu's statement has gone down in history as part of the tapestry of demonstrable untruths that have vitiated a sensible, objective and balanced debate on the tragic events of those days.

One particularly motivated charge is that the train fire at Godhra Junction was started either as the result of an electrical short circuit or passengers cooking in the cramped carriage and had nothing to do with a mob throwing petrol bombs at the train. This account was dismissed multiple times – by the Justice Tewatia Committee, the Special Investigation Team (SIT) and the Supreme Court that reviewed its report, as well as by the Nanavati Commission. Forensic scientists demonstrated, according to the laws of physics, exactly how the combustible accelerant thrown into the train carriage by the accused spread and did its deadly work.

Only one investigation, the Banerjee Committee of 2004, consisting of a single judge in Bihar sitting at the request of Lalu

Prasad Yadav – who needed the local Muslim vote for an upcoming election – decided that the attacking mob had nothing to do with the fire. The Banerjee report when published, two days before Lalu's vital election, was widely discredited for its one-sidedness. It, however, remains a potent weapon in the hands of those who regard, rightly or wrongly, the Modi administration as being either complicit or at the very least negligent in the matter of the riots.[57]

All this should not minimize the real horror of Muslim suffering – and Hindu suffering too – in the days and even months after the riots. But to ignore incontrovertible, documented facts and instead purvey unconfirmed, motivated accounts is both unprofessional and indefensible.

According to one such account, the Godhra atrocity preceding the riots was either an 'accident' or the result of provocation by Ramsevak hooligans. Justice Tewatia, after observing that 'the editorial pages of local and regional newspapers maintained a balance in projecting all viewpoints', went on to say: 'Newspapers published in English from Delhi invariably editorialized the news. Direct and indirect comments in the news writing were so telling that the personal likes and dislikes of the news reporters were too obvious to be missed.'

What exactly were these likes and dislikes? Justice Tewatia carefully enumerated them:

English language newspapers published from Delhi appeared to have assumed the role of crusaders against the State Government from day one. It coloured the entire operation of news gathering, feature writing and editorials.

The edit pages of English language press carried comments that clearly indicated biases:

- Against the State Government of Gujarat,

- In favour of Congress, leftist parties and the secularist intellectuals,

- Indifferent to the carnage at Godhra,
- Against the Hindu organizations, and
- Against the NDA government at the Centre.

Using unusually candid language, Justice Tewatia also charged that a large number of editorials and articles 'projected Godhra as a reaction to provocation by kar sevaks and riots in the rest of the state as "state sponsored terrorism"'. TV channels ignored warnings from officials 'and kept telecasting communal riots like infotainment' and in doing so 'contributed in spreading the tension to unaffected areas'.[58]

Disinformation was rampant. For example, in early March 2002 there were protests about the initial level of victim compensation. Money for the families of the dead at Godhra had been increased, while the amount paid to Muslims remained pegged at the previous amount. The Gujarat government quickly admitted the fault and announced on 9 March that the entitlement of every victim, Hindu or Muslim, would be equal. One month later a Congress politician visiting the US was still loudly denouncing the discrepancy. Although his accusation was reported in the press, no journalist pointed out what they very well knew: that it was no longer true.

Anger among locals was meanwhile beginning to come to a boil, but not against minorities. Justice Tewatia had become 'alarmed at the intensity of hostile attitude among the people of the state for the Delhi press and television news channels ... Even the Tribals [victims of Muslim aggression before and during the riots] complained that the media had no time to hear the tale of their agony and was spreading canards against the Hindus.' He concluded that 'Telecasting images that spread hatred and instigated violence is unhealthy, but their repeated telecast is lethal. The media acted as an interested party in the confrontation, not a neutral reporter of facts.'[59]

The one element of the riots that truly united Gujaratis in anger was this sort of reportage which sought to portray them as saffron stormtroopers and their chief minister as a genocidal mastermind. The fury was felt by both BJP- and Congress-supporting Hindus, and by a significant number of civic-minded Muslims – of whom there were very many more than the media calculated. As a whole the population felt humiliated by the attitude of several TV channels and newspapers as well as politicians in Delhi.

Out of power in 2002 for six years, the Congress under party president Sonia Gandhi had seen in Modi and the 2002 riots two dangers. One, the emergence of a strong nationalist leader. Two, the potential of 2002 to polarize voters in Gujarat and later across India in the BJP's favour. Shrewd and single-minded, Sonia and her advisors decided to treat Modi as a key future electoral threat to Congress hegemony. An ecosystem of activists and media to demonize him relentlessly soon emerged. Modi's success carried too high a price.

While it is important to rebalance slanted reportage around the 2002 Gujarat riots, the unavoidable truth is that Modi was chief minister and the carnage happened on his watch. He has always refused to apologize in the form of words demanded by many reasonable people but that does not mean he feels no remorse or responsibility, for guilt is not the same as responsibility. There is plenty to suggest that it was the most shocking episode of his life and that Modi was shattered by the experience as he desperately attempted to deal with the rapidly unfolding events. Even without the hostility of the media and politicians he was a man alone, and he was forced to call on all his reserves of character to hold himself together.

But the reason for his refusal to apologize, while it may owe something to politics – the Right would slay him, as Modi himself has pointed out – is mainly that he believes an apology accomplishes

Young Narendra, a boy
with dreams

Narendra, a young cadet

As an RSS pracharak

Sharing a meal
with co-pracharaks

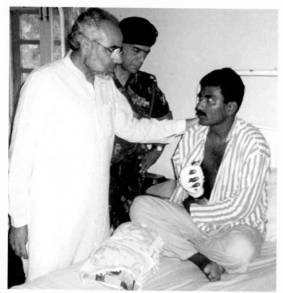

Comforting jawans in Kargil

Interacting with children in a Gujarat school

With specially abled girls at the airport

A quiet moment with Sri Sri Ravi Shankar

Greeting the Dalai Lama

With the late Syedna Saheb

With Amritanandamayi (Amma)

With Sathya Sai Baba

A mass leader

Meeting the governor of
Astrakhan (Russia)

In discussion with former President
A.P.J. Abdul Kalam

In conversation with President
Pranab Mukherjee

With senior BJP leader Lal Krishna Advani

Standing behind Prime Minister Atal Bihari
Vajpayee and Russian President Vladimir Putin

Meeting N.R. Narayana Murthy, Executive Chairman, Infosys

With Lata Mangeshkar's family

Speaking animatedly with Amitabh Bachchan

During a visit to China

On a visit to South Korea

With Japanese Prime Minister Shinzo Abe

Model of the ambitious Gift City project

At the inauguration of the new solar park, Khadoda

With mother Hiraben

nothing. His enemies on the Left would only redouble their efforts to condemn and convict him. He says that if he is guilty he should be hanged. He means it. Speaking in 2003, Modi reflected:

> This blot happened during my tenure and I have to wash it off. People told us Modi never says sorry. I said, what does sorry mean? We have a criminal justice system in this country which does not accept sorry. What will Narendra Modi's sorry mean to us? We will judge his sorry from his actual doings.[60]

Although the deaths from the riots occurred during his tenure and although he must carry the remorse for the rest of his life, the facts show that Modi did not want them to happen, did not help them to happen, and did everything within his power as quickly as he could to stop them happening. It is irrelevant to him that he performed better than any Congress chief minister.

In our lengthy and candid conversations, where neither he nor I held anything back, the subject came up often but his answer was always: 'I feel sad about what happened but no guilt. And no court has come even close to establishing it.' That is true. No FIR or chargesheet has been filed against Modi in over a decade since the riots, and the Supreme Court–monitored SIT has exonerated him, though legal challenges continue in the lower courts.

Modi learned the hard way in 2002 that part of leadership, as anthropologists tell us, is sometimes to be a sacrifice or scapegoat. This is what is meant when it is said that all political careers end in failure, because a politician eventually always suffers for the wrongdoing of others if not for his own. Except in Modi's case the career was not yet over.

Modi says he wanted to wash the blot away publicly by virtue of his future actions, and deal with his remorse privately. On the other hand, he was increasingly beginning to feel that his presence as chief minister of Gujarat was not helping its people.

Leaders have no friends when things go badly wrong, and this was the position Modi found himself in following the 2002 riots when his party, completely rationally, was mulling the idea of asking him to step down. The BJP national executive was due to meet in Panaji, Goa, on 12 April 2002, and everybody knew what – or rather whom – the unofficial focus would be on.

Vajpayee, despite all that had happened, had not condescended to visit Gujarat until 4 April and apologized for his tardiness when at last he arrived. He had a message for Modi that the chief minister should 'follow rajdharma', which of course means that a ruler should treat all of his subjects equally and without prejudice. Modi quietly replied, 'Even I am doing so.'[61]

This can either be seen as an affectionate exchange between a prime minister and his younger protégé or as a deadly warning. It was neither. Vajpayee simply implied in his avuncular way that if Modi were to survive politically he would have to ensure peace in the state. There was no second option on the table.

Vajpayee's visit would certainly have underlined to Modi the danger his career was in. Yet on his home ground of Gujarat, Modi was not wrong in thinking that there was a groundswell of support for him. Modi would also have been correct in believing that he had a chance of survival at home, if not in Goa, where big problems could await him.

But did Modi particularly want to survive? The truth was, he confided to me, possibly for the first time in an on-the-record interview, that he no longer wanted to be chief minister after the riots because he had decided it was unfair on the people of the state, who were being subjected to extreme abuse in the media because of him. Modi thought it would be better to offer his resignation in Goa, and that was exactly what he intended to do.

The results were not what he expected.

On arrival in Goa, when all were foregathered the first afternoon, Modi announced, 'I would prefer to sit here as a general executive member and not as a chief minister.' This was not officially a resignation but was as close to one as could be, and it set the cat among the pigeons. Instead of reconvening the morning after the inaugural meeting, the BJP national executive decided to begin its order of business that very evening – lest a night of plot and counterplot, rumour and faction-mongering throw the conference into chaos and result in unpredictable casualties.

Modi's resolve to step down was clear. BJP president Jana Krishnamurthi then delivered a mildly panic-stricken speech condemning 'the hue and cry of those who demanded the head of the CM'. Krishnamurthi was referring to the media and the Congress but Modi now knew he was also betraying the feelings of some in the party. The president followed up with some boilerplate rhetoric about being tough on terror and the causes of terror but Modi was not interested in listening.

He waited politely until the president had finished and then stood to deliver his short speech:

> I want to speak on Gujarat. From the party's point of view this is a grave issue. There is a need for a free and frank discussion. To enable this, I wish to place my resignation before this body. It is time we decided what direction the party and the country should take from this point onwards.

Modi couldn't make it any more plain: he wanted to resign. He was prepared to leave the room as an ex-chief minister and continue as a party worker. At this point it was what he wanted: he had had enough. 'But the background is this,' he told me. 'I wanted to leave this position but my party was not ready to leave me, the people of Gujarat were not ready to leave me – this situation is what I had (to deal with). It was not up to me. And I was not ready to go against party discipline; I don't want to fight against my party. What my leaders say, I must follow it.'

The BJP had to calculate what consequences might ensue from Modi's resignation, including renewed communal chaos in Gujarat, quiescent after the riots, and national humiliation for the party.

Modi had inadvertently conjured an existential moment for the BJP. His offer of resignation had the effect of revealing to his colleagues that the future was in their hands. They all knew the true background of the riots – Krishnamurthi had announced in support of Modi that the fingerprints of the ISI were all over Godhra. Now the assembly had to decide whether they were happy to be lectured about Hindu brutality by the Congress–media conglomerate, whose brand of secularism they believed pandered to sectarianism, or whether they were going to take a stand on behalf of Modi.

Prime Minister Vajpayee suggested that it might be better to wait until the next day to make a decision on Modi's offer but Pramod Mahajan, then parliamentary affairs minister, backed up by Sanjay Joshi, who briefly overcame his loathing of Modi in the emerging spirit of the hour, insisted a decision be taken immediately. Soon, even Vajpayee had breathed in the electrifying atmosphere, and one journalist describes how, suddenly and miraculously young at heart, 'he delivered a speech that could have been a replay from his heady Jan Sangh days'.[62]

Modi's resignation was rejected. The Goa session closed and as a stream of leaders headed back to the airport, *The Indian Express* breathlessly wrote on 16 April: 'Hardline Hindutva is back on the party's agenda, but there's a new face – Narendra Modi.'[63]

But the *Express* had got it wrong. What came out of Goa may have been a rejuvenated Modi, but it certainly was not hard-line Hindutva. Having assented to the will of his party and withdrawn his resignation, Modi was deliberating his next step. It involved dissolving the state assembly and seeking a fresh mandate for his leadership.

> Within three or four weeks, after brainstorming, thinking, thinking
> – I never discussed it till then with any of my colleagues – we had
> a cabinet meeting. In the cabinet meeting I put this resolution,
> and all my cabinet colleagues accepted it, that we will dissolve the
> government.[64]

He concluded that leaving it to the voters would be the best, most democratic way to decide his future. He had already stepped back, detached, and was content to let events now take their course.

For the time being Modi carried on as chief minister and life in Gujarat returned to normal with surprising calm over the summer and monsoon. It seemed as if a poisonous gas, long bottled up, had escaped and dispersed upwards and away. There was something different about the state in the aftermath of the bloodshed that was hard to put one's finger on. The riots were terrible, but similar to countless others that had gone before.

Something was different; but something else was the same. On 24 September 2002, less than seven months since the Sabarmati Express had burned, Islamist terrorists struck again in Gujarat.

The Akshardham Temple in Gandhinagar, a stone's throw from the chief minister's bungalow, is a popular tourist attraction. It encloses a seven-foot-high gold-leaf–covered murti of Lord Swaminarayan. Outside the shrine and within a fenced perimeter is the Sahajanand Van, a blend of contemplative garden and children's park including rides and games, a herbal garden, a lake and waterfall. It was consecrated in November 1992.

At four-thirty on that peaceful September afternoon, two heavily armed terrorists scaled the fence and once inside began shooting indiscriminately and throwing hand grenades at families enjoying the gardens. In all twenty-nine men, women and children died along with the two terrorists who were shot after a night-long firefight with National Security Guard (NSG) commandos swiftly flown in from Delhi. One commando and one state police officer also died. Seventy people were wounded.

And nothing happened. There were no riots, no massacres, no communal uprisings at all. An investigation proceeded and conspirators were arrested – yet again, the fingerprints of the ISI were all over the attack – and the law took its course. The people and the government conducted themselves in a civil and mature manner despite their grief and anger, as Modi had pleaded with them to do back in February. Pramukh Swami Maharaj, the spiritual leader of the temple, asked for clemency for the accused.[65]

Something had definitely changed in Gujarat, and much more was about to change.

8

FIGHTING FOR GUJARAT

The image that has been built, that I went into a reactive
mode because of Godhra, is wrong.
— Narendra Modi

N THE MONTHS AFTER the post-Godhra riots, normality appeared
to resume. The worst of the riots were over and 122 out of 129
relief camps had been closed.[1] But to Modi's mind a fresh start
demanded a fresh election. In July 2002, having mulled over it since
returning disappointed from Goa, he dissolved the state assembly: if
the BJP wouldn't allow him to resign, the will of the people might
still release him. He would abide by their decision.

Modi's position within the BJP was settled for the time being,
but he wanted to renew his mandate in Gujarat — to discover
whether its people, who had borne so much trauma, were content
to retain the chief minister who had been universally blamed for it
in the media. 'I am not saying I want to be in power. I am already
chief minister. I want elections because allegations have been hurled
at me,' he told *Outlook* on 20 September. Modi was in search of
redemption and the polling booth was where he naturally went to

seek it. Many said there was cynical calculation behind the move: Gujarat's post-riot polarized environment presented a unique electoral opportunity.

Modi's growing legion of opponents had of course been incessantly calling on him to resign in the wake of the riots. But as soon as he volunteered to resign, they changed their tune.[2] The Congress suddenly realized that Modi was very popular among Gujaratis and began to worry that a snap election could put him back in power for another five years. This was unthinkable, and therefore his opponents decided that elections must not be allowed to take place until much later, possibly in 2003. They argued that the state was still in chaos and fair elections could not be organized under such circumstances.

Modi's new security advisor K.P.S. Gill had by now been in Gujarat for over a month and felt differently. 'Today, I feel the shock about Godhra is over. There is a realization that there should be peace in the state,' he told a journalist who interviewed him on 20 May. 'The desire has come into the minds of people, and converting that desire into actuality is not a difficult task ... The state can face an election. Because if you look at the state today, the disturbed areas are very limited.' He added that if Godhra had happened in 1992, 'the whole of UP, Bihar and Rajasthan would have gone up in flames. This time it has not happened.'[3]

Gill's point that 'the process of an election reasserts democracy' was pertinent. Given how loudly Modi's resignation was being called for by voices in the press, the Opposition and even in sections of the Central government, the polity of Gujarat was in danger of being undermined. A fresh election would settle the matter and allow the state finally to return to normal.

The latest sitting of the state assembly had been in April 2002 and elections were traditionally called within six months of the previous legislative session. This spelled out a timetable for elections to take place some time in October 2002. Modi knew very well it was best to take advantage of the popularity he now enjoyed before it dissipated. If his planned programme of economic reforms and development was successful, it would add to his electability, but only after a considerable period of time had elapsed. Now was the time to go to the people.

❧

The Congress, not surprisingly, wanted to postpone elections for as long as possible. Despite, or perhaps because of, Gill's wise summation of the situation on the ground, a team headed by the chief election commissioner (CEC) was dispatched from Delhi. It declared that under present conditions voting was impossible.

'I said, "That is not fair to me,"' Modi recalls. '"I do not want to be in this post, we must do something." But it was a constitutional compulsion that I had to carry on as chief minister for six more months.'

The Election Commission ruling was based on the assertion that minorities, comprising 10 per cent of the state's population, were deemed unlikely to vote, even though 95 per cent of them were by this point back at home rather than in relief camps.[4]

The CEC, J.M. Lyngdoh, would not reveal how he arrived at his conclusion. Modi though saw the situation as clear-cut:

> For several months, the Opposition has been after me to resign. When I did, they did not know what to do and started running to Delhi to seek Madam's help. They realized that James Michael Lyngdoh, the Chief Election Commissioner of India, is their only saviour.[5]

At any rate, Lyngdoh now found himself in a battle of wits with Modi. Lyngdoh may have had the power, but Modi had the guile. Lyngdoh was likely a prisoner of the widespread assumptions, kept alive over the years, that Gujarat was deeply communalized by the riots. But a dystopian economic and social landscape was a long way from the truth. Again, in the interests of objectivity, we must divine the facts.

On 29 April 2002, *India Today* reported: 'According to estimates by the Gujarat Chamber of Commerce and Industry (GCCI), the loss to commerce and industry is a whopping Rs 10,000 crore.' Businesses were apparently on their knees, with hoteliers particularly affected: 'So severe is the impact of the violence that many of the hotels face certain closure,' said one owner, claiming that occupancy rates were down from 70 per cent to 20 per cent. Ten thousand hotel workers were soon to be cast out of jobs amidst immediate financial losses to the industry of over Rs 250 crore, according to Narinder Saini, general manager of Class Gold Hotel.[6]

This is how it may well have looked amidst the flames of the first week of rioting, when the future appeared bleak. But the GCCI soon revised its figures in light of the swift end to most of the violence and a return to near normality. It concluded that 15 per cent of small and medium enterprises (SMEs) had been affected to various extents, but that the vast majority had carried on trading as normal.[7] The hotel business did not lose the Rs 250 crore it had feared, and instead of 600 establishments it found that only 220 had suffered, incurring losses of just Rs 10 crore – a small fraction of the hoteliers' guesstimate in the first ten days after the riots.

In all, 4,767 insurance claims – a somewhat reliable means of measuring actual losses – were registered, adding up to Rs 168 crore rather than the feared rupees ten thousand crore! Clearly there were many personal, uninsured losses, but not from businesses. Some analysts argued that banking statistics underline the resilience of the economy in the heaviest period of rioting in February–March 2002. If the levels of banking activity – numbers of cheques cleared and amount of funds transferred between accounts – are compared pre- and post-Godhra, the figures are similar in terms of money velocity. Total cash dropped only slightly from about Rs 17,700 crore to Rs 16,700 crore.

These are dry and bloodless numbers and take no account of what the dreadful situation looked and felt like at the time. But they are hard figures, and show that the situation by no means approached Armageddon. Fewer cars were sold in March–April 2002, down to 1,000 from an expected 3,000, because nobody wanted to buy a car only to see it go up in flames. But when the riots ended the delayed purchases were made, and overall sales stayed much the same subsequently.

Similarly, Gujarat's second biggest share of overall national investment remained steady at a little over 16 per cent in 2002.[8] Reading contemporary media reports one can detect how every negative statistic was slightly exaggerated and spun. For example, the GCCI's hoteliers said occupancy rates had fallen to 20 per cent, whereas *The Hindu* of 5 May changed it to 10 per cent.

Modi had this to say on the matter in an interview some time later:

> You must keep in mind that after Godhra, not for a single day did any industry remain closed. No banks were closed for even a day after the incidents; this is the reason why I say that any evaluation of my tenure cannot be done on the basis of what has been written or said in the media. What should be the parameter of evaluation – did schools run, were exams held, did shops stay open, did markets remain vibrant? Everything was running but still there was so much (of a) negative campaign.[9]

If Gujarat was still open for business, the next item on the critics' agenda was future investment which must surely have been derailed, for what sane businessman would dream of investing in a communal tinderbox?

As soon as he became chief minister in October 2001, Modi began to work assiduously towards holding a business–industry summit with a view to attracting new investment – especially foreign direct investment (FDI) – into the state. He involved the GCCI as well as its parent national federation, and attracted delegates from Asia, Europe and the US. It was titled Resurgent Gujarat and was the prototype of what would later be his series of larger, two-yearly Vibrant Gujarat summits. Modi had hosted it from 8 to 10 February 2002, a mere fortnight or so before Godhra.

In the wake of the bloodshed, it now appeared obvious to the media that investors would be rowing at full speed back to their own countries. *The Hindu* pointed out at the time that investment promises generated by the first Resurgent Gujarat summit, worth Rs 12,360 crore, would just about cover the losses incurred during the riots. Its analysts declared: 'Investors are not only likely to shy away from future investment but the existing industry may also leave the state.'[10] But three months after the riots foreign investors turned their boats around and announced new projects in Gujarat worth Rs 75,800 crore.[11]

The chief election commissioner's inflexibility over holding early elections meanwhile prompted an aggressive response from Modi that August, starting at a public meeting at Bodeli, near Vadodara, where Modi referred to him using his full name: *James Michael* Lyngdoh. This was deliberate. Lyngdoh, Modi was telling the people, was an 'outsider' who should not be allowed to order local Gujaratis around in such a way. Modi regarded Lyngdoh's attitude as elitist and supercilious. Lyngdoh's response to Modi, calling his words 'the gossip of menials', only added to this perception.[12]

When Arun Jaitley informed Lyngdoh of the Gujarat government's decision to dissolve the assembly on 19 July, Lyngdoh refused his subsequent request for early elections with the remark that Modi's was a 'discredited government'[13] and that the call was from 'a few mad people who were saying it without authority'.[14] As the icing on the cake he also called Gujarat officials 'a bunch of jokers'.[15]

Modi confirmed to me exclusively, and for the first time publicly: 'He told one of my officers he was a joker,' instantly recalling the incident twelve years later.

To Modi's ears this did not sound like impartiality, and it was certainly an odd way for a civil servant to express himself. His suspicion that the chief election commissioner was prejudiced against him, or at least against the BJP, increased when Lyngdoh decided that month, amidst 'wide publicity', to appeal to Gujaratis who had fled the state for other parts of India during the riots to vote from wherever they now were.

Modi says of Lyngdoh today:

> As far as a career officer, he was a good officer, but because of some political reasons, or because of the media perception, he had something against me ... he did what he could do, everything he could try. For the first time in the history of the Indian electoral system, under the rules and regulations, if you want to vote, you will have to go to a particular place to vote. But in my case he opened voting for the Gujarat assembly elections from anywhere in India.

Lyngdoh's rhetoric of 'taking into account the large-scale movement and migration of the affected people from the riot-torn areas to safer havens',[16] was disingenuous. It implied that Gujarat was indeed the combat-wracked wasteland the media had made it out to be several months after the riots. Modi suspected that Lyngdoh was utilizing a legal but rarely enforced rule to boost the anti-BJP vote when elections eventually took place – since those who had fled Gujarat were less likely to be sympathetic to him.

Modi pointed out with satisfaction that despite erecting polling booths across India for the state assembly elections, 'One cannot imagine this ... but what happened, not a single vote was cast outside the state.' This is interesting as it implies that there was very little traumatized migration away from the state after the riots, and that Lyngdoh's dedication to the image of chaos may indeed have been inaccurate.

Modi made a pointed reference to Jammu and Kashmir, whose elections Lyngdoh was also overseeing and where the situation was far worse: 'If elections could be held in the terrorist-infested state of Jammu and Kashmir, why not in Gujarat where normalcy has returned?'[17]

No answer came from Lyngdoh, but on 28 October 2002 the Supreme Court in Delhi issued a ruling. It said that because the Gujarat state assembly had been dissolved prematurely, the six-month mandate between sittings did not apply. This apparently undid Modi's ruse for a snap election, which did not now have to take place as soon as October.

Yet Chief Justice B.N. Kirpal also had some stern words for the Election Commission, which appeared to have inquired whether President's Rule could be imposed after a period of six months without a sitting of the state assembly. The Supreme Court bench observed that as there was no infraction of mandate to hold elections within six months of the latest sitting of the assembly, the application of Article 356 of the Indian Constitution did not arise.

The bench also thundered that Article 324 of the Indian Constitution casts a responsibility and duty on the Election Commission to hold polls 'at the earliest', adding that timely elections were the essence of democracy and that law and order should not be grounds for deferring them.[18] *The Hindu*, no friend of Modi, reviewing Lyngdoh's own account of the election, reported that 'Oddly, while Lyngdoh sets out the EC's case in detail, he glosses over the fact that the Supreme Court strongly disagreed ... Moreover, it held the EC's advice about the invocation of Article 356 as "gratuitous" and "misplaced".'[19] This final point referred to Lyngdoh's 'observation' concerning the possibility of President's Rule. If it was a political ruse to neuter the BJP in Gujarat, the Supreme Court was having none of it.

Elections were finally set for 12 December 2002, which still suited Modi. Critics complained that this would give Modi time to 'consolidate his Hindu vote bank'. This was obviously not entirely untrue.

In June, well before the decision of the Supreme Court, Modi had initiated preparations for a series of yatras designed to draw the people of Gujarat to support the BJP. Modi was a yatra veteran, even a yatra addict, having organized statewide, interstate and pan-national yatras in previous years. He knew the powerful political effect such multi-location, many-staged journeys could have, with their opportunities for remote voters to feel a close proximity to their leaders, and be reassured that their concerns were being listened to.

In June 2002, Modi flagged off the 125th Jagannath Rath Yatra. It set off on its 35-km route from the Jagannath temple in the Jamalpur Gate area of Ahmedabad on the morning of Friday, 12 June. The yatra was led by a dozen elephants and followed by thirty-three trucks carrying devotees, ten bhajan mandalis and fifteen sects of akharas, with supporters walking behind the chariots in a procession 1.5 km long.[20]

After that a Shobha Yatra was taken out in Rajkot on Janmashtami day (Krishna's birthday), 31 August, with a 'Fight against Terrorism' theme. This was well-timed, as it turned out, because the police soon after claimed to have foiled a plot to assassinate both Modi and VHP president Pravin Togadia. Its general secretary, Jaideep Patel, was shot and wounded on 3 December 2002.[21] It is telling that at this point some people still bracketed Modi and Togadia together. Within years, Togadia and the VHP would be marginalized in Gujarat by Modi whose antipathy towards religious extremism was not then widely recognized. He could have capitalized on majoritarian sentiment by aligning with Hindu fundamentalist forces but did not do so.

Next came the festival of Ganesh, and then the Gaurav, or Gujarat Pride, Yatra – by far the biggest, during which Modi proposed to traverse the length and breadth of the state, visiting all twenty-five districts and 182 assembly constituencies before October (at the time dates for the elections had not yet been fixed).[22] The yatra was delayed twice. The first occasion was immediately before its proposed launch from the Bhathiji Maharaj temple in the village of Fagvel, which happened to be in Shankersinh Vaghela's constituency. This was because of opposition from the Congress, which claimed it would be provocative. After pressure on Modi from a nervous Vajpayee, a revised date was set for 3 September.

Vaghela, clearly a man of ambition rather than principle, had by now defected to the Congress, and on 19 July was appointed its party president in Gujarat. Vaghela also raised a local rabble at Fagvel, which he called the Bhathiji Sena (Army of Bhathiji), and promised a fight if Modi pitched up at what Vaghela began to describe as his own yatra, coincidentally set for the same departure date, from the same location as Modi's Gaurav Yatra.

This political comedy was enjoyed by Modi, and he composed a gracious letter to Vaghela, the import of which was, 'Please, after you ...', which not only gave him the moral upper hand with Vaghela but called his bluff and also instantly destroyed the Congress party's agitation against the Gaurav Yatra: how provocative could it be if the Congress was planning one of its own?

After Modi had given way to Vaghela, a final, definite date of 8 September was announced and the Gaurav Yatra duly commenced from the temple at Fagvel to much fanfare. According to press reports it was a dismal failure, indicative of horrific defeat in the polls to come. But the report of the additional director general (ADG) of the Gujarat State Police to the additional chief secretary (ACS), Home Department in Gandhinagar, says otherwise. Almost 150,000 people attended Modi's initial address. Then the yatra trundled off. The official police record stated:

> Later, the Yatra pursued its scheduled route and at Kapadvanj (Azad Chowk), a public meeting (15,000) was addressed. Thereafter, public meeting at Bayad of Dist. Sabarkantha (12,000), (20:34 hrs), at Dehgam of Dist. Gandhinagar (12,000), (22:45 hrs), at Talod (Sabarkantha) (10,000), at Prantij (8,000) were addressed. On dated 9/9/2002 (1:30 hrs) a public meeting at Himmatnagar (15,000) was addressed by Hon'ble Chief Minister, Rajendrasinh Rana, etc.[23]

The police report reveals that the attendance was similar throughout the route, and that although precautions were taken, there was no violence whatsoever.

On 24 September, in the midst of the Gaurav Yatra, the Akshardham Temple terrorist attack took place. But far from provoking more riots, the peace held, and after an interruption of ten days a sombre but even better-attended Gaurav Yatra resumed on 5 October and drove on without mishap to its conclusion. Modi adjusted his trademark angry rhetoric to attack 'Miyan' Musharraf, the Pakistan dictator whom Modi blamed squarely for the terrorist attack.[24]

Since Modi had been parachuted into Gujarat from Delhi the previous October there had been almost nothing but turmoil – he was forced to deal with the aftermath of an earthquake, two major terrorist attacks and vicious riots, win his first-ever election (for his MLA seat in Rajkot), resign and prepare to fight another. There was also a terrible drought. Most surprising, though, and what he was probably least prepared for, was the way in which he had become a public figure, and hence public property, catapulted onto the stage of national attention from relative obscurity in the BJP's political 'back room'. And that attention was almost universally vituperative. It seemed the media took an instant dislike to Modi. He also had plenty of enemies within his own party.

The Congress high command had by now identified Modi as its principal threat in future elections, both in Gujarat and nationally. Party president Sonia Gandhi had shrewdly seen in him the most fiery of the BJP's young leadership after Vajpayee and Advani. Modi was fifty-one and Sonia, who herself had taken charge of her party only four years ago in 1998, aged fifty-one as well, knew how important it was to neutralize his potential.

An outward sign of the strain Modi had been under for the past several months was his brief hospitalization on Friday, 22 November, just hours after Lyngdoh finally concluded that the Gujarat police had proved themselves 'quite professional' and went on to confirm 12 December 2002 as the date for the polls. 'He is perfectly all right,' said Dr Dholakia of the Civil Hospital who treated Modi, 'but needs rest.'[25]

Perversely, Modi seemed to thrive on the abuse he received. He became more eloquent as the elections approached and the criticism intensified. By now the press was bursting with predictions of doom for the BJP in the December 2002 assembly elections. The entire party was supposedly tearing itself apart in frustration at Modi's failures. As *The Financial Express* put it:

In fact, highly placed Bharatiya Janata Party (BJP) workers here maintain that the caretaker chief minister is fast becoming a liability, both for the BJP as well as for the Rashtriya Swayamsevak Sangh (RSS) ... even die-hard BJP supporters seem to [be] losing confidence in the party's ability to wrest back power in the state in the forthcoming battle of the ballot.[26]

An opinion poll on 6 December predicted that the election would be a close thing, with the BJP and Congress each likely to win between eighty-five and ninety-five seats in the 182-member assembly. It concluded that while the BJP might attract 49 per cent vote share, the Congress was on course for 48 per cent, making the outcome too close to call. Research apparently showed that Modi's Gaurav Yatra was a flop and had no effect on 34 per cent of people, with only 32 per cent of respondents voicing an opinion that Gujarat's pride had been restored after the riots.[27]

Outlook, with its prediction of 100 seats for the Congress, foresaw Modi's eclipse.[28]

The December 2002 Gujarat state election was described as 'driven by hatred' of Hindus towards Muslims.[29] More likely it was driven by the media's dislike of Modi and in turn the Gujaratis' dislike of the media. 'Little did they [the media] realise they were creating a constituency that would later buy into the logic of the Gaurav Yatra that Mr Narendra Modi so successfully enlisted in the cause of route-mapping his election campaign,' wrote Debraj Mookerjee in his coruscating post-election condemnation of 'pseudo secularists'. They failed to understand that 'the triumphal march posited Hindu pride only in the derivative. What really was being rallied to a pitch was Gujarati pride.'[30]

The net effect of the general hostility directed at Gujarat and its chief minister was to precipitate a voting landslide for the BJP. As

Modi said on the eve of polling, 'I think we are fighting the Congress only in the media. On the ground I don't see any battle; we remain unchallenged. Rather, I see a frenzy in favour of the BJP wherever I campaign.' [31]

The signs of victory were very much in the air. But ever cautious, Modi was still not certain of success. Swapan Dasgupta recalls a rare moment of doubt for Modi while flying back to Ahmedabad with him one night after a rally:

> Leaning across the aisle, he asked: 'What do you think?' 'Looks very encouraging,' I replied. He nodded and then lapsed into a reflective silence. Then, quite abruptly, he shot me another question: 'And what if we lose?' I smiled warily and he too smiled back. 'But at least I fought a good campaign. I gave my best.' [32]

December 2002 was probably the final time in his career that Modi experienced doubt regarding his fate. Were he to win a majority in the assembly, the political landscape of India would begin to alter. It was Modi's first election campaign as leader of his state. He had joined the BJP a bare fifteen years earlier from the RSS and had fought his first election (a by-election) only in February 2002 to become a debutant legislator after having been catapulted into the chief ministership in October 2001. And yet he now campaigned like a veteran.

By the evening of 12 December 2002, with a turnout of 61.5 per cent, exit polls were predicting between ninety-three and 109 seats for the BJP and up to eighty-eight for the Congress. Muslims had voted in large numbers. There had been some anxiety in Gandhinagar that the BJP's middle-class voters might stay home, put off by having to queue at polling stations. On the other hand, a winter election day meant that the scorching sun would not be a deterrent.

As the results trickled in, the scale of Modi's victory became clear. L.K. Advani declared, 'I have never witnessed such a campaign during the last 20–22 years since the BJP was formed or in the fifty years of the Jana Sangh's existence.'[33]

The BJP won 126 seats (it would eventually rise by one to 127) and the Congress was more or less annihilated, securing only fifty-one seats. Modi's government now had two-and-a-half times as many MLAs as its rival. It was a clean sweep, maybe the biggest ever: even in its great win of 1998 the BJP had notched up a tally of only 117. It lost a few seats in Saurashtra and Kutch, possibly because of the previous administration's ineptness after the earthquake. But to the dismay of the Congress, the BJP did extremely well in central Gujarat and surprisingly dominated the tribal belt in eastern Gujarat.

The Congress's caste-based tactics had come undone, and this was an omen of the future for Gujarat. 'When the result came it was a surprise for Lyngdoh also,' says Modi today with a smile. 'I have never met the gentleman, but after his retirement he took an assignment with the Congress party.'

Modi's long-term strategy was to work towards an inclusive political community through development and efficient governance and neutralize the Congress's KHAM agenda. The 2002 poll gave an early but important signal that it could work.

The only shock from the poll was that former chief minister Suresh Mehta lost at Mandvi – one of the Kutch casualties. But the overall victory had a rationale and Dasgupta summed up Modi's triumph concisely: 'He successfully established a direct correlation between demonology and adulation: the more he became a hate figure in cosmopolitan circles, the more his popularity soared in Gujarat ... This was only incidentally an election centred on ideology; the real issue was leadership.'[34]

For all the fiery speech-making, the election campaign had not been about Hindutva or even about terrorism. Thanks largely to the media, it had been about Modi.

With hindsight, Sonia had accurately recognized the long-term threat Modi's politics posed to the Congress. Over ten years later, with a barely reduced majority in the Gujarat assembly, Modi was elected for the third time. Few Muslims had voted for him in December 2002. But in December 2012, 31 per cent did ('The Muslim vote now was more than 25 per cent, in some constituencies 34 per cent,' Modi said to me).

Would the Congress belatedly realize that its tactics had backfired and that for every insult it aimed at Modi it handed him another thousand votes? Or would it double down on its losses and bet more heavily on demonizing him? Time has proved that it would choose to do the latter – with interesting consequences.

By the time of his 2002 election victory, the narrative of Modi as the progenitor of the Gujarat riots was already being laid down as an unalterable truth. The initiating Godhra atrocity had been carefully airbrushed out of the picture.[35] During the campaign Shankersinh Vaghela went so far as to accuse the VHP of engineering Godhra to provoke riots against the Muslim community. Even the Congress, among whose members were some of the true culprits, thought this an accusation too far: 'It's a suicidal statement that can harm the Congress in the polarised atmosphere,' said a local leader at the time.[36]

Modi was once again sworn in as chief minister on Sunday afternoon, 22 December 2002, at the Sardar Patel Stadium in Ahmedabad. Over 100,000 people were present, not many more than the huge majority he had received in his new Maninagar constituency. K.P.S. Gill was present. And for the first time in Indian history, a sitting prime minister – Vajpayee – was in attendance at the swearing-in of a new state chief minister.

During the election campaign, ominous signs from erstwhile colleagues were evident. Vaghela, despite all his efforts to play spoilsport, had only ended up being helpful to Modi and the BJP. In 1998, Vaghela had leaped from what he thought was a sinking BJP ship. Vaghela destroyed the Congress's credibility in the election with his imitation yatra. This helped Modi enormously. Closer home, another malcontent, Keshubhai Patel, taking advice from Sanjay Joshi back in Delhi, was manoeuvring.

Under Keshubhai the BJP had lost ground to Vaghela's Congress party – dramatically so in the local elections of 2000 and then in a Lok Sabha by-election in 2001. Modi had made it plain in off-the-record comments to journalists what he thought of Keshubhai Patel's administration from its inception in May 1998, and especially in the wake of the 2001 Kutch earthquake.

Keshubhai felt undermined by Modi's comments, and soon after was unceremonially dismissed by the BJP high command. If he was humiliated by Modi's return, insult was added to injury by having Suresh Mehta second Modi's uncontested nomination for the chief minister's position. But the situation had now changed: seatless after the December elections, Suresh Mehta was marshalling his forces to join one flank of Keshubhai's battlelines.

On the other flank was the RSS, similarly dissatisfied with Modi. It may seem unbelievable that after such a conclusive victory Modi should have any enemies at all within the Sangh Parivar, but Modi always had enemies, partly because of his single-minded attitude.

With the RSS the problem was partly formal, partly familial. Modi had been an RSS man. Normally, once you are in you never leave, but Modi had moved on and become a BJP chief minister. The RSS on the other hand still believed that he was their man in the BJP. In truth Modi was nobody's man, but the argument at this point was about who should call the shots in Gujarat. The RSS assumed that as the ideological parent of the BJP it should be consulted on decision making. Modi merely smiled and nodded and listened politely.

There was also the matter of the VHP, headed by Pravin Togadia, who had been a friend many years ago, but had matured into a raging extremist. Despite Modi's anti-terrorist election rhetoric, he was no extremist, and time would prove he was not anti-Muslim either.

The dialectic whereby relentless criticism from the Congress and the media safeguarded Modi against sanctions from the Right and allowed him to slowly detach himself from the Sangh Parivar orthodoxy is fascinating. It began to matter in earnest in 2003. With Modi's declaration that 'the nation is more important than the party',[37] he could start to proceed in his own direction.

Belief in the priority of nation over party is central to the dedicated work of RSS members but it means something more when an RSS-bred chief minister reasserts it. At this time, fresh from his election victory, Modi was preparing to point at himself, turning away from the old RSS orthodoxy and to an extent away from the older, stratified BJP as well. As he confessed to me: 'In a way I am an apolitical person. I am in the political system and that is why people know me as a politician.'

Modi's ideas and ambition were bigger than anyone in the party had envisioned. He had dreams to remake India, and he was to test his ideas in the laboratory of Gujarat. Many of the policies he wished to implement would, however, only be approved of by the RSS and the BJP after they were shown to be electorally beneficial and economically successful. For example: Modi's further alignment of Gujarat with industry, private enterprise and free-markets. This approach was still somewhat alien to the RSS, which placed Hindu nationalism and therefore soft-socialist policies at the heart of its economic theory.

After the 2002 electoral victory, Modi made significant changes. He first removed Gordhan Zadaphia, who had been minister of state for home affairs, from the cabinet. In exchange for his support when Modi returned from Delhi to become chief minister in October 2001, Togadia's acolyte Zadaphia had been placed in charge of police postings. Many compromised officers were implicated in the 2002 riots (as was Zadaphia himself), and it looked as though extremism had wormed its way into the heart of government. Modi had shouldered the blame for the riots. But to the extent that some of the violence was encouraged or allowed, he knew who was really to blame.

Even those who were not actively involved in the riots were sidelined if their performance during the crisis was seen to be below par. Ashok Narayan, at the time the additional chief secretary (ACS) of the Home Department, was overlooked by Modi for promotion despite his seniority because he 'was unable to do a competent job of controlling riots'.[38]

One journalist[39] relates a rumour: Togadia complained after the election that Modi was garnering all the credit when it was Togadia's men who had done all the hard work of butchery. He apparently said this to make Modi look bad, but it had the opposite effect. It also summed up his attitude to extremists in his own party and their unwanted efforts, because suddenly, Zadaphia was out. This sent a message to Togadia that he was finished too. Modi ceased consultations with the VHP and also other Sangh Parivar organizations such as the Bharatiya Kisan Sangh (BKS).

This course of action was behind much of the insurgency aimed at Modi from the far Right – especially around 2003–04 when mutinous plotting was afoot – and was a result of Modi disavowing religious extremism which he had come to see as bad for Gujarat and bad for India. The idea of a religious state was anyway anathema to Modi. When the BKS retaliated to its marginalization by starting a farmers' agitation, Modi evicted its members from their state-provided accommodation. One of Togadia's aides, Ashwin Patel, sent an angry SMS saying that Modi had betrayed Hindutva.

When Modi was re-elected he saw with renewed clarity that his real supporters were not the extremists who had led the riots and in the process almost destroyed him as a politician. Rather they were the peaceful citizens of Gujarat who had recently voted for him in droves.

The cleansing was an ongoing operation. Even in 2008, five years after he had turfed the mutinous BKS out of their taxpayer-funded homes, he looked around Ahmedabad and saw illegal shrines erected haphazardly all over the city in defiance of planning regulations. These were often built on paths where citizens could no longer walk. They were a perfect illustration of the conventional Indian belief that once your party was in power, you could get away with whatever you liked: rules were now for other people.

Modi had made it clear that he was against illegal encroachments of any kind. This applied equally to structures of all denominations. His demolition drive was 'agnostic' – rules were rules.[40] Modi demolished several hundred illegal shrines that violated the law. Not unnaturally, this attracted opposition from leaders of various religious communities as well as civic officials hitherto unused to going by the rule book. In the end, the demolition exercise proved successful. Modi had made his point: rules were for everybody to follow.

'Modi's political problems, including within his own party stem from the fact that he is not willing to shield any wrongdoer,' writes Madhu Kishwar, editor and publisher of the feminist women's magazine *Manushi*. 'Earlier the Congress and BJP used to be in riots together and so they dutifully protected each other. Modi has severed the umbilical cord that connected anti-social elements within both the BJP and the Congress.'[41]

One of the most memorable comments to arise from the furore over the temple demolitions was when VHP President

Ashok Singhal likened Modi to Ghazni, the Islamic invader who had destroyed the Somnath temple in AD 1026. Modi had also demolished an illegal Sufi dargah that enraged local Muslims, but he stuck to his guns, citing the system of 'anushasan' – of enforcing the law 'irrespective of which community is affected'.[42]

The 'Ghazni' jibe was another example of how criticism helped Modi, for it served publicly to put distance between him and Hindu extremists, and even caused Gujarat's cynical Muslims to take note. Modi had been accused of using the 2002 riots as a cover to destroy an important Islamic tomb. The destruction of illegal Hindu temples, and the caricature of Modi as an Islamic invader, could only help the slow, careful rapprochement he had in mind: an unbiased friend to Muslims, and an enemy of extremists of every hue.

If the VHP and Bajrang Dal were puzzled by Modi's ingratitude for their efforts during the riots, and offended by his high-handed treatment of them after he was sworn in again as chief minister, they were about to discover the situation would become a lot worse. The normal way of dealing with the aftermath of riots was to pretend that nothing had happened and that the party had not been involved, the 1984 anti-Sikh pogrom in Delhi being the template. But even if Modi had wanted to follow the Congress's example after the 2002 Gujarat riots, he would not have been allowed. The media's attention was focused like a laser beam on him and it sought every day, in the court of public opinion, to indict him on charges of mass murder – an ordeal that Rajiv Gandhi never had to endure.

The Supreme Court had ordered the original, cursory police investigations into the riot killings to be reopened. It convened a Special Investigative Team (SIT) to go to Gujarat and re-examine all the evidence. Modi says he welcomed this. He felt he had done everything he could have to deal with the violence as fast as possible under the circumstances. He also knew who the guilty were. Seeing extremist members of the VHP, Bajrang Dal, BJP and Congress prosecuted for their murderous acts would give

Modi leeway to differentiate his governance from their thuggish actions. In the long term it would aid his rehabilitation. It was a high-stakes risk but in the end it was no gamble because Modi had no choice. Hence his statement: if I am found guilty of anything I should be hanged.

Over the next few years stunned and baffled rioters from every political party in Gujarat began to find themselves in court, and then in prison, as the SIT ground away with its exhaustive investigations into the 2002 riots. Why, then, was the extreme Right in Gujarat, in alliance with dissident elements in the BJP – not only Keshubhai Patel and Suresh Mehta, but Sanjay Joshi and K.N. Govindacharya as well – unable to topple Modi or at least reassert its control?

It was because of two factors, one of which drove in the wedge between Modi and certain elements of the BJP even further. This was the 2004 Lok Sabha election. The BJP had been enjoying its first and – from today's vantage point – its only sustained period of national government. It had won the twelfth Lok Sabha election in 1998 with Vajpayee as leader and secured 182 seats to the Congress's 141. Vajpayee's National Democratic Alliance coalition survived for a year before falling out with one of its partners, the All India Anna Dravida Munnetra Kazhagam (AIADMK).

In the thirteenth Lok Sabha election in 1999 the NDA acquired twenty-four allies and established a more stable NDA-2 coalition that enabled it to serve almost a full five-year term. That Vajpayee had recently visited Pakistan as part of successful peace negotiations which led to the Lahore and Islamabad Declarations[43] had not hurt him in the eyes of the BJP.

Hopes were high that the BJP had broken the decades-long hegemony of the Congress and that a new era in Indian politics was dawning. One of the elements that contributed to this hope had of course been Modi's election in 2002 halfway through NDA-2's term of office, and then successes a year later in other state assembly elections in Madhya Pradesh, Rajasthan and Chhattisgarh.

All this was taken as an augury for the 2004 Lok Sabha election. Yet, paradoxically, these victories encouraged a complacency within the BJP that led to its surprise defeat when it called an early general election in April–May 2004. It was a decision that ended Vajpayee's political career. 'The party has lost under my leadership and I don't mind stepping down,' he said, and did so, handing over to L.K. Advani.

The BJP had looked at encouraging economic indicators, backed by glowing reviews from opinion polls that seemed to guarantee an easy victory. It launched its 'India Shining' campaign in October 2003. But many sections of India's population felt excluded from the country's prosperity and the Congress played on their frustration with its slogan: 'What did the aam aadmi get?'

> One of the seminal moments of the campaign occurred in Lucknow. During a rally celebrating a BJP leader's birthday, 22 women died during a stampede for free saris. While the BJP has tried to disassociate itself from the incident, the event was a gift for opposition parties who were able to ask why, if India was shining, would people die in an attempt to get a sari worth Rs 40.[44]

In May 2004 the BJP was crushed at the polls, winning only 138 seats. As M.D. Nalapat wrote, it changed from a party with a difference to an organization happy to adopt classic Nehruvian ways.[45] In other words, once in office the old socialist tendencies – a sort of political default position in India – had crept back. The Congress won only seven seats more that the BJP – 145 – but formed a coalition government with support of the Left Front's sixty seats and other allies. The 2004 general election marked not so much a victory for the Congress as a defeat for the BJP central leadership.

After the Lok Sabha election, Modi and certain leaders in the BJP were suddenly at odds, and calls for his removal were widely made. Nonetheless, it actually worked in favour of Modi in two ways. First, he no longer had to pay as much attention to the humbled, shell-shocked national party as he had in his first two-plus years as chief minister.[46] Out of power and unpopular, it could exert far less pressure on him. In contrast, he was consolidating his power base in Gujarat.

Modi's growing power was being noticed as was his style of exercising it:

> This was a criticism increasingly voiced: Modi is not the BJP. He is a lone wolf. He may make all the right noises but he reports to no one, is accountable to none. That's why he takes the kind of decisions a party man may not, being forced to balance countervailing forces.[47]

The BJP drifted to the Left and seemed content for a while to echo the Congress. Economist Arvind Panagariya recently argued:

> Part of the problem in this is that the BJP has taken the 2004 defeat as the defeat of reforms. It is a damaging reading of the election verdict. Except for Narendra Modi, a large part of the BJP leadership has not come out of it. What is the point of an opposition which simply goes along with what the ruling party is saying?[48]

The BJP seemed to turn away from some of the economic liberalism of its six years in power between 1998 and 2004 and returned to a sort of negative orthodoxy, playing the parliamentary role of Opposition only by trying to block Congress legislation without saying what it was in favour of as an alternative. It seemed to have run out of ideas and lost direction, and retreated into a self-defeating comfort zone. Modi, meanwhile, was engaged on his project of turning Gujarat into a prosperous, business-friendly and economically progressive state.

While it had been kept at bay by Vajpayee, Advani allowed the RSS to return to centre stage, and he paid the price after making complimentary remarks about Jinnah in Pakistan in 2005. The RSS had now supplied two successive BJP presidents: it was calling the shots at the national level, which in terms of the popular vote could be termed risky. Modi by contrast kept on the right side of his RSS mentors but ensured minimal interference in governance.

> The VHP was, however, implacable: 'More than the BJP, the greatest opposition to Modi – paradoxically – is from the VHP in particular. The VHP top brass, from Ashok Singhal to Praveen Togadia, detests him ...'[49]

There was a second factor besides the BJP's post-election depression that guaranteed Modi a free hand in Gujarat and kept his enemies within the Sangh Parivar at bay. This was the progress he was making in terms of economic and social development early on in his second term.

In October 2001, on the day after he was sworn in, Modi had enacted his first practical and also symbolic decision as chief minister by directing the diversion of waters from the Narmada River to the dry river bed of the Sabarmati.[50] It had been made possible by the completion of the Sardar Sarovar dam to a height of 100 metres, but had taken decades of bitter struggle to achieve. The Narmada flows from Amarkantak in eastern Madhya Pradesh all the way to southern Gujarat, through the plains of Bharuch and into the sea. The idea of building a dam on it, which would eventually irrigate almost 7,000 square miles of arid land and supply water to more than 3,000 villages in Gujarat and Rajasthan, was first mooted in the 1960s. The project was eventually given the go-ahead in 1979. After that a political war ensued between environmentalists, left-wing activists and the governments of four states, which often fought or obstructed one another during the process.

Now fresh water was beginning to reach those who thirsted for it, and Modi used the flooding of the Sabarmati to inaugurate a new phase in the development of Gujarat. In a semi-desert state, the change from dry to wet was a powerful metaphor. The success of the dam to date was of course not his doing, and Modi was not claiming credit for it, although later he would achieve a significant heightening of the dam to increase its radius of influence. Now, though, he used the occasion to inform everybody that change was here and was going to happen fast.

Part of the reason for sidelining the VHP was that Modi wished to push the ideological and rhetorical aspects of religion to one side. He had seen ample evidence of where religious-nationalist agitations led, and although he was a nationalist he claimed to follow the tenets of genuine secularism: justice for all, favouritism to none.

As always, Modi was looking two ways, both forward and back. He wanted to rejuvenate and make relevant to modern India its vast backwater of Hindu culture and identity, seeing it as full of energy and potential. He intended to do this by allowing them to flourish in a modern, liberal context, not to install a 'fortress India' economically or culturally.

But by defining Hindutva as a way of life rather than religious dogma, Modi was going to put it into practice by incorporating principles of India's ancient philosophies and modernizing them to create a state which was prosperous, demonstrated good governance, was honest and put citizens first.

To tackle the deeply embedded communalism evident in the 2002 riots, Modi knew that he needed to prove to Gujarat's angry and frightened Muslims what he stood for in deed rather than word. He remained relentlessly tough on terrorism and law and order in general because, as Sardar Patel had pointed out, government means nothing if it cannot protect its citizens.[51] This was part of Modi's penitential quest after the riots, as well as being one of his key political beliefs moving forward.

Modi next turned his attention to reforming government. He wanted to make his administration more streamlined and efficient, even if he could not shrink it. He reasoned that the half-million government employees had families to look after. So even having inherited over-employment in the civil and public services, he would not start sacking people en masse. Instead, he decided to look at public servants as a resource, and try to improve their performance at the same time as he improved their lives and careers by enthusing them and granting government employees more autonomy.[52]

Modi began to hold brain-storming sessions (chintan shibirs) and let it be known that bona fide mistakes would not be punished. Usually civil servants hesitate to speak their minds or query their bosses. Modi changed that and said that because he wanted everyone to do their best, if a sincere idea went awry or failed it would not leave a black mark; in fact the opposite.

'In my first meeting with my government bureaucrats I said, "Don't bother about the punishment; in my office there will be no punishment. You have to take the risk, you have to perform. If any problem arises, I am responsible."'

It would be proof that the employee was trying to innovate and improve, and the person's career would benefit by learning from a mistake. This was a radical and previously untried step and had a miraculously liberating effect on the work ethic of the civil service. Soon, everybody felt involved. Government employees would gain from training courses and the chance of better job satisfaction in return for working more conscientiously and efficiently. As he describes these initiatives, Modi's face lights up: clearly innovation – doing things better and smarter – engages and animates him.

Modi started a programme that allowed civil servants to work with the public according to their own personal interests, reasoning that this would make them happier and more enthusiastic about their jobs. 'I told them, "You choose any project you like, which gives you satisfaction, and implement it in your way. Don't worry about the resources, I will give you all." What happened? The government officials were doing their duty, but in a new way – like one officer who was interested in music, but it was not a part of his duty. I said, "If you are not satisfied with this work, do something else." So he called on poor people and tried to give them education in music. It gave him satisfaction. I gave him full freedom to do this. He was satisfied and because of this satisfaction his performance and ability in his other work improved.'

Above all, the jungle of red tape was slashed. The undergrowth of triplicate forms was hacked back so that more could be accomplished and more quickly. The Internet would be taken full advantage of in a push towards e-government, and the lumbering beast of Indian bureaucracy tamed. But there would be a stick to accompany the carrot, as Pravin Sheth said in 2006:

> Officials, small and high, in his administration have surely become alert about the work they are expected to carry out. It may not mean that there is a significant behavioral transformation in bureaucratic tradition. But they know that if files are not disposed of expeditiously, or tardiness is noticed, the officer liable for his non-action will be transferred to an inhospitable position or will face some penal action.[53]

Journalist Prem Shankar Jha, in his essay 'Jha's India: Where Democracy Has Gone Wrong', said that the country had suffered since Independence from 'the failure to enact provisions that could convert a bureaucracy that had been schooled over a century into believing that its function was to rule the people (rather than be its servants)'.[54] Modi began in Gujarat to change the ossified mindset of the bureaucracy. Thus it was hoped that governance would improve and the 'consumers' of government – benighted citizens with no choice in the matter – would begin to understand for the first time that customer satisfaction came first.

While this is common in the West, nothing as reformist had been attempted before in India. Modi didn't stop there. Corruption was also going to end – 'Hoon khaato nathi khaava deto nathi' ('I don't take bribes and don't allow anyone else to take bribes either'). Such a claim sounded bizarre in a country where bribery, graft and embezzlement are often lubricants that encourage the cogs of authority to turn reluctantly.

As with unemployment, corruption will never fall to zero anywhere. But what Modi meant was that the culture of administration would change so that the government would become the servant of the people instead of its master; that the voter would be placed in charge. Modi had power, but only because it had been vested in him by voters.

The personality of an administration depends on the character of the leader, and he will eventually influence its culture all the way down the chain, for good or ill. Modi let it be known in no uncertain terms that anybody accepting bribes was to be sacked, with no exceptions. This filtered through the arteries of the political system rapidly. Because Modi was acknowledged to be personally not corrupt – something even his worst enemies admit – his words carried weight. The idea was to spread a new spirit of integrity and diligence through the Gujarat civil service, with the best being promoted and the worst sidelined or dismissed. Once that process was underway, Modi turned to more pleasant matters.

This is how he put it to me: 'I told each and every department, and every secretary, "Think that you are the chief minister of this department – what are you going to do in five years? I will give you the full authority as a chief minister. You are a chief minister. Think about it. What resources do you have? What is your aim, what is your goal? What is your roadmap, and how are you going to implement it and how are you going to achieve it?" They each had to present their new and innovative plans so that all could see what the others were planning and how they were thinking.'

Modi believed a major problem in government was lack of communication. 'In governance, the major problem in our system is that the mentality is one of secrecy. One person who is sitting at the table thinks that no one should know what he is doing. All is compartmental thinking and in watertight compartments, psychologically and physically. I wanted to change this environment.'

To this end Modi assembled all his senior officials. 'Every day, in the evening, we used to start our workshop. It went on till late night, ten o'clock. And it was for months together. The top 250 members of the team sat with one officer giving a detailed presentation, and then we discussed the issue. In the audience there were six agricultural representatives, five industry representatives, so they had their own ideas.'

Once each department began to understand the direction in which the others were moving, they began to adjust their own plans to coordinate better. 'So in this way, in each and every department, rethinking started. If this department is doing this, I will have to adjust myself.'

The biggest problem, a barrier all departments faced, was the perceived negativity and intransigence of the treasury. Modi elaborates:

Always in government, the finance department is on one side, others are on the other side. They are always fighting against the finance department, they always complain against the finance department: 'They are not helping, they are not giving.' So many complaints. And always they think the finance department has this secrecy – it cannot be opened up. I said, 'No, nothing doing! let my whole team have knowledge about the financial situation, let them know.' And the finance department gave a presentation. They spoke in detail about their limitations, their problems, everything. Then what happened? The people who were always against the finance department, they said, 'This is the situation? We will cooperate, we will find a way, we will reduce our expenditure.' So self-discipline came out of it. And because of that the thinking process was in a single direction. And they were all feeling, 'Yes, I am a chief minister of my department, I have been given all the authority.' So it anchored people, and that's why this is the basis of good governance.

What Modi had done of course was empower civil servants and give them a sense of responsibility and ownership of their respective domains. And yet the criticism that Gujarat's administration was authoritarian remained. Critics said nothing moved without Modi's go-ahead. He held several ministerial portfolios and, despite the attempt at empowering bureaucrats, micromanaged all important decisions.

This is a criticism valid for most chief ministers who routinely hold up to a dozen ministerial portfolios and keep a tight rein on the bureaucracy. But if Modi wants to be different, decentralizing authority must be high on his list of priorities. In another way though, Modi has improved the efficiency of civil servants in the state. The 'transfer industry' among bureaucrats is rampant in India with large sums of money exchanged for transfer of government officers. In Gujarat, however, the transfer industry has been systematically done away with and transfers are made on merit.

Many civil servants stay in their posts for up to a decade or more, ensuring continuity and oversight across development programmes.

Gujarat was now officially open for business. The prototype Resurgent Gujarat exposition Modi had hosted a fateful fortnight before the 2002 riots was to appear in its next incarnation as a business summit designed to attract both domestic and international companies: Vibrant Gujarat. During the next decade, up to Vibrant Gujarat 2013, which saw for the first time a large presence by the Chinese,[55] these events were held biennially. Despite the unquestionable success they have attracted a lot of derision. The charge: many of the memoranda of understanding (MoUs) never materialize. This is partly true, and a fair examination of the reality is necessary.

The original pre-riot summit in 2001 raised Rs 12,360 crore. The September 2003 meet resulted in eighty MoUs signed (thirty-three of these would remain unfulfilled) adding up to Rs 66,000 crore.[56] The FDI element of this was only 20 per cent and many of the pledgers were domestic companies already operating in Gujarat.

At the 2005 summit of Vibrant Gujarat, 'a more organized affair', Rs 106,160 crore worth of MoUs were signed, with eighty-nine of 227 eventually falling by the wayside. The gross investment was nonetheless nearly twice that of 2003. Furthermore, this time foreign investors were more numerous. That was more important, to Modi's mind, than the absolute levels of financial promises.

The 2007 Vibrant Gujarat summit differed in that it had the backdrop of approaching elections to lend it a certain reflected colouring. There was also, related to the elections, another internal plot to dislodge Modi hatched by disaffected colleagues. It was vital for him that a success could be hailed, and he unveiled the slogan, 'In Gujarat there is no red tape, only a red carpet'! In 2007, 343 MoUs[57] quadrupled investment to Rs 461,835 crore in value. It was a good springboard for the election campaign and gave Modi ammunition to use against any potential coup: Gujarat had never before experienced such a large intent for investment and industrial development.

Critics pointed out that most of the MoUs remained on paper. Officials countered that investment proposals, especially in infrastructure, had long gestation periods.

In 2009, a humungous sum of Rs 1,200,000 crore was raised, nearly three times the amount of the previous event, and in 2011 it almost doubled again, to Rs 2,083,000 crore. This time 8,662 MoUs were signed[58], compared with only eighty in 2003. In 2013, 17,719 MoUs were signed – the final investment figure is still being calculated.

Critics routinely mock the MoUs as 'paper investment' and some of this criticism is clearly justified. However, the interest foreign participants have shown in successive Vibrant Gujarat summits has drawn significant investment to the state. Modi's own visits to China and Japan have meanwhile served to strengthen the state's relationship with global investors.

Modi's refusal to engage in the traditional culture of patronage stung many. This was clear as the 2007 assembly election approached. Several were forced to sit on the sidelines, powerless, even as they basked in the reflected glory of Modi's apparent developmental and economic progress in Gujarat. Such figures ranged across the spectrum: members of the VHP, whom Modi had first punished and then kept at arm's length; some of his own MLAs, whose low estimation in Modi's eyes was painfully obvious to them; elements of the BJP who were still in disarray after the 2004 Lok Sabha debacle; and most of all the man Modi had replaced in 2001, Keshubhai Patel.

Keshubhai, blind to his own faults and woeful track record of endemic corruption and inefficiency, still fancied that he was destined to dislodge the 'upstart tyrant'. He regarded Modi as autocratic who had converted Gujarat into a 'police' state with a slew of alleged fake encounter killings between 2004 and 2006. Keshubhai had a large constituency among the Patels of Gujarat. He thus carried a powerful caste wedge that could be inserted into Modi's majority.[59] His behind-the-scenes dissent gradually grew louder. It broke out into the open by August 2007. Five MLAs were promptly suspended on Advani's orders. Soon after, Keshubhai denounced Modi as a 'dictator', to the delight of the Congress. It suited their efforts to fight the Gujarat election by splitting the vote caste-wise. It seemed the only tactic to counter Modi's popularity.

The Congress was pushing its KHAM agenda again, and welcomed Keshubhai's 'Patels', which in effect created a KHAMP. Suresh Mehta added to the pressure when he announced he would not support Modi in the election campaign. After the election nothing was ever heard from Mehta again.

But the Congress was taking a big risk fraternizing with BJP dissidents. Just as Vaghela's maladroitness had damaged the Congress in the 2002 assembly election when it brought him in as its star player, so Keshubhai and the group of malcontent MLAs that trailed after him threatened to muddy the distinctness of the Congress's offering to the electorate. Part of preserving that distinctness meant not letting Vaghela anywhere near the campaign. But then without a clear leader, it was also confusing to the electorate exactly what the Congress *was* offering.

The Congress was especially worried as Modi's approval rating settled at an alarmingly high 60 per cent – remarkable for a chief minister approaching the end of his second term, and in Gujarat the BJP's third consecutive term. Unsurprisingly, while the Congress targeted small voting pockets, Modi decided to turn the election into a referendum on himself. 'Whom do you want for the next five years?' he asked voters again and again. 'Me, or ...?' All he then did was roll his eyes.

The Congress countered by attempting to enlist to its cause farmers they thought were angry about Modi's decision to charge them for previously free electricity (they had shared a patchy supply with the main industrial cables). Yet it turned out that ordinary farmers, enjoying their own newly installed domestic power supplies, did not resent paying for a steady and reliable service.

This demonstrated the logic behind Modi's free-market reforms and exposed the obsolescence of the socialistic philosophy that the state should provide everything, no matter how shoddy or intermittent.

Realizing that there was unrest among extremists marginalized by Modi, the Congress even attempted to make common cause with disaffected elements in the VHP. The Congress had fatally allowed Vaghela to sink its ship of secularism in 2002 and now risked doing the same again in even more spectacular fashion. It conveniently forgot that to have any chance of success or even credibility in the campaign, all mention of Hindutva had to be kept out. It afforded Modi the opportunity to damage them by pointing to the company the Congress was keeping while at the same time consolidating the larger, moderate Hindu vote behind him.

A sting operation by *Tehelka* recorded Babu Bajrangi of the Bajrang Dal – who would later be imprisoned for murdering Muslims in 2002 – boasting about his deeds and claiming that Modi was complicit.[60] The exposé backfired on the Congress when the programme was criticized both for revealing nothing new (it was all in the Nanavati Inquiry that had already exonerated Modi) and for using people known to be his enemies. It was also lambasted for partiality, being broadcast so close to the elections.

After the official period of electioneering had begun in November 2007, a visit by Sonia Gandhi to Gujarat, which local Congressmen believed would sprinkle some magic dust on their campaign, upset their fragile edifice of voting alliances. In a speech at Navsari on 1 December to a large crowd of the Congress faithful, she called Modi *maut ke saudagar* (merchant of death), which clearly breached the Election Commission code and led to an uproar. The party quickly attempted to retreat from the outburst by saying that it was not directed at Modi, although it obviously was. Digvijay Singh, who had refused to send aid to Gujarat to help quell the 2002 riots, then made things worse by referring to 'Hindu terrorism' at a press conference.

In truth it was yet another instance of criticism working in Modi's favour. It now gave him the ideal opportunity to harangue his opponents for ignoring Muslim terror while they demonized the ordinary people of India – and especially Gujaratis – by invoking Hindu terror. Terrorism, he declared, has no religion. Things had slid back to 2002, exactly where the Congress had not wanted them to go. Now at rallies Modi would ask the adoring crowds, 'Do I, a son of Gujarat, look like a maut ka saudagar?'

'No', the crowds shouted back. And with every resounding 'No', the Congress was reminded of the fatal error Sonia had made.

Modi's critics, however, were unconvinced. *The Hindu* made a confident assertion:

> Gujarat 2007 is tailor-made for a Congress victory. The caste equation favours it. Sections of the RSS and the VHP are indirectly supporting it. The police seem to be with the Congress and against the BJP. As many as 50 BJP rebels are in the fray, many of them strong in their constituencies. Teachers are angry, bureaucrats are unhappy. It just cannot get any better for the Grand Old Party.[61]

Others were equally dismissive of Modi's chances: 'Democracy is taking revenge on Narendra Modi,' wrote *The Indian Express*. 'This election may well be the long deferred moment of truth for the man who invoked popular mandate to bypass norms, laws or the Constitution'.[62]

This echoed one TV anchor who said: 'I will be happy that a dictator has lost. In a democracy, there is no space for a dictator.'[63] A nearby example of an actual dictator had recently been available in Pervez Musharraf across the border in Pakistan, but the media seemed uninterested in talking about him. Swapan Dasgupta observed acidly: 'The election was held in a peaceful atmosphere. There was no apparent tension and no fear of large-scale intimidation – although some secular visitors from Delhi and Mumbai insisted there was.'[64]

The Election Commission certainly had no complaints and an optimistic media seemed happy with how it thought the polling was progressing. 'All exit polls after the first-phase voting in 87 constituencies (of 182) forecast a vote-swing away from the BJP,' noted the journalist Praful Bidwai. 'Such a defeat will be a seismic shock for the BJP and a historic setback for the Sangh Parivar.'

The reporting on most TV networks went along the same lines, having discovered that 'In a dramatic last-day swing in the satta bazar, bookies there have swung suddenly against Narendra Modi. In fact 24 hours before the vote count, they now give the Congress the edge over Modi in the race for power.'[65]

As they say at the race track, you should never argue with the bookies. Then again, as one TV anchor concluded, 'Remember the old adage, the one who is the most proud always finishes last.'

Hindsight is all very well, but Modi's impending victory was nevertheless plain for all who wanted to see. He had done well in Gujarat during his second term, and though it remained a work in progress, his mantra of 'less government, more governance' was gaining traction. The BJP won 117 out of 182 seats, upsetting most forecasts. More than that, Modi seemed to have captured the popular mood not only of Gujaratis as in 2002, but of much of the country. At the same time, it was clear that people were enamoured of Modi but not necessarily of the BJP, a phenomenon that would persist and have consequences in the future.

The BJP's tally of 117 seats was only ten fewer than in the post-riot atmosphere of 2002 when Gujarat was galvanized against outside influences. This time, even with a concerted media campaign and a whole bag of tricks unleashed by the Opposition against Modi, he had still won a handsome overall majority, with an unprecedentedly low anti-incumbency vote share decline of 0.5 per cent in north Gujarat.[66] Modi's majority in his own constituency increased from 75,000 to 87,000 votes. The Patels had proven indifferent to Keshubhai's brand of scheming discontent.

Modi also wrecked the Congress party's KHAM strategy. In Saurashtra and Kutch, where it had been predicted that farmers, Dalits and tribals would vote against him, Modi had taken twenty-six seats from the Congress, with the BJP gaining eleven of the thirteen seats reserved for scheduled castes. Even Muslims had begun to vote for Modi: it is believed that up to 25 per cent of Muslims voted for the BJP, a percentage that would rise further in the 2012 assembly poll. Something was clearly happening that the media and the Congress could not yet comprehend.

Asifa Khan was a journalist before taking on a job as spokesperson for the Gujarat Congress party. She worked for it for four years before crossing over to the BJP shortly before Modi was re-elected for a third time in 2012. As a Muslim, she had been puzzled by why so many Muslims were voting for the 'enemy'.

It was, she discovered, because of two things: under Modi, development was happening everywhere and poorer Muslims were benefiting hugely from it – it was the wealthier Muslims who still felt hesitant to vote for the BJP. Secondly, the BJP was responsive at the grass roots to Muslim concerns – unlike, says Asifa, Congress councillors – and they were given their full rights as citizens rather than being treated as a minority.

'As an opposition party, your job is to blame and criticize the BJP,' she says. 'My job was to find faults with Mr Modi and I couldn't find any. In fact, I started finding faults with my own leaders and saying why aren't we doing what they are doing? ... Because the leader works, everybody under him is functioning. Why else would people come out in such large numbers to vote for the BJP? The Muslims did so because they developed an active interest in governance.'[67]

According to one estimate, during the 2007 campaign Modi addressed 155 Gujarat constituencies and spoke directly to crowds totalling thirty million people – a plain majority of voters in the state.[68] No Congressman achieved the smallest fraction of this. Modi tailored each of his speeches to its particular audience, proving that he knew whom he was talking to. As one observer pointed out: 'To fishermen he spoke about his Sagar Khedu scheme, to tribals he described his Van Bandhu plan, and the subject of his talk to women was Mahila Sammelan.' Speaking of women, all of the Congress party's female candidates lost, while fifteen of the twenty-two BJP women standing for the 2007 election won.

In addition to personally addressing crowds, Modi had summoned the growing power of social media and crafted an online campaign movement to contact predominantly young voters who used the Internet in their daily lives. At one point 6,500 members of the Orkut Internet community led a silent march through Ahmedabad protesting against the treatment of Modi in the mainstream media. Modi was building loyalty through trust and communication in every way he could even in a pre-Facebook and pre-Twitter era. It was a strategy that would, in years and elections to come, multiply manifold across exploding social media.

For Modi the 2007 victory was more important than his career-saving 2002 win. The earlier election had been an angry one with voters standing behind him against the hostility to Gujarat coming from the media and political opponents. This time voters were judging him far more impartially, on a record of five years of governance.

Since his days as an RSS worker and later BJP back-room planner, Modi had shown he was thorough and methodical. He used these qualities along with his intuition to get his policies executed. He often went against convention and as a result frequently created friction with those who opposed him. For that reason Modi always had, and probably always will have, enemies: emollience is not his middle name.

Wit and self-possession were usually enough to see him through – he is an exceptional orator – and even when they did not, as with his 'exile' from Gujarat in the 1990s, he always had a fallback plan. Modi believes that if a specific task is done with the correct pressure applied and in the right order, a predictable result will occur. That was the reason the riots shook him to his core. The sequence of events unwound chaotically and his actions did not lead, at least to begin with, to expected outcomes.

That experience marked Modi, and he dedicated the years of his second term as chief minister to carefully applying his customary methods to the economy of Gujarat, to development and to governance. If it didn't work, his whole understanding of politics and government was flawed. Since December 2002 the measures he had put in place appeared to be functioning and much had been achieved, but ultimately the only proof of that was in the ballot box.

Was Modi doing the right thing? Were his theories and assumptions, not only about politics but about people, correct? Were his deeply held beliefs the right ones? Modi is not a man given to self-doubt, but even so, everything was riding on the result of the

2007 election. If the people had rejected him, he would have been finished as a politician of consequence.

After he won in 2007, Modi was observed for the first time to have somehow softened. He did not gloat but thanked voters and all the thousands of party workers who had contributed to the victory. He said that if they were invisible to others, it was because the media did not have cameras 'with good enough resolution to spot them'. Modi even forgave the mutinous Keshubhai Patel, not that he expected kindness in return, and sure enough received none. During his various speeches of thanks Modi would often stumble and be left speechless. He would stand in front of his audience, silently looking at the ceiling, before resuming.[69] It showed that beneath the clinical façade lay a man with complex emotions.

What was the effect of Modi's victory at the national level? It had only a superficial effect on the BJP outside Gujarat. The party was delighted and confident in the wake of the 2007 election, but ultimately Modi's purposefulness and success was his and not theirs. Nationally the BJP remained without definite direction and it was inevitable that the heady impact of the 2007 assembly election would wear off.

With the 2009 Lok Sabha election looming, the BJP made the fatal mistake of deciding that emulating Modi's tactics of winning in Gujarat would work for them at the national level with L.K. Advani as prime ministerial candidate. The campaign for the fourteenth Lok Sabha poll made use of all the technologies Modi had pioneered: Advani became the face of the party on all the posters, as Modi had in Gujarat. The cartoonish 'Modi masks' had been a joyous, spontaneous craze in the Gujarat elections and everybody tried to get their hands on one to the point they became rare and coveted.

Advani made masks available too, but not this time in response to any public demand. Instead, dutiful party workers wandered around

with the mask of his face on theirs. In an attempt to 'get down with
the youth', official websites and blogs were launched. The party
mapped out an exhaustive Internet strategy to hoover up online
attention votes.[70] The celebrations that accompanied Advani's
crowning as the BJP's prime ministerial candidate were scarcely
less than if he had already become prime minister, so infectious was
the feeling of inevitable success. What could possibly go wrong?

A lot, came the answer. Modi's communications had grown
organically out of years of interactions with the citizens of Gujarat.
His methods had developed organically and voters knew they were
backed by action. Modi had worked consistently hard to earn the
trust of people. Advani was a much-respected figure but he was
not getting any younger. During the Lok Sabha campaign, Advani
called Prime Minister Manmohan Singh 'weak' – and he was – but
in 2009, ahead of the corruption charges that would engulf him
in UPA-2, Manmohan Singh was a middle-class icon. The BJP's
campaign was woeful, and each foray against the Congress resulted
in a speedy counterpunch. Modi sat out the 2009 Lok Sabha
election and concentrated on Gujarat, biding his time.

It wasn't only Advani's age that was against him. As Sanjeev Nayyar
pointed out,[71] the key error of the BJP campaign was its betrayal of
the things it had previously stood for. Advani had coined the term
'pseudo-secularism' to define the way that the Congress pandered
to the minority vote bank, giving special dispensation to Muslims
and other groups. The BJP had valiantly upheld the principle that
all citizens should be equal under the law, even if in practice this
meant losing the minority vote. Now, though, Advani went for a
softer position, thinking that it would draw the minority vote from
the Congress.

All that happened was that the BJP's core constituency drifted
away. Muslims did not trust Advani – either despite, or because of,

his visit to the Jinnah Mausoleum in Pakistan and the remarks he made there. They stayed with the Congress. An electoral catastrophe ensued. The BJP won a mere 116 seats, twenty-two fewer than in 2004. Its national vote share plunged to 18.80 per cent – the lowest in two decades.

Indian politics is so labyrinthine that ironies can be found wherever one cares to look. But surely one of the richest in 2009 was that while the BJP toiled against the Congress, Modi in Gujarat was transforming his concept of 'India first' into a supple, all-embracing and attractive national identity that would have inclusiveness in its governmental and philosophical DNA. Modi had made the simple decision that the job of government was to work for citizens, not to enthrone politicians and line their pockets or to indulge in extremes of prejudice.

The Congress saw that Modi and not Advani was the existential danger to the Delhi dynasty. This was why, as soon as the election was concluded, the big guns on its foredeck swivelled in the direction of Gujarat.

9

DEVELOPMENT AND GOVERNANCE

When a man is educated, one individual gets educated, but when a woman is educated, an entire family gets educated.

– M.K. Gandhi

A 2011 SURVEY CONDUCTED BY Political and Economic Risk Consultancy of Hong Kong found that India was the most over-regulated country in the world, and that its rules 'were complex and non-transparent, while standards and certifications procedures were onerous'.[1]

The Peruvian economist Hernando de Soto established an index to rate the economic freedom of countries – with a strong correlation to their growth and prosperity – by measuring how long it takes to overcome various bureaucratic hurdles. The least prosperous countries are almost always the most rule-bound and are usually autocratic, dictatorial, African, or a mixture of the three.[2]

For a free and democratic country, India's metrics are extremely poor.[3] The World Bank's 'Doing Business Survey', which takes its cue from de Soto's research, found that in India it can take six weeks to register property or a business (a matter of days in the UK and the US), 'almost 200 days to obtain a construction permit, over 1,400 days to enforce a contract and seven years to close a business'.[4]

Bad governance impedes individual aspirations and restrains the country from maturing as a world power. Ordinary people in India know what the problems are and badly want them solved. But their powerlessness in the face of aloof authority grates the most. Repeatedly, across the country, across demographics, the complaint is of poor and corrupt governance.

When opaque and selectively applied regulations are in place, bribery and corruption thrive. One reader's comment in the *Economic Times* about the World Bank survey explained the situation with vexed and touching clarity: 'They could have added that apart from being over-regulated, India is also the most under-governed country. The laws and regulations are only for those who want to follow them, others use the "rupee" license to freely do what they wish to do. One big reason is lack of accountability among bureaucrats, who have enormous discretionary powers vested with them.'

This situation obviously could not exist without the tacit approval of politicians in power – otherwise, over a period of decades, they would have worked to at least amend Article 311 of the Constitution which guarantees effective immunity to government employees.[5] While governments of different ideological stripes have remained comfortably ensconced, governance has decayed.

If substantial change is to occur and allow higher standards of governance, several steps are necessary: one, ensuring greater economic freedom through slashing a burdensome bureaucracy; two, reducing discretionary powers to minimize corruption; three, enhancing transparency; and four, mandating time-bound decision making. Yet the opposite is the case across the country and so a governance deficit continuously widens.

Modi called himself 'a non-political chief minister'. His favourite slogan is 'less government, more governance'. But was this true?

When Modi became chief minister of Gujarat in October 2001, he immediately embarked on what were essentially 'supply-side' reforms. This refers to the idea that by making it easier for people to produce goods and services – to *supply* the needs of individuals and industry – the economy will be stimulated and growth will occur, along with lower prices and higher incomes, or at least relatively higher incomes.

The best way in which growth can be stimulated is not deficit funding but reducing taxes and regulations – by slimming down government and reducing its influence and reach. The state can also help by investing in infrastructure and incentives that allow people to work more easily and more efficiently: roads, irrigation, education and health care. By stimulating growth it can then sustain investment-focused budget deficits, as Gujarat has tried to do.[6]

Supply-side economics is regarded as right-wing mainly because it implies smaller government or less regulation. The state steps back from trying to do everything and trusts its citizens and the markets to make the correct decisions. It is axiomatic among those on the Right – such as America's Republicans or Britain's Tories – that the individual knows best how to spend his money, allocate capital efficiently, and that government spending other people's money leads to poor spending choices and waste. Thus the Right favours empowerment over entitlement, or development over doles.[7]

Left socialists distrust supply-side economics because it believes ordinary people need government direction and involvement on every level to protect them from the arbitrary power of capital that has no 'social conscience' and profit as its sole motive. The Left or Centre-Left, broadly speaking, believes that market-driven growth will inevitably be unequal and serve only the owners of capital. Any 'trickle down' benefits to the poor will be small and disproportionate and public assets will fall into private hands.

The government, the Left believes, must therefore plan and provide to fulfil the rights of its people to food, employment and housing, and to thwart capitalists with taxes and regulations. Social progress through big, responsible government is the objective.

In contrast to this system of benevolent entitlement, the Centre-Right believes that small government is empowering and that the tendency towards ever-greater government control and legislation strangles growth, inhibits free trade and results in diminution of individual rights. But as the US political commentator P.J. O'Rourke remarked caustically: 'The Republicans always say that big government doesn't work. Then they get elected and prove it.'

Clearly there are two sides to the story.

Modi rose from within the broad Centre-Left economic consensus that dominated politics in India since Independence. However, his economic philosophy has changed since he took over as chief minister of Gujarat. He is interesting because his background is in the RSS whose political outlook remains culturally conservative and yet economically socialistic. The RSS has shown little ideological interest in espousing free markets. It believes in the authority of the group, not the individual, which has caused Modi problems in the past.

Yet clearly he had been impressed by the reforms enacted by Manmohan Singh and Narasimha Rao in the 1990s. He arrived in Gujarat already bubbling with supply-side energy full of ideas about individual empowerment, the basis of his emerging political and economic philosophy. What he attempted to do over twelve years in Gujarat was remove government from people's lives and replace it with governance.

'When I first took charge, the problem I was facing here in Gujarat was the same problem my country is facing [now],' says

Modi contemplatively. 'The problems are not new. The problems were there in Gujarat. The confidence levels were very low.'

Yet arguments continue to rage over whether significant improvements in overall development in Gujarat actually took place under Modi.

Human rights activist Shabnam Hashmi recently issued this summing up of Modi's time in Gujarat:

> Modi projects himself as the man who is developing Gujarat in a very fast pace. But he is pumping in huge amount of money for this publicity propaganda. Almost 40 per cent of population there is under poverty. Minority groups including tribals, Dalits and Muslims are considered as second grade citizens in Modi's Gujarat. He is no different from Hitler.[8]

The focus on Modi's development and governance record is important because it could be the 'model' his putative prime ministership could soon adapt for the rest of India. But has the model worked in Gujarat?

As the general election approached, the perpetual controversy surrounding Modi shifted from his 'masterminding' the 2002 riots to the role he played in the development and progress of Gujarat since 2001. Is Hashmi correct in claiming that almost 40 per cent of Gujarat's population lives in poverty, or that Muslims and Dalits are treated as second-class citizens? It is necessary to examine the official figures to discern objectively the actual state of affairs, free of political or ideological bias. But first it should be explained how Modi changed things and what policies were implemented to bring about, for better or worse, the changes he made.

Modi first announced publicly in Delhi in early 2003, a fortnight after his December 2002 election victory, what for many years had been brewing in his mind. He travelled to the capital on 9 January for the inaugural Pravasi Bharatiya Divas – the Non-resident Indian (NRI) Day. There, in a meeting with NRIs, he unveiled his plan to take advantage of new computer technology to develop e-governance with which he sought to bring transparency to his administration. In other words, with his first post-election announcement Modi was placing governance at the apex of his ambitions in office. Politics was not mentioned. Next, he outlined five pillars of a development policy for Gujarat. The five were: water, energy, people, education and security.

Gujarat naturally already had in place policies that dealt with all these areas. But Modi wished to transform them. Specifically, his development agenda brought to Gujarat the concept of an inclusive 'India first' ideology. It had been evolving in his mind, he says, for a while. Modi called the five pillars 'shaktis', Sanskrit for 'sacred force': the originating energy and perpetual dynamism of the universe. It is imagined as feminine and personified through the goddess Kali. Notably, it is the feminine force of shakti that is responsible for all change and liberation.

As Sandeep Singh points out in *Third Curve*, it is this idea of the feminine force that has actually been at the heart of all the change Modi has tried to bring about in Gujarat. He has even reduced transfer tax on properties and businesses if they are registered to a woman instead of a man. Modi often emphasizes how India suffers from its wastage of the intelligence and talent of 50 per cent of the population when women are unable to make their full contribution to society.[9]

Modi translated his proposed programme of change and development into terms that would be instantly understandable at an almost subconscious cultural level, entwining the mythological with the technological – an organic conception that he calculated would bud and then blossom over the next decade.

Taking the five shakti pillars, he grouped them under a collective name, 'panchamrut'. Unlike 'shakti', which is as universal as concepts get, panchamrut comes from everyday life and holds within it the elements of the daily puja, or domestic offering: milk, dahi (yogurt), ghee (clarified butter), honey and sugar. The mixture of these ritual ingredients is called 'panch' ('five': English retains the Indo-European root in words such as 'pentagon') but the individual ingredients carry their own symbolism and guide the evolution of the soul.

Modi took the idea of these five nectars of the daily devotional and inserted it into his development programme so that each shakti took on the identity of one of the elements of the panchamrut. He named the development of water resources Jal Shakti; the energy programme was Urja Shakti; people, or 'human resources', became Jan Shakti; Gyan Shakti was to refer to the power of knowledge and education; and security would be Raksha Shakti. As each was a shakti, constant movement and improvement was implicit in them. And as part of a cohesive development 'puja', it implied that they were all interrelated and dependent on one another for overall effect.

Development in Modi's conception was dynamic and interrelated and enfolded into a civilizational ethos, but at a sub-religious level – related to cultural ideas familiar even to the non-religious Indian, in fact to anyone irrespective of religion. As he told me reflectively:

> I am aware that water, and other natural things in society, from centuries the thinking on these is well ingrained in our society, in Indian culture, our lifestyle. I wanted to use the same ideas. If I used the same ideas, I would get change. If I am going to inject something new with which they are not familiar it will take a lot of time, so I will have to use their natural thinking.

In 2003, fresh water was flowing along the Sabarmati river through Ahmedabad, transforming the prospects of the city and hinting at a wider transformation of the landscape of Gujarat. The economic transformation had been set in process, even if with small steps, at the Resurgent Gujarat exposition in 2002 and would continue with Vibrant Gujarat, scheduled for September that year.

Now it was the turn of rural areas to be given a fillip. Already, the damming of the Narmada had allowed irrigation of thousands of hectares of arid farmland – a first instance of Jal Shakti in action. Water is for everyone but the roughly four million farmers of Gujarat, a predominantly agricultural state, also needed power. For this, under the Urja Shakti aspect of the panchamrut, Modi launched his 'lighted village' Jyotigram Scheme (JGS) in September 2003 to bring dependable and steady electricity to every single one of the 18,000 rural villages of the state.[10]

Such ambition was not only physically and technologically daunting, it also flew in the face of accepted political wisdom. Indian farmers everywhere constituted a vote bank, and still do. They had been bribed with free electricity across the country for decades. This supply was 'industrial', for powering pumps and other machinery. It was also typically ramshackle, and much produce was ruined by surges and cuts in the supply that meant, for example, irrigation pumps could not be depended on. In addition, the official blind eye allowed farmers – the wealthier ones at any rate – to steal electricity from the main industrial supply for domestic usage.

Indian agriculture absorbs a significant portion of total electricity generated, so giving it away for nothing to farmers meant huge financial damage to the power sector. Yet charging farmers for power seemed electorally impossible: they could easily hold politicians to ransom through their influential rural vote. An expensive (because it was free) and inefficient system of distribution ensured that governments could not afford to improve the country's power grid infrastructure. It also meant most power companies were in effect bankrupt and therefore state-subsidized, while citizens often lived in darkness caused by erratic and weak supplies, if they were even connected to the grid in the first place.

Modi's plan to change this was counter-intuitive. First, he decided that because electricity was valuable people should pay for it – including farmers. This strategy may have seemed like political hara-kiri even after a major election victory, and the details appeared suicidal: not only would he charge farmers for their electricity, but instead of allowing them to have it for all the daylight period he would restrict the supply to only eight hours out of twenty-four. It was almost designed to provoke an insurrection.

The plan, costing Rs 1,250 crore, was to lay another complete network of power lines – a domestic one – alongside the agricultural supply. The overall system would use powerful 400-volt three-phase electrical power (instead of the rickety single phase) which would stop ruining farm and pumping equipment, while also providing previously 'dark' villages with a reliable and continuous supply at a single or 220-volt two-phase level.

'We are giving farmers a subsidy of Rs 1,700 crores every year,' the minister for energy, Saurabh Patel, reported at the time. It was simply unaffordable. Now energy would cost farmers money but if the plan worked they would have reliable, uninterrupted power.

For a time it seemed as if revolt was indeed on the cards because the power famine was linked to an already acute water shortage. Without continuous power free of charge for drawing water from tube wells, how would the crops survive? 'The can of worms has been opened. For how long will the Modi government be able to contain the crisis?' wrote Dionne Bunsha in *Frontline* in February 2004, shortly after the Jyotigram Scheme had gone live.[11]

'Actually,' recalls Modi, 'when I took charge as chief minister, I had a lot of friction with the farmers.' He adds:

And even some people who belonged to the Sangh Parivar were also against me, because here in Gujarat, the farmers are always fighting for electricity. I told them that this is not the real solution. Forget about electricity; think about water. If you want to fight against Modi, please fight on the issue of water, not on the issue of electricity, because for the last thirty or forty years you are always doing agitations for the requirement of electricity and not a single government is in a position to provide you with sufficient electricity.

Modi held fast and faced down the farmers' rebellion. Metered electricity soon proved the sceptics wrong.[12] The new infrastructure, after limited trials in the most needy districts, was put in place across the entire state in the space of 1,000 days. Many farmers at first disliked the restricted hours, and there was undeniable hardship for certain marginal farmers who found it temporarily more difficult to buy water from tube-well pumpers when prices rose as a result of metering and restricted supply. Yet something happened that changed their attitude:

> Farmers found they could not make unauthorized use of power; they also disliked the effective rationing in force. But then, for the first time they enjoyed largely uninterrupted power supply at full voltage along a strictly adhered schedule. Farmers were also happy that they were spared the very high repair and maintenance cost that poor power supply imposed on them.[13]

In 2001, when Modi came to power, Gujarat faced a shortfall of nearly 2,000 MW. From a power deficit state, Gujarat is now a power surplus state. By providing uninterrupted power to all households, Gujarat under the Jyotigram Yojana has transformed lives in rural Gujarat. The scheme, launched in 2003, covers 18,000 villages.

In rural areas where milking buffalo mechanically had been a hit-and-miss affair because of power cuts, there was now regular electricity supply and a surge in production. The animals reportedly even gave extra milk because they were comfortable standing beneath cooling electric fans. Schoolchildren also found themselves able to concentrate in classrooms that summer heat usually made insufferable.

Likewise, workers in shops and homes, hospitals, colleges and workshops discovered that in addition to feeling cool for the first time, their equipment functioned reliably. Tailors were surprised that despite the new charges they could profit by bolting electric motors onto their sewing machines. New businesses such as diamond polishers were started (or moved out from towns for the lower rural rents), and existing businesses increased their profitability not only because of dependable power but also because they could plan and schedule efficiently.

This had a knock-on effect that slowed the rate of migration from rural to urban areas as the countryside became more prosperous to live in: drinking water and street lighting improved, and people began to enjoy television, labour-saving devices in the kitchen, refrigeration to preserve food, and of course the cooling breeze of electric fans in Gujarat's searing summers.

Secondary agribusinesses such as rice and flour mills saved money thanks to the new electrical supply – as much as a third of their power bills – while simultaneously becoming more productive. A 2008 report on the Jyotigram Scheme concluded that it 'offers a case study of astute political management by intervening in an arena surcharged with animated mass politics'.

In our assessment, JGS has pioneered the real-time co-management of electricity and groundwater irrigation. It has unshackled domestic and non-farm rural electricity supply from the clutches of an invidious political economy of farm power subsidies ... JGS has transformed what was a highly degenerate power-pricing-cum-supply regime into a rational one.[14]

The Gujarat State Electricity Corporation Limited (GSECL) recouped its infrastructural outlay in only two years. 'When I took charge,' says Modi, 'my electricity company had an annual loss of Rs 2,500 crore. We have not increased any tariff. We now have the highest power generation in India. There are so many states, they don't even have 5,000 megawatt power. In only one district of this state we generated 10,000 megawatts power – one district.'

As a point of comparison, Pakistan produces just over 13,000 megawatts (MW) of usable power. 'Yes,' Modi smiles. 'One district in Gujarat produces nearly as much power as Pakistan.'[15]

As Saurabh Patel summed it up: 'Gujarat has achieved 149 per cent increase in power generation since 2001. In 2001, our installed power generation capacity was 8,657 MW, which increased 149 per cent in the past 12 years to reach 21,567 MW now.'[16] In 2012–13, total power generation was more than 23,887 MW.[17]

From being as good as bankrupt, GSECL's revenues rose from Rs 850 crore in 2004–05 to Rs 1,473 crore in 2008–09. In 2010, its surplus was Rs 123 crore. People were happily spending more on electricity because they were making much more money from their businesses with reliable power: overheads were up but profit more so. Growth was occurring. They were working and also entertaining and studying more because the evenings were no longer dark. A civic (as well as economic and even psychological) revolution had taken place: people saw that paying for electricity was far superior to having unreliable electricity free of charge. And Gujarat now had so much electricity to spare it began to sell it to other states, which helped to keep domestic costs down.

Jyotigram was the beginning of the panchamrut transformation of Gujarat. But the five shakti pillars were inseparable in Modi's plan. So it was that when electrification, part of Urja Shakti, had been conceived, it was twinned with Jal Shakti, the transformation of Gujarat's water resources. Electricity was congruent with water because of tube wells, which were being pumped dry before people had to start paying for electricity. Besides, power cuts often reset irrigation processes back to zero so that water was consistently wasted. By linking electrification with a plan to revolutionize the husbanding and distribution of water, a related and self-reinforcing positive change – a virtuous circle – could be set in motion.

As with all the shaktis, it was done with the essential cooperation and involvement of ordinary folk themselves. Enthusiasm, commitment and support were redoubled by people feeling linked to the improvements they saw happening around them. Modi's appeal on Doordarshan, in the midst of the worst phase of the 2002 riots, comes to mind: hands folded, he had pleaded, 'Come, help the government.' Now people understood it was in their interests to do so.

Gujarat enjoys only 80 cm of annual rainfall and just eight of its 185 rivers stay wet all year round. The state covers 6.39 per cent of India's territory but has only 2.28 per cent of its water, and that too mostly in the south. It was worse before the Sardar Sarovar dam was activated in 2001. Lack of water was a principal contributor to poverty and underdevelopment in the state. Droughts were endemic.

The way power was being used only exacerbated the situation and further depleted the water table: a negative resource loop. Often there were water riots. The state treasury was being drained by supplying drinking water by truck and even train to its citizens and cattle (recall Modi's youthful idea, described in an earlier chapter, to move the cattle to the water instead).

As the water table slowly sank, the remaining liquid became more polluted with greater and greater concentrations of minerals, chemicals and trace elements. Fluorosis had become a major problem, leading to illness and deformity. Modi's Jal Shakti was to act on both the potable and agricultural water problems.

Soon after his election win in 2002, the 'State-Wide Drinking Water Grid' began to be laid across Gujarat. Almost 2,000 km of water mains, 115,000 km of subsidiary pipes, 11,000 water towers and an equal number of sumps and reservoirs were, like the Jyotigram electricity grid, speedily installed. Over 150 water treatment and filtration plants, and more recently coastal desalination plants, ensured that 2,250 million litres of drinkable water reached 10,000 villages on a daily basis. Again, nothing on such a scale or with such speed had been seen or even attempted in India before. Fluorosis rapidly declined, and reverse osmosis before long rendered the water safe again.

Depopulation was averted. 'We were thinking we had minus growth in the desert district of Kutch,' Modi says. 'Minus growth – people were leaving the district. Today they are coming back.' The infrastructure quickly paid for itself through savings on road and rail distribution. Costs fell from almost Rs 43.6 crore in 2000–01 before Modi took office to under Rs 1.4 crore by 2008–09.[18]

Again the help and involvement of citizens were encouraged. The Water and Sanitation Management Organization devolved responsibility to the local level, enabling village committees to manage their own facilities and water conservation schemes.

As drinking water supply improved, agricultural supply was also replenished. A programme was begun to construct 113,000 check dams (small dams across water channels that irrigate a maximum of 10 hectares, built through the Sardar Patel Participatory Water Conservation Scheme), stockpiling 56,000 sandbag stores – 'bori bunds' – for use in the event of floods to trap water, digging quarter of a million new farm ponds and erecting 60,000 other structures.[19]

Every drop of water was newly classified as precious. Farmers were educated to see the transformative effects of effective water conservation, or paani bachao. It has been estimated that if India conserved just 30 per cent of its rainfall, the country would have no water shortages.

After the initial infrastructural effort of 'micro water harvesting', the next phase began – of teaching farmers how to micro-irrigate, using far smaller quantities of water to attain the same effects. Drip irrigation was the message spread by the newly created Gujarat Green Revolution Company. The technology saves both water and fertilizer by allowing water to drip slowly to the roots of plants through valves, pipes and tubing. Its genius is to moisten only the minimum necessary amount of soil around the plant itself.

Modi sold the idea to farmers by using language they could understand. 'Imagine,' he said, 'trying to feed a baby by dunking it in a pail of milk.'

I told them, if your child is not well, his weight is not increasing, and you have one bucket of milk, and if your child is taking a bath in that milk, will his health be improved? No. If you want to improve the health of your child, you will have to give him a drop of milk every hour. Then the milk will go into his body and good health will be there. Simply if he bathes in the milk, the body will not get any benefit. In the same way, when you grow the crop on the farm, don't think that the floodwater will strengthen your plant. Only the drip will strengthen your plant, so if you want to strengthen your plant you will have to use the same technique which you are using for your children.

As he speaks, Modi becomes animated. It is clear nothing pleases him more than reflecting on how even simple innovation can improve peoples' lives.

⁓

Drip irrigation requires special equipment, even if it's only specially adapted hoses. A loan system requiring just 5 per cent down payment from farmers and a 50 per cent state subsidy ensured its rapid spread. It not only saved vast quantities of water and improved agricultural yield, but cut electricity consumption yet further. In 2009 alone, 74.1 million kWh were saved. Orchards have now been planted in what was until recently barren desert soil.

In 2001, the water situation in Gujarat was as bad as, if not worse than, the power supply problem. Prone to drought, 70 per cent of Gujarat's land is classed as arid or semi-arid. Before the Jyotigram Scheme began, the water table was dropping by 3 metres every year. The further it fell, the more electricity was needed to drive the pumps to bring water to the surface. Today, Gujarat is the only state in India where the water table is actually rising, by 4 metres annually.

Meanwhile, Modi carried on fighting to raise the permitted level of the Sardar Sarovar dam. He knew that with every extra metre of height a proportionate radius of land could be made fertile. In early 2003 permission was given to raise it to 95 metres, and construction began one hour later.

It was raised again, to 110.64 m, in 2004.[20]

On 16 March 2006, Modi eventually received permission to increase the height of the dam to 121.94 metres. This was after battling to get four fractious states to agree,[21] despite fierce attempts by NGOs and green activists to oppose it.

Some, like the author and activist Arundhati Roy, opposed the dam per se:

> Big Dams are to a Nation's 'Development' what Nuclear Bombs are to its Military Arsenal. They're both weapons of mass destruction. They're both weapons Governments use to control their own people. Both Twentieth Century emblems that mark a point in time when human intelligence has outstripped its own instinct for survival. They're both malignant indications of civilisation turning upon itself. They represent the severing of the link, not just the link – the understanding – between human beings and the planet they live on.[22]

Modi ignored the apocalyptic warnings. Instead, he began to use the new water made available by the dam to multiply its effect on agriculture by building a series of canals.

The aim was to dig thirty-eight canals, stretching 2,538 km. To date twenty-nine canals (stretching 2,000 km) are in operation, with a projected 5,112 km of distribution canals, branching off the main conduits, planned for the near future. The canals are in the process of being 'roofed' with photovoltaic solar panels which will give the twin benefits of preventing evaporation of water from the canals, while simultaneously generating electricity. A pilot project by GSECL is generating 1 megawatt on the Sanand branch canal at Chandrasan in Kadi.[23]

By conceiving of irrigation and electricity as related, both were greatly improved. And as part of the panchamrut, they led inevitably to yet more improvements in related areas: Urja Shakti grew Jal Shakti, and both in turn helped to transform Jan Shakti – people: their abilities and potential. In agriculture this meant that the exposure of farmers to new and efficient methods to improve their lives could be taken advantage of. The education of farmers would further embed and improve agricultural production and the quality of rural life.

Thus in 2005 the Krushi Mahotsav scheme was inaugurated – a travelling roadshow and mobile education centre that visits every single village in Gujarat annually. It comprises an arrangement of booths and displays manned by government employees and representatives from agricultural colleges and businesses, domestic and foreign, who advise farmers and demonstrate new methods of improving land productivity and the production of crops.

Some officials used to complain of having to work outside in searing heat during the Krushi Mahotsav. But Modi led by example, travelling to many villages himself, which he does every year. The complaints soon stopped.[24]

Farmers were issued with soil cards to test the state of the soil and were educated about how best to nourish and improve it. Further improvements in agricultural practice were aided by Modi's decision to split Gujarat's agricultural university into four separate institutions to encourage a wider scope of research and greater specialization. With more expertise and assured water, farmers have increasingly switched to higher-value crops such as mango, banana and wheat, and their production has risen year on year.

The International Food Policy Research Institute (IFPRI) in Washington DC reported: 'While Gujarat's dairy success is well known, which is growing at 6-7 per cent per annum on sustainable basis, the recent phenomenon of high growth comes from fruits and vegetables (dominated by banana, mango, potato and onions) that has grown at almost 12.8 per cent.'[25] Those figures are from 2000–01 to 2007–08, but they have remained on trend since then.

Seed companies encouraged better strains to be planted, including bajra (pearl millet, which is high in iron) and castor for oil. The adoption of Bt cotton, immune to several common diseases of the plant, has meant that the yield of that crop particularly skyrocketed from 3.05 million bales (of 170 kg each) in 2002–03 to 11.2 million bales in 2007–08 – again, it has not slowed down since.[26] According to 2009 figures, Gujarat was producing 35.5 per cent of India's cotton production from only 26 per cent of the area under cultivation. Neighbouring Maharashtra was nowhere near as efficient.[27]

To raise the standard of living of the poor, Modi realized that while policies could be made and implemented, it was important to ensure that benefits reached intended recipients directly. There were concerns about 'middlemen' who pretended to act as a link between the government and intended beneficiaries, but actually hustled the rewards away. It was using this insight that he envisioned the garib kalyan melas.

An ambitious programme for social transformation, the garib kalyan mela has integrated benefits from multiple schemes and eliminated middlemen so that benefits reach the neediest. Reversing the process of beneficiaries seeking government officers, now government officers go in search of eligible beneficiaries to provide assistance. The government thus went to the doorstep of people to bring about a significant change in their lives. The Gujarat government has so far conducted 1,000 garib kalyan melas and distributed Rs 13,000 crore assistance to around eighty-five lakh beneficiaries.

Modi's idea of governance and its role in devolving administrative autonomy to local levels away from state government led to innovations that awoke the moribund gram sabha (village administration) committees. 'For me,' says Modi, 'development is a mass movement. People think that development is a government agenda. I say no, development should be the agenda of the common man. Unless and until the common man's agenda is development, government can build the buildings, but that is not development.'

The drift towards a centralized bureaucracy was reversed by Modi offering a bounty, under his Samras Yojana programme, of one lakh rupees to any village that could unanimously elect a representative. With money as the bait, over 60 per cent speedily did so. This ended the sort of gossipy disagreements among petty village cliques that had held back decisions being taken at a local level. It additionally revitalized rural life as people for the first time saw local improvements being made around them thanks to their own decision making, turning entitlement into empowerment. 'The change in Gujarat happened because every Gujarati feels that he is part of the development process,' says Modi.[28]

The government's idea was that unleashing the potential latent in people's lives should extend across all aspects of society, urban as well as rural. 'Development is a mass movement,' Modi says. 'Each and every citizen of my state is the initiator, creator, implementer; this is what the citizen is doing. And because of that reason, we can actually set a goal.'

For instance, it is universally accepted that justice delayed is justice denied, and the sluggishness of the Indian legal system in dealing with its litigants is a national scandal and a disgrace to democracy.

'In Gujarat we took the initiative: we started evening courts,' says Modi. 'The same infrastructure, which was not used after 5 p.m., could be used. I started evening courts from 6 p.m. to 10 p.m. I gave special pay to the judges and all court staff. Because of that reason, pendency came down.'

In only four months, between November 2006 and the end of March 2007, 50,000 cases were disposed of.[29] The state now has the lowest proportion of outstanding cases in India at 2 per cent, though it has 5 per cent of India's population.

The health improvements generated by clean, plentiful water (often meaning clean drinking water on tap, a rarity in India) and steady power were buttressed by many schemes that aimed to add 'health to wealth'. These included improved standards of food, education, hygiene, and a drive for cleaner air and a general reduction in pollution.

The state government kept up its role of facilitator, leading to other related improvements. Roads continued to be built, until over 98 per cent of rural habitations at village level were connected.[30] When critics mocked that in one year, contrary to Modi's 'propaganda', only 10 km of roads were constructed in Gujarat, they neglected to point out that it was because the entire annual highways budget was being spent upgrading the ample roads that were already built over the decade – something anybody who travels around in Gujarat cannot fail to notice.

In 2005, Modi presented Gujarat with the first revenue-surplus budget in its history.[31] Red tape meanwhile was slashed for companies that wanted to set up facilities in the state, and word quickly spread globally that a helpful administration which did not expect bribes existed in the west of India. Investment began to flow into Gujarat, shepherded by Vibrant Gujarat, culminating in emblematic fashion with the relocation of Tata Motors' Nano manufacturing plant from Singur in West Bengal to Sanand in Ahmedabad district in 2008.[32]

The arrangements once the company's decision had been made were completed within ten days owing to Gujarat already having an established land bank in reserve for industrial projects. This was an innovation Modi had put in place. It drew criticism of crony capitalism with allegations that land was being sold to industrialists at throwaway prices. But the employment these new manufacturing plants generated and the wealth they created in local communities muted much of the criticism.

The Nano project in West Bengal had been bedevilled by worker agitation, bandhs and even violence as Tata attempted to ready the plant for production. The Left Front state government, which acquired land from unwilling farmers for the proposed site – perversely, the most fertile area in Hooghly was chosen – and the opposition Trinamool Congress, which led an agitation against Tata, had not helped matters. In despair at the attrition, Ratan Tata decided to call off all development at the Singur site and move the business elsewhere. When Modi heard of this he texted the industrialist a single word: 'Welcome.'

At the time West Bengal's chief minister was the communist Buddhadeb Bhattacharjee, with Mamata Banerjee leader of the Opposition. Soon after the Nano's arrival in Gujarat, Modi did a most outrageous thing by writing open letters to both Bhattacharjee

('I'm doing this after due deliberation ...') and Banerjee ('You are like a sister to me ...'). Although he assured them that he wasn't gloating over their loss, he actually was. To Bhattacharjee he confided, 'The fact of the matter is: despite your efforts, Bengal doesn't yet have the work-culture to produce a Nano.' Modi signed off by explaining that it was 'the commitment of the people of Gujarat towards industrialization, work-culture, and joint effort by all regardless of political affiliations, that the project came to our state. I'd hope that some day a similar climate would come into existence in your state too.'

If anything he was even more direct with Mamata, chiding her for 'opposition for the sake of opposition' and issuing a brotherly warning that, though she claimed to be fighting communism, she must not 'become an ultra-communist [yourself]'. His message was that West Bengal's Luddite policies were the equivalent of shooting itself in both feet. The state, he reminded them, had attempted to keep out job-destroying computers. 'Rather, take the rightwing route to build an alternative in Bengal,' he wrote. 'Please make demands for more industry, more roads, and more jobs in your state.'[33]

His correspondents' replies went unrecorded and were probably unprintable. Why did Modi send the letters? Was it helpless exuberance or a declaration to more than the recipients and readers of the letters – a declaration to himself? By 2008 the developments and infrastructure he had put in place in Gujarat were already bearing fruit and all the indicators suggested that growth would not only persist but accelerate. Modi's reference to the 'rightwing route' was by now a reference not to chauvinistic Hindutva – how distant, even irrelevant that now sounded – but to the idea of the free market and innovative governance.

The open letters stood not only as advice to West Bengal but also to elements in the Sangh Parivar. They announced how far Modi had travelled from his roots. They even implied the difference, or rather the gulf, that implicitly separated his economic outlook from that of the old BJP guard. The party had remained rudderless and relatively policy-free since its defeat in the 2004 Lok Sabha poll, falsely believing it was their 1998–2004 reforms that had lost them the election.

~

In 1994, the southern Gujarat city of Surat, then with 1.2 million inhabitants, fell victim to pneumonic plague, a complication of bubonic plague. Hundreds died while hundreds of thousands attempted to flee the city, which by all accounts had become an impoverished hellhole (the plague was spread by fleas) and whose emergency and medical infrastructure was quickly overwhelmed by the *Yersinia pestis* bacterium.

But by 2006 when the city suffered another disaster, being inundated by catastrophic floodwaters, it was a different place altogether. There were now 500,000 high-tech looms in use by its weavers and 10,000 diamond polishing units. For in the meantime the city had risen to the top of the league in the diamond industry and produced annual exports worth Rs 55,000 crore, representing 90 per cent of the industry's world trade and practically all of India's own. A state-of-the-art, all-weather seaport was being constructed by Shell, and it would be well served by the new roads and flyovers lacing together the busy city.[34]

Unlike the plague that struck in 1994, Surat's floods were handled reasonably well by the authorities, though there are conflicting reports of delayed help. Normality – by now normality in Surat meant growth and prosperity – swiftly resumed. Critics say that Modi was initially slow to react. But once relief operations got under way, documents and anecdotal evidence suggest the local administration moved relatively swiftly.

It is useful to examine the full facts before studying the claims of both critics and the government. Today, Surat has water distribution which, like its drainage system, is computerized. Surat even operates a sewage treatment plant which transforms waste into energy, as well as one of the best water treatment plants in India.[35]

Every street in Surat now has drains beneath its sidewalks and pavements, with street lights above them. Over 95 per cent of its autorickshaws and mass transit vehicles use compressed natural gas, helping to keep the air clean. E-governance is in place almost everywhere, speeding up and slimming down interactions and processes between Surtis and the state, and cutting out many of the opportunities officials previously enjoyed to ask for 'donations' to help get routine things done.

Not surprisingly, as the economy boomed and the standard of living rose, so did the city's population, which more than trebled from 1994. Surat of course is exceptional. It had the fastest growing GDP in India until recently and currently ranks eighth in terms of city GDP (it basically doubled in size from 2001 to 2008). Nevertheless, Surat exemplifies the cross-fertility of Modi's panchamrut development. With its modernized manufacturing in clothing and jewellery, Surat has been transformed from the plague-ridden city it once was.

'I said we must have a five-step formula,' says Modi. 'Farm; farm to fibre; fibre to fabric; fabric to fashion; fashion to foreign. Then the farmer will be the beneficiary. So we must have a value-addition chain right up to exports.'

This demonstrated how a dirty, chaotic eyesore with hopelessly inadequate infrastructure and an inefficient municipal government – and even visitations of medieval mass death – only two decades ago can be changed under reformist municipal commissioners who receive support but also independence from the state government. 'Surat was known as the dirtiest city of India,' Modi says. 'Today it is the cleanest city in India.'

Development is Modi's favourite topic of conversation. He likes it because he believes that apart from making individuals' lives better, development makes everybody's life better. Modi is a politician and this translates into votes. Does Modi, in modernizing Gujarat in the energetic manner he had done, not fear he is following the Western path? What is the cost of cultural tradition being hammered into oblivion by relentless change for material benefit alone?

Modi's answer to my question about India rushing forward but leaving behind its heart was a simple one: 'Modernization without westernization,' he says. It certainly sounds better than westernization without modernization, of which India already has a surfeit. But what does it really mean?

Modi firmly believes in remaining traditionally Indian while embracing modernity, and especially technology, of integrating it with cultural traditions rather than destroying tradition with progress, as arguably the West has done. In other words modernization without westernization: remember that you are Indian, and go forward in an Indian way; find a way to renew your old relationships as you learn new ones.

This lies behind Modi's deepest inspiration for his development shaktis: they are characterized as feminine because this allows progress to be held within the traditional 'mamta', the nurturing maternal ethos of the home that carries within it the traditions and reassurances of Indian family life.[36]

'The Ganga is an incarnation of the Mother, so is India,' Modi said. 'Even the cow is revered as a Mother. The position of women has always been supreme, there are no two views on this.'[37]

It has to be stressed how fundamental the idea of the feminine is to Modi, something that is not immediately apparent to the observer, especially because the media embellishes Modi's image as exceedingly masculine. But at the heart of all his development philosophy is a strikingly feminine ethos, as the word 'shakti' suggests. For as Jan Shakti nurtured the talents and resources of

Gujarat's farmers, so the educational development ran directly within the Gyan Shakti, knowledge power. And here, the emphasis on improving educational institutions – especially science and technology – is juxtaposed with an emphasis on the most traditionally neglected aspect of Jan Shakti – the people power of women, whose abilities and potential Modi decided were underused everywhere. It was, he said repeatedly, a shocking waste of the talents of half the population. Hence the concentration on educating girls.

Education though is precisely one of the areas where critics deride Modi for Gujarat's lack of social development, so the record needs to be carefully examined. Again, his programme began early in his tenure as chief minister. A drive for school enrolment (spearheaded by initially reluctant bureaucrats who found themselves out of their offices and in distant village schoolrooms) was quickly launched, with attention paid especially to girls. Beginning in 2002 a 'Narmada Bond' was issued, worth Rs 1,000 for girls to put away towards their educational expenses. The assumption was that society must improve organically and sustainably over the long term, and that FDI in industry would not alone accomplish an even spread of prosperity across Gujarat.

So is Gujarat's progress illusory? Or, is it simply that Gujarat was always prosperous, even before Modi arrived on the scene? What can be done to logically settle the argument is to compare various socio-economic parameters from before Modi was chief minister with the same parameters after he took charge. Comparisons with indices of advancement in other states can also yield factual information. The rate of progress over time, more than current snapshot indicators, reveal true performance.

For example, back in 1991, a decade before Modi became chief minister, Gujarat stood in sixth place in the human development index (HDI) of Indian states. The HDI was invented the year before, in 1990, and is a composite statistic of life expectancy, education and income.[38] By 2007–08, when Modi was re-elected for the second time, Gujarat's all-India state ranking in HDI had slipped by five places to eleventh, apparently a steep decline. But this figure needs to be examined more closely. It must be remembered that in 1991 states such as Delhi, Himachal Pradesh, Goa, Jammu and Kashmir, the north-east states, Uttarakhand, Jharkhand and Chhattisgarh were not included in the rankings – and three did not even exist.[39] If they are removed, Gujarat rises to exactly where it was in 1991 – sixth.

The figures reveal that Gujarat's HDI actually rose from 0.431 in 1991 to 0.527 in 2007–08, an increase of 22.3 per cent. Is that impressive? The 1991 all-India value was 0.381, lower than Gujarat's at the time. In 2007–08, the all-India HDI which took into account the newly included states and territories – all small and relatively well developed that pushed Gujarat down the table – was 0.467, well below Gujarat's 0.527, meaning Gujarat was still above average.[40]

Even including all these new small states, the all-India increase in HDI had been 22.5 per cent, almost exactly what Gujarat's was over the same period. When Modi is accused of being laggardly with regard to poverty, health, malnutrition and education, he can in all fairness reply that it is consistent with the nation's fortunes, which were (very slowly) on the rise throughout the period 1991–2008. Without some of the new, smaller states, and their sometimes extremely high HDIs, which in part are a function of their size, Gujarat's statistics would look even better. This does not absolve Modi from failing to get Gujarat's HDI to rise faster. But tendentious interpretations lend neither balance nor objectivity to an important debate.

It is true that in the real story of growth and development that Gujarat has experienced under Modi's stewardship, education, health and other social indicators have not done as well compared to other indices such as GDP growth, which has far outrun Indian averages. While it is relatively easy to start up a factory and begin producing units of economic value, the more difficult areas of improvement are the human ones of education, health and hygiene, which can take at least one generation, possibly more, to show significant transformation. They depend upon a change of outlook, habit and behaviour, often in the private sphere of the bathroom and kitchen where it is most difficult for the government to exert a positive, or at least measurable, influence.

It is also true that Gujarat spends less on education (13.9 per cent of its budget) than it should. Bihar spends 18 per cent. But because of poor governance, success is not always about absolute levels of spending; it is rather the efficacy of the spend.

To illustrate this, literacy levels should be examined. The official Indian government figures[41] are also used by Professor Bibek Debroy of the Centre for Policy Research in Delhi in his book, *Gujarat: Governance for Growth and Development*, referred to here.[42]

Going back again to 1991, the average rate of literacy in India was 52.2 per cent. Twenty years later, in 2011, great strides had been made: it had risen significantly and stood at 74 per cent overall. In Gujarat, over the same period, literacy rose from 61.2 per cent to 79.3 per cent, well above the national average.

Debroy points out that in the increase in literacy among females, the differential growth between Gujarat and India as a whole is even more pronounced[43] – underlining the points already made concerning Modi's drive to emancipate women into a larger and more fulfilling role in India's economy and social life.

In the two decades since 1991 Indian women have improved their literacy from 39.3 per cent to 65.5 per cent and in Gujarat from 48.9 per cent to 70.7 per cent. Gujarati women are thus more literate than the Indian female average. While average literacy for

Indian women increased between 2001 and 2011 – during Modi's tenure – from 54.2 per cent to 65.5 per cent, it increased from 57.8 per cent to 70.7 per cent for Gujarati women. The increase in female literacy in Gujarat – though higher than the all-India average – must be tested qualitatively as well to arrive at an objective conclusion. The effect of lagging indicators can't be ignored: Gujarat has a tradition of not educating girls. Modi had to overcome cultural prejudice and change conditioned behaviour.

There is further evidence of overall improvement in educational outcomes from school dropout rates, argues Debroy. Again the improvements for girls have been especially significant. Dropout rates for girls in primary school plummeted by 90 per cent during Modi's, tenure, from 20.81 per cent in 2001 to a very low 2.08 per cent in 2011. The later years of school are naturally more difficult for pupil retention, especially girls, but under the Modi government the dropout rate for girls in Standards I–VII fell from 36.90 per cent in 2001 to 7.82 per cent in 2011-12, meaning over 90 per cent of older girls now remain in education. This suggests that in the near future a further improvement in female literacy is to be expected as the lag effect disappears.

These official figures are at variance with the criticism levelled against Gujarat – that while it is hospitable to industrialists, it is less so to women, the poor and Muslims.

Another lagging indicator is health. Here again, it is important to compare Gujarat's average or slightly substandard infant mortality rate (IMR) with all-India statistics from 1991 to 2011, and then make a further comparison under Modi's leadership from 2001 to 2011.

In India, baby girls are less favoured than baby boys, and sometimes undergo foeticide because of their sex, resulting in more births of boys than girls. Debroy notes that this situation worsened nationally between 2001 and 2011, from a ratio of 927:1,000 girls:boys to 919:1,000. That initially strikes one as strange in a rapidly developing country, but perhaps a reason could be that medical scans identifying the sex of the foetus have become more common.

In Gujarat for the same period (2001–2011) the ratio improved marginally, from 883:1,000 girls:boys to 890:1,000. That remains below the national average, and is anyway poor, but it is a problem Gujarat specifically has suffered from for a long time. Modi was well aware of this, and in 2005 began his 'Beti Bachao Andolan' ('Save Our Daughters') campaign.

In a speech in April 2013, he said that in the eighteenth century, baby girls were often drowned in milk. 'Sometimes I feel we have become worse than the eighteenth century, where at least the girl child was allowed to be born. In the twenty-first century the girl child is killed before she is born.'[44]

The impact of government policy on redressing the imbalance in sex ratios among children is best observed in the statistics for sex ratio at birth. This measure shows a significant improvement in Gujarat from 837 to 909 under Modi's stewardship compared with 894 to 906 nationally between 2001 and 2011. State figures for child malnutrition in Gujarat between 2007 and 2013 (oddly, no national statistics exist before 2005–06) fell from 71 per cent to 29 per cent, which correlates with the positive effects of agricultural progress in the state. These are still high, though lower than in other large states, and Gujarat clearly has much work to do to improve child malnutrition and gender ratios.

Does Modi's chief ministership look as if it deserved Prof. Amartya Sen's comment that 'Gujarat's record in education and health care is pretty bad?'

The figures used here are all official central government statistics. Jagdish Bhagwati and Arvind Panagariya of Columbia University disagree with Prof. Sen's conclusions. 'Critics who insist on viewing everything related to Modi through the 2002 lens and, thus, fail to separate their economics from politics have fallen short of 20/20 vision,' says Prof. Panagariya, perhaps drawing nearer to what the argument is really about.[45]

Panagariya concludes that 'critics frequently deride the exceptional growth in Gujarat by pointing to its lack of achievement in social sectors. But they often do so by focusing on selective indicators. A consideration of a broad set of indicators hardly offers an indictment of the state, even in social sectors.'

Compared with contentious social indicators, there is less debate on economic growth in Gujarat since 2001. Even Rahul Sachitanand, writing an otherwise critical piece in the *The Economic Times*, admitted: 'In the five years before Modi took charge, the state's average growth in GSDP (gross state domestic product) was 2.8 per cent. Under him, between 2002-03 and 2011-12, it was 10.3 per cent. Only three small states – Sikkim, Uttarakhand and Delhi – have grown faster. Gujarat is ahead of the national average (7.9 per cent).'

Consider now the poverty figures. In 2004–05, 31.8 per cent of Gujarat's population was defined as living in poverty. By 2011–12 that had fallen to 16.6 per cent, almost halving the number of people below the poverty line. During the same period, Nitish Kumar's Bihar, which critics often compare favourably with Gujarat under Modi, saw its own levels of poverty fall from 54.4 per cent to 33.7 per cent. Some, such as Sachitanand, contend that there has been little 'trickle-down' effect even though Gujarat's per capita income has trebled under Modi. Yet a halving of poverty in the seven years under review looks entirely in keeping with the state's 10 per cent annual GSDP growth. Some sections of the population have done better than others – OBCs better than tribals, for example – but the trend is positive and it is of course a work in progress.

In an elegant analysis in *The Times of India*, a senior journalist demolished Nitish Kumar's arguments while stressing that it is a futile and irrelevant contest. Though perhaps still underestimating Gujarat's social sector achievements, he pointed out that Bihar's levels of poverty remain twice as high as Gujarat's (33.7 per cent vs 16.6 per cent) and showed the dangers of 'mixing apples with oranges' – of drawing misleading inferences about the performances of states by ignoring their demographics, sizes and populations. He discovered that when the ten most populous states are compared in terms of per capita income (PCI), only Maharashtra ranks higher than Gujarat. Bihar is tenth and last. When the 'unfair weightage' of India's financial capital, Mumbai, is removed from the calculation of Maharashtra's average PCI, Gujarat moves above it into first position. Bihar remains anchored at the bottom of the list.[46]

Modi, through the several interviews we had, continuously stressed that he personally had no interest in growth for the sake of growth. 'Inclusive' development gave better rewards, he stressed. Other states such as Maharashtra and Tamil Nadu may have grown as fast, but 'the real story of Gujarat's relative underperformance compared to its obvious peers – Maharashtra and Tamil Nadu – may be explained by the simple fact that Gujarat's growth is based on manufacturing, not services.'[47]

In terms of general prosperity the focus on manufacturing rather than services is very important. For example, under Chandrababu Naidu, chief minister of Andhra Pradesh from 1994 to 2004, the software industry grew rapidly. Yet outside of Hyderabad and beyond its high-tech clusters, development in the largely rural state was neglected.[48] Unalleviated droughts and unevenness of progress, mixed with the despair of farmers who committed suicide in the thousands, contributed to his electoral defeat. In 2004 Naidu's Telugu Desam Party (TDP) won only forty-seven of 294 constituencies in the state assembly and five out of forty-two Lok Sabha seats.

What manufacturing does steadily, rather than speedily like IT and financial services, is to create layers of jobs in the community, and thus successive, cumulative, sustainable waves of prosperity. Back-office IT companies employ people whose salaries are mostly paid directly into their bank accounts, with relatively little local 'spillover' benefit. A new car factory (basically an assembly plant), on the other hand, will create work for many local suppliers of all the bits and pieces needed for the cars. Their employees in turn will create demand in the area for shops and other services as wages are spent locally.

A ripple effect develops. At 27.4 per cent of GSDP in 2009–10 (against a national average of 15 per cent), Gujarat has the highest manufacturing-to-GSDP ratio among the states,[49] and this is an important element in its overall development: it does not simply have high-tech islands of prosperity as in southern India, or a concentration of banks and financial institutions as in Mumbai. The industrialization, and the employment it creates, is more widespread.

It is also worth asking to what degree Gujarat's prosperity has percolated down. There has indeed been a large increase in incomes, and though there are disparities in prosperity they are not extreme: all boats, including even the leaky ones, are rising with the tide. Most importantly, everybody is aboard one boat or another. The disparities in income levels are further ameliorated because much of the prosperity in Gujarat is in the form of 'public goods': roads, electricity, water, education, jobs – all of which arise from development projects that aim to benefit the whole population, not only those fortunate enough to already have the best start in life.

By concentrating first on agriculture and manufacturing –

Gujarat's traditional strengths – and only after that on technology and latterly finance, Modi planned to ensure a wide and roughly egalitarian base of progress. This is a point many critics of the Gujarat model have missed.

The fifth and last pillar of Modi's panchamrut is Raksha Shakti: security. The prosperity and quality of life that accrue from the common benefits of infrastructure affect other areas as well. Foremost among these collateral benefits is that for twelve years Gujarat has seen no riots. People of all communities now go about their daily lives without the ever-present fear that used to haunt their steps. No comparison can be made between Gujarat now and the ghettoized tinderbox Modi inherited from Keshubhai Patel in October 2001.

Life is a daily struggle for many Muslims still living in closed, segregated communities twelve years after the riots. But the shadow of mass violence has melted away – alongside strictly unprejudiced treatment from the administration towards every citizen in accordance with the Constitution. In trying to treat citizens 'blindly' as equals, ignoring pleas for special treatment for minorities, Modi believes he has done what he said he would do: demonstrating through action rather than words his idea of secularism.

Civic peace and security helps the poor and Muslims who suffered disproportionately during violent disturbances in the past. It was always their homes and businesses and loved ones who were hurt the most. It was they who suffered most from hunger and deprivation as curfews made it impossible for them to go out and earn a living. Now, with some exceptions, they can work and get on with their lives. And as they do so, the tension eases further, because where hope and opportunity exist there is less inclination to resent or fear one's neighbours.

Some believe that 'under Modi's clean image and administrative ethics, corruption has rather gone underground.'[50] It is true that in India corruption will not disappear, and Gujarat is not an island. But by common consent far less corruption exists in Gujarat now than before, and far less than it does in other states or at the Centre.

In a sense Modi was lucky ('I am a lucky fellow,' he agrees with a smile). Today in India, it costs an average of Rs 15 crore to be elected an MP. Few aspiring politicians possess that sort of money and must rely on donations, usually in cash, to help them on their journey to the Lok Sabha. Once they are there this money, and all other sorts of favours received along the way, have to be repaid with interest. This is fertile breeding ground for corruption.

Modi, by contrast, never had to raise any money to fight an election simply because he had never considered standing for political office. Modi became chief minister in October 2001, at his party's behest, without ever having fought an election. Not owing anything in favours or cash, he was beholden to nobody. As a result his ideas and principles remained intact. He says: 'God has given me this opportunity to serve the people, not to serve Modi.'

Modi seems uninterested in amassing personal wealth. His net worth at the time of his re-election in 2007 amounted to a little more than Rs 40 lakh, Rs 30 lakh of which was tied up in a small property he had bought in Gandhinagar, probably in case he was turfed out of the chief minister's bungalow. At the time of his re-election in 2012, his wealth had trebled to Rs 1.3 crore, but Rs 70 lakh of that was accounted for by the rise in the value of his still uninhabited house.[51] He had under Rs 4 lakh cash in the bank. In comparison to any other Indian politician, Modi is a pauper.

In politics there is the corruption of money and the corruption of favours, with one normally leading to the other in both directions. Modi, from the start of his time as chief minister, made it plain he would tolerate neither. He assumed people around him accepted his opinion regarding the grave illegality of taking bribes and rarely mentioned it afterwards. But woe betide any member of his party or any administrative officer found to be financially corrupt. Favours and influence on the other hand, endemic in the way that government and political parties did business, were previously unremarkable and everywhere visible in Gujarat. Modi's zero tolerance on that score came as a great shock to nearly everybody. It soon aroused resentment and sedition, eventually outright mutiny.

Shortly after he was sworn in as chief minister, Modi gathered his officers and legislators and told them that they should not come to him with any requests that were not strictly relevant to their work, or were in any way unethical. 'You should talk about the interest of the party (BJP). I cannot entertain a wrongful demand. Don't do any work which will flout ethical norms, even though important political leaders approach you and try to influence you.'[52]

Next, he visited the BJP headquarters in Ahmedabad and made it clear that in an important way he was no longer one of them. 'You should support me and my government for implementing our party's programme, but you will not come to me with unrealistic and unreasonable expectations.'[53]

For Modi the citizens of Gujarat now deserved his loyalty, and this meant that the interests of friends and party colleagues were sublimated. He acted so decisively in this regard that it shocked those around him and stirred such keen emotions of betrayal in some colleagues that they curdled into hatred.

'As a young energetic Sangh pracharak, Modi was quite popular in the BJP circuit, but after he became CM, he has not remained that popular in his known circles,' says Pravin Sheth, Modi's old tutor from the time he took an MA in political science. 'One reason is that he would not submit to use his position to do any unfair work.'[54] But Modi knew from the beginning that if he did not take this harsh course of action, his plans for reform would go nowhere. They would inevitably be dragged down by the endemic culture of privilege and corruption that had eaten away at Indian politics and civil society.

Sheth also says that Modi had an 'abrasive manner of saying "no" to seekers of undue favour' and would even 'run down a minister for coming to him for a palpably improper demand – sometimes in the presence of their supporters from their constituency in the very precinct of Sachivalaya. All this was unheard of in previous governments.'[55]

What then is the verdict on Modi's governance and development? Is the Gujarat model a myth? Can it, with modifications, be adopted nationally? Beyond the statistics of GSDP growth, HDI, heath care, infant mortality and poverty levels lies the principle of economic freedom without which no society can be called fully evolved.

In 2012, the Fraser Institute, a Canadian think tank that measures the degree of economic freedom in the world's nations in its annual Economic Freedom of the World (EFW) survey, ranked India 111th out of 144 countries. In 2005, soon after the Congress led UPA-2 government had come to power after defeating the NDA, India had stood in seventy-sixth place. India is quickly travelling in the wrong direction.[56]

In contrast, Gujarat was fifth in the rankings of economic freedom across Indian states in 2005. In 2012 it was in first place. Bihar was last, below West Bengal.[57]

PART 4

The Future

10

AND NOW, PRIME MINISTER MODI

I am lucky that I do not belong to the Delhi club.
In my case it is true that I am not from the Delhi club.
I belong to the common man.

– Narendra Modi

N SEPTEMBER 2006 A party member spoke anonymously to journalist Saba Naqvi at the BJP national headquarters in Delhi. 'We're just biding time till the real leader can take over and fix the mess,' he told her. 'Narendrabhai is the only one who can save us.'[1]

Seven years after the whispered admission that the BJP needed Modi to 'fix the mess', and after several months of speculation following his appointment as chairman of the BJP election campaign committee for the 2014 Lok Sabha poll, Modi was declared the party's official prime ministerial candidate. The autumn of 2013 thus saw one of the BJP's cardinal rules – that no member shall hold more than one office at the same time – broken not once but twice, by a man who already held office as a chief minister. A new chairman of the election campaign, Rajnath Singh, was subsequently appointed – again breaking the one-job rule, as he remains BJP president – because Modi could not after all campaign for himself. But it remains true that at the heart of the BJP something fundamental has changed.

As usual Modi had to fight the intransigence of the system, which distrusts mavericks and free thinkers, and whose mills grind not only slowly but grind exceedingly fine.

The anti-Modi camp in BJP calculated that by advancing slowly, and eventually securing just enough seats in the May 2014 Lok Sabha poll, it would be able to form a coalition only slightly larger than the Congress-led UPA. This would guarantee the smallest tilt in the see-saw of power and ensure business as usual in Delhi.

Furthermore, by turning away from the challenge of winning well over 200 Lok Sabha seats that would give the BJP and its pre- and post-poll allies an overall majority, a compromise prime ministerial candidate would emerge acceptable to 'secular' political allies.

At the age of eighty-six and having lost the previous general election, Advani saw the possibility of political resurrection. But after Modi's elevation, as one commentator put it, Advani is now revered as a mentor, a role he should have chosen himself rather than allowing it to be foisted on him. And yet, Advani to his credit has been fulsome in his praise for Modi once the issue was settled with a nudge from the RSS. The BJP's top leadership, including Sushma Swaraj, too has presented a united front under Modi's leadership.

Ram Jethmalani, the maverick politician and lawyer, pointed out succinctly: 'Many in India have become so accustomed to dynastic succession that a democratic succession exercised through contest in the true spirit of democracy is construed as a great aberration, or an indication of a dysfunctional political party.'[2]

The 'quiet' internal contest for leadership in the BJP was unlike the robust primaries in the US and party ballots in the UK, but it reflected, in the end, popular opinion of who should lead the party into the 2014 general election.

~

It is said that in India voters usually vote against the candidate they dislike rather than in favour of the candidate they like. This favours the mildest and least offensive politician and would usually rule out a figure such as Modi. It is also said that 'voters in India dislike ambition and are pulled towards renunciates', and that this worked against Advani in 2009, when he clearly nurtured the illusion of himself as India's ablest candidate as prime minister.[3] Such reasoning should mean that Modi is also likely to suffer from self-promotion, if one believes what part of the media says about him. Yet there were clear signs that 2014 would be very different from other elections.

The BJP's choice of Modi reflected a change of tactics: unleashing a daring cavalry charge against the Congress instead of sticking with the safer, attritional trench warfare, advancing and retreating yard by yard. It may be seen as a revolution of youthful optimism – or impatience – and perhaps a sign that the Indian people, if not its politicians, crave change. It is also a sign that the centre of gravity of Indian politics is shifting from Delhi to the states.

Dr Manmohan Singh was prime minister for ten years despite never having won a Lok Sabha seat, although he contested and lost in South Delhi in 1999. Modi, on the west coast, has never won a Lok Sabha seat either, but has been chief minister for four terms over twelve years, winning three state elections. Who has the greater claim on democratic legitimacy? During that time Gujarat progressed while the country slid backwards and Manmohan Singh, dutiful to dynasty rather than nation, remained in place to silently witness his previous economic reforms unravel. When Singh visited the US in September 2013, as the Republicans were locked in battle with President Obama over the budget ceiling and public services ground to a halt, the joke in India was that Dr Singh went to America and even America's government shut down.

Whatever policies the BJP espoused during the charged and polarized election campaign are flavoured by Modi's own combative personality. The Congress still does not realize (or perhaps it does) that giving poor people free food will not abolish poverty; and neither apparently does the BJP, which helped to vote the Food Security Bill (FSB) through the Lok Sabha in August 2013. The FSB is officially estimated to cost Rs 1.25 lakh crore, but is likely to cost the exchequer at least twice that, including infrastructural, storage and logistical expenditure. It mandates grain and rice handouts to over 800 million of India's 1.2 billion people, much of which will be misdirected, stolen or left to rot.[4]

Critics have argued, among other things, that anyway it is not grain that poor people need, and that ending malnutrition requires a diet including milk and vegetables, which many destitute Indian children have never tasted. Creating an ecosystem of sanitation, hygiene and clean drinking water rather than just handing out cheap wheat and rice is what is needed to tackle malnutrition in India.

An opinion poll in Karnataka before the assembly elections in May 2013 showed that 62 per cent of voters backed Modi as a prime minister, while only 25 per cent wanted the BJP to return to power in the state.[5]

The voters were not bluffing, and the Congress went on to win an absolute majority over the BJP in Karnataka. It was widely assumed that the spectre of Modi-as-PM was to blame, despite it being common knowledge that assembly elections are determined by local issues and that the Congress, in spite of anti-incumbency and a vote split among BJP supporters due to B.S. Yeddyurappa's breakaway party, had increased its own vote share by only 1 per cent.

Modi's opponents in the party began to argue that he should be announced as the prime ministerial candidate (if at all) only after the five state assembly elections scheduled in November–December 2013 since Modi would be tainted if the party did badly. Yet, every opinion poll showed that Modi was the country's leading choice as prime minister and would spike the BJP's Lok Sabha seat tally significantly.

The sixteenth Lok Sabha election was now *faute de mieux*, a presidential-pattern election. M.J. Akbar, the veteran editor, who joined the BJP in March 2014, wrote that Indians are desperate for decisive leadership: 'If Mrs Indira Gandhi were seeking re-election today, she would win 400 seats.'[6]

That suggests at present ideology is second to character. But is a character such as Modi's – brusque, decisive, combative – what is needed? In Modi, India will certainly have a decisive leader, and that is what worries many people. It certainly alarms Delhi's status quo elite.

Several years ago the British writer Frederick Forsyth noted that Left and Right were outdated labels, relics of twentieth-century conflicts between labour and capital, no longer suitable as compass or anchor points in a new technological era. Henceforth, argued Forsyth, from the dissolving of the old battlelines would emerge a situation where radicals on the Right shared more in common with radicals on the Left than with conservatives in their own parties.

If a complacent Congress and BJP are replete with conservatives who want nothing to change, Modi appears as a radical who wants to transform the country. His sort of administration, with bureaucracy minimized and governance maximized, potentially has appeal across the political spectrum, especially to the young. It is a new formulation, and along with its success in Gujarat, is in large part responsible for Modi being hailed as a leader – the sort of figure, good or bad as only time may tell, that a major reorientation of politics calls forth.

If Forsyth is correct, Modi could attract support from reformers from every quarter (including Muslims) and, ironically, disapproval from conservatives from all parties including occasionally his own. It does not matter if anti-Modi ideologues think of themselves as liberals or believe they are the only guardians of minorities: that is only one of the current contradictions as politics itself realigns to new poles of power and absorbs unconventional ideas.

Those who seek dramatic reformation and change will be found across political ideologies because people with all sorts of political persuasions will recognize that no one party is completely correct and that the system itself must be transformed for the greater benefit of the nation. One could call these people pro-India rather than pro-party and it is partly why individualistic political figures instead of parties are increasingly popular with voters.

India is growing weary of ideological bickering and point scoring, which leads only to stasis and stagnation. Instead, its young thirst for a kind of sweeping change that threatens every vested party interest. They will probably not get it until leaders go beyond party boundaries and enthuse a sufficient number of voters to break the mathematics of coalitions. The success, though short-lived, of the Aam Aadmi Party (AAP) spearheaded by Arvind Kejriwal in the December 2013 Delhi assembly elections, is a sign that a new kind of politics – and politicians – is gaining traction in India.

The electoral effectiveness of appealing to a minor but significant section of the population has meant in recent decades that vote-bank politics slowed down the rate of political and social progress. Modi explained his view of vote banks to me as follows – it is probably the first time he has expounded on this publicly and at some length in his characteristic colloquial, earthy style:

In India we have average 60 per cent polling. One hundred per cent of the people are not going to vote. Out of 60 per cent if you want to win the election you need only 30 per cent, and if four or five parties are there it will require only 25 per cent or 26 per cent. So out of 100 per cent, the person who is only having 25 per cent or 26 per cent is ruling. In this situation he is always taking care of the combination of two sets of voters. He is always thinking that I have to take care of these 26 per cent of people. Whatever government benefits go, will go to these 26 per cent. Whatever schemes he will bring, he will bring for these 26 per cent.

And because of this reason, 75 per cent are left without any benefit. Because of such vote-bank politics, the whole country is not represented. Always that 75 per cent is left out, so I am against vote banks, but it is nothing to do with religion. I am against vote-bank politics and I say, whosoever voted for you is not simply for you, and you are not for them only. You are a part of the democratic system. So you work for those who have voted for you, but you should also work for those who have *not* voted for you, and even for those who have not voted at all. You have to take care of 100 per cent people.

⁓

'Enthuse' is an important word, and is being used increasingly as the election approaches, because the message must be optimistic. If voters choose Modi, it will not be because they like him but because he makes them feel secure about themselves and their future prospects.

Paradoxically, it is because he has been painted as a 'divisive figure' that Modi might be the man who unites voters sufficiently to continue coming close to the 30-35 per cent vote share mark that could marginalize vote-bank politics in the future. In the UK, Margaret Thatcher was just such a figure and her elevation to leadership of the Conservative Party was fiercely opposed within her own party and mocked by her political opponents. But she won a landslide – coming to power in 1979 with 43.9 per cent vote share. It changed the political geography of Britain forever.

In his book, *Breakout Nations,* Ruchir Sharma writes about the conditions countries need to breach a particular economic benchmark. Stretching the analogy, Modi needs to make himself be seen as a 'breakout leader' who breaches old electoral trend lines and sets new ones.

Modi's take-charge personality is part of who he is and has been, as we have seen, from a young age. But it is useful to look one last time at what exactly that personality consists of, because it may help us to understand what will happen in the forthcoming election and beyond.

Every observation made about Modi ultimately reverts to the riots of 2002 as definitive evidence about his personality and politics. Initially, the evidence was presented to suggest that the accusations made against Modi, even allowing for exaggeration because of political reasons, would contain some substance. There was simply so much of it, and so much of it in 2002 was unanimous: the riots were labelled Modi's pogrom. He had risen through the ranks of the RSS and then the BJP in an era dominated by the loud and angry adolescence of the Hindutva movement. Those were the post–Babri Masjid days when India bred a generation of kar sevaks upset at the marginalization of Hinduism in national life and afraid for the future of what they saw as India's true identity. Those were the days too when L.K. Advani was a gimlet-eyed hardliner.

It was a time of regular and frequent communal riots across the country. These led to ingrained resentment between communities. Tensions from outside India added to those within. In the Muslim world, radical Islam was on the rise – from Shias after the Iranian revolution under Khomeini and from Sunnis in the wake of the Soviet invasion of Afghanistan and the outrage of American armies on holy Arab soil during the liberation of Kuwait. Wahabbism was on the march. Pakistan was turning itself from a defeated military aggressor into a terrorist facility, and still pursuing 'imperialistic Islamic fantasies'.[7]

This was the political landscape Modi operated in, mostly below the media radar and before India's economic reforms truly began to modernize the country in the 1990s. It was also a period before the BJP had come to power at the Centre and learned what it was to govern instead of merely oppose.

But violence does not only reside with individuals, it resides within organizations, and ultimately within the state itself. This was clearly observable in the 1984 Delhi genocide of Sikhs after the assassination of Indira Gandhi. Not only the police but Congress politicians encouraged and actively took part in the slaughter. For the entire period of the pogrom there was no countervailing police force deployed on the part of the authorities, and little attempt at investigation or justice in its aftermath. It showed how doing nothing can sometimes be the most violent act of all.

Likewise, but not so extremely, the state apparatus in Gujarat when Modi took over was psychopathic. The authorities – police and political – were infected with communal hatred. This was the outcome of a long process, a thousand years of antagonism since the destruction of the Somnath temple, and the more recent period of communal rioting from 1969. The 2002 riots were sparked by the Godhra atrocity, a slaughter of Hindus by Muslims which few would even have heard of if they read only the English-language press: many people abroad who know of the riots still know nothing of Godhra.

Yet in conclusion, it is clear to me beyond any reasonable doubt after my extensive research that Modi did everything he could to make the violence cease and abate – but that he faced resistance on several fronts. These were within his own party and administration as well as in the Congress and the media. To state this is merely to echo official judgements, reports and inquiries that have already been quoted and which found Modi innocent of all charges levelled at him. Yet it is undeniable that for over a decade Modi has been subjected to an unprecedented campaign of propaganda that seeks to blame him exclusively for all that happened. Regardless of one's opinion of Modi – and there can be conflicting ones – including those which hold him negligent if not complicit in the 2002 riots, this appears excessive. M.D. Nalapat summed it up concisely:

> There has been a well-planned effort to define Narendra Modi by the six days in his 12-year rule which saw riots across Gujarat where both Hindus as well as Muslims died. ... Although he has been condemned for his lack of success in preventing the riots, the fact remains that they took place at such speed and with such virulence that it was doubtful if anyone else could have done better. At that time, Modi had spent just a few months in his new job. However, he clearly learnt from the experience, for since then there has not been a single communal flare-up in Gujarat, nor a single individual losing his or her life as a result of the madness of communal hatred.

But even Nalapat assumes that the worst of the riots endured for six days, although they did not. They began the day after Godhra, on 28 February, and were largely under control by 2 March. Modi said to me that people always seem to forget February has only twenty-eight days not thirty-one, and that as a result they unconsciously extend the period of the bloodiest clashes. Disturbances rumbled on after 2 March of course, but the army was already on the streets. By then, in contrast to the Delhi pogrom, justice was already in the process of being administered despite a partially communalized police force – an old legacy.

One of the important things Modi is never given credit for is keeping safe the witnesses – often illiterate Muslim migrants to Gujarat – so that later they could testify against their tormentors. His government is routinely accused of influencing witnesses but not of protecting them for which voluminous evidence exists. It is one more sign of how the debate over 2002 has become hostage to vested interests.

On the publication of his autobiography *The Paramount Cop* in late 2013, K.P.S. Gill defended Modi over the 2002 riots. 'In law and order situations, it is the police leadership which has to respond and not the political leadership,' he said,[8] which is clearly a policeman's view. But was not Modi the chief minister in overall charge and ultimately responsible for the police?

'Mr Modi had become the CM only a few months back,' Gill stressed. 'The administration and the police force were not in his proper grip and it takes time to develop such a grip ... From my first-hand experience of the Gujarat situation, I can say with conviction that the Gujarat riots were not the failure of Mr Narendra Modi; instead it was the failure of the Gujarat cops as well as the intentions of the neighbouring states which had then denied forces to Gujarat when the riots started.'[9] Gill also confirmed that it was Modi who, following the 2002 riots, asked him to come to Gujarat – not, as is commonly believed, the Union government.

The starkly different versions of the extent of Modi's culpability for 2002 will not disappear. The fact that after twelve years of the most thorough investigations, not even an FIR, much less a charge sheet, against Modi has been filed shows the weakness of available evidence. Dozens of convictions, including those of ministers close to Modi as well as Congressmen involved in the rioting, have taken place. And yet investigations, monitored by the courts, continue in order to give closure to the victims of the tragedy.

Is the long period of peace Gujarat has enjoyed under Modi attributable to the fact that he has browbeaten Muslims into sullen silence? Or is it rather that conditions have improved to the extent that, in the 2012 assembly election, it is said around twenty-five per cent of Muslims voted for him?

In the 2013 by-elections held shortly after Modi's third victory in the assembly elections, the BJP won six out of six seats formerly held by the Congress, a feat only feasible with Muslim votes. Likewise, six out of eight Muslim-majority assembly seats in Gujarat are represented by the BJP. But Modi clearly needs to bring Muslims into the assembly as he has done in local corporations.

M.J. Akbar points out: 'Muslims believe that they enabled the Congress to win two general elections, and in return got illusions wrapped in cheap rhetoric instead of jobs. The discovery that Narendra Modi's government had more Muslims on its payroll than Bengal did not help Modi much, but it certainly destroyed the Left in Bengal.' The number of Muslims in public service in Gujarat simply reflects the composition of the population. There are no reservations, no special treatment – in consonance with Modi's philosophy of equality for all, preference for none.

'Now Muslims learn that Modi's Gujarat has many more Muslim constables in every police station than any Congress state, or indeed Mulayam's UP,' concluded Akbar.[10] What he states is true, but can life for Muslims in Gujarat truly be as benign as it should be?

Following the Supreme Court's acceptance in 2011 of the SIT's report exonerating him in the Gulbarg Society case, Modi had gone on a series of sadbhavana fasts – a gesture of reconciliation.

But it was only after the metropolitan court on 26 December 2013 upheld the SIT report and decisively rejected Zakia Jafri's protest petition against the report, that Modi opened up in a blog he wrote the day after the judgment:

I had appealed to the people of Gujarat on the day of the Godhra train burning itself; fervently urging for peace and restraint to ensure lives of innocents were not put at risk. I had repeatedly reiterated the same principles in my daily interactions with the media in those fateful days of February–March 2002 as well; publicly underlining the political will as well as moral responsibility of the government to ensure peace, deliver justice and punish all guilty of violence. You will also find these deep emotions in my recent words at my Sadbhavana fasts, where I had emphasized how such deplorable incidents did not behove a civilized society and had pained me deeply.

However, as if all the suffering was not enough, I was also accused of the death and misery of my own loved ones, my Gujarati brothers and sisters. Can you imagine the inner turmoil and shock of being blamed for the very events that have shattered you!

The Gujarat Government had responded to the violence more swiftly and decisively than ever done before in any previous riots in the country. Yesterday's judgement culminated a process of unprecedented scrutiny closely monitored by the highest court of the land, the Honourable Supreme Court of India. Gujarat's twelve years of trial by the fire have finally drawn to an end. I feel liberated and at peace.

On Sunday, 27 October 2013, sixteen bombs were planted, and many exploded, at Modi's Hunkaar rally in Patna, Bihar, killing several people and wounding scores more. Chief Minister Nitish Kumar, despite being alerted by Delhi to the possibility of a terrorist attack,[11] failed to provide adequate security – or indeed much security at all – for the event, which several lakhs of his own citizens attended. Visit my state at your own risk, seemed to be Kumar's message to his old foe.

The Patna rally was a test of Modi's character. Though live bombs had exploded minutes before he arrived at the rally venue, Modi kept calm, delivered a powerful speech in which he exhorted Hindus and Muslims to fight poverty, not each other, and ensured at the end that the massive crowd dispersed peacefully. A few days later he visited the families of those who had died in the explosions.

Modi's rallies across the country have drawn large crowds, running into several lakhs, unprecedented in recent years, with most paying to attend – a stark reversal from most political rallies where crowds are paid to attend. However, on the same day as his Patna rally, *The New York Times* in its 'Sunday Review' ran an extremely hostile article about Modi. Among other accusations it claimed that Muslims were mired in poverty in Gujarat to a far greater extent than in other states. This animosity was routine: the US worries about Modi as prime minister because, unlike the Congress, he cannot be relied upon to act indulgently towards America's client state Pakistan whenever it launches a proxy terrorist attack on India just in order to protect Washington's interests in Afghanistan.

But the point made in the article about Muslim poverty in Gujarat is important to inspect, because it can settle the argument about Modi's decade or more of development in the state. There is an anecdote about the time a journalist confronted Modi and asked him what he had done for Muslims:

'Nothing,' Modi answered.
The journalist was scandalized: 'So you admit it?'
Modi said, 'Ask me what I have done for Hindus.'
'What have you done for Hindus?'
'Nothing. Everything I have done has been for Gujaratis.'

But if Gujarat's Muslims have not in fact enjoyed comparable progress, have not been included in the general prosperity, then in a way all Modi's claims about inclusivity are hollow, and perhaps all his other claims as well. His actions towards Muslims, as he explicitly stated, were supposed to speak louder than any words of apology for the 2002 riots.

The New York Times quoted figures issued by the National Sample Survey Office (NSSO) based on the Tendulkar Committee's poverty cut-off line. They showed poverty levels for Muslims in Gujarat at 39.4 per cent in 1999–2000 and still 37.6 per cent in 2009–10. Considering the growth that had occurred in India over that period it is an astonishing, anomalous figure, a remarkable outlier, although nobody seems to have questioned it. For Gujarat's

Muslims not to have improved their fortunes at all – to have experienced by comparison a catastrophic decline as overall poverty in Gujarat fell by 47.8 per cent from 2004–05 to 2011–12 – was surely a searing indictment of Modi's policies.

In fact, the NSSO had already released a newer set of data for 2011–12 that showed the number of Gujarati Muslims below the official poverty line at only 11.4 per cent compared with a national average of 25.5 per cent.[12] This was the fifth best performance by a state in India. In rural areas the number of Gujarati Muslims living in poverty was now only 7.7 per cent, almost the very lowest of any state in the country. Poverty for them had been falling at a rate of 7.6 per cent per annum, not at the rate of 0.18 per cent that the original decadal figures implied.[13] This proved exactly the opposite of the point made by *The New York Times*.

It meant in only two years the numbers of the poorest Muslims in Gujarat had supposedly plummeted by 26.2 percentage points, from 37.6 per cent to 11.4 per cent, such that two-thirds of the state's Muslims previously in poverty had been suddenly lifted above the Tendulkar line – and this after a decade of near stasis. Had Modi travelled around handing out suitcases full of rupees or had the high 2009–10 estimate been wildly inaccurate?

Almost unnoticed, somebody had indeed questioned the 2009–10 figure of 37.6 per cent. In a recent paper,[14] Professor Arvind Panagariya and Vishal More of Columbia University discovered that there had been a consistent decline in Muslim poverty in Gujarat throughout Modi's period as chief minister. By using other sources and by casting their research net wider than the NSSO, Panagariya and More discovered a decline among Gujarat's Muslim minority below the Tendulkar poverty line 'of 23.3 percentage points in rural areas and 27.7 percentage points in urban areas since 2004–05'.[15] These figures 'flatten the curve' considerably and place them much more in line with other statistics of Gujarat's development over the period, proving that Muslim poverty had actually fallen slightly faster than the average.

So why had nobody else noticed, and why was the 2009–10 figure being taken at face value?

In December 2012, Surjit S. Bhalla wrote an article, 'The Modi Metric', in *The Indian Express* severely critical of Modi. The article took its cue from the NSSO's 37.6 per cent figure for Gujarat Muslims in poverty. 'Inclusion is another word for good governance and good governance generally implies equitable growth,' he said, and continued: 'An argument for prime ministership that all can respect, including all contenders, is that the best choice for PM is one who can deliver the most inclusive growth.' Although Modi had delivered growth for Gujarat, Bhalla added, 'such growth has been neither equitable nor inclusive. It is unlikely that availability of data for the last two years, 2010 to 2012, will change any of the findings.' [16]

This analysis represented the conventional view of Modi's stewardship of Gujarat since 2001: he had enabled a heartless capitalist expansion that had ruined the poor, and especially poor Muslims, exactly as it was designed to do. Modi was thus unfit to be prime minister.

When the findings changed to the 11.4 per cent figure in the NSSO data for 2011–12, Bhalla wrote another article. 'Today,' he admitted in October 2013 in *The Indian Express*, 'the contours of the debate have changed somewhat.' There followed an honourable mea culpa and another admission: 'The Gujarat development model has come under increasing criticism. Sometimes, this criticism comes in the form of fantasy' – not least from Digvijay Singh, who had claimed the number of poor had actually increased under Modi, and from the Congress's Bhalchandra Mungekar, who in 2012 asserted that 31.8 per cent of Gujaratis lived below the poverty line, even after figures were released showing the actual level was half that. [17]

'There is a considerable amount of molestation of statistics going around', Bhalla now agreed, although he did not go so far as Panagariya, who said Modi's ideological opponents 'want to turn the best into the enemy of the good to give a walkover to the bad, but that won't work'.

The resistance against accepting evidence of progress under Modi's regime, especially progress amongst Muslims, appears to be linked not to conspiracy so much as to an ingrained impression left in the public mind about the 2002 riots. Many people simply refuse to believe that Modi is capable of benign behaviour, especially towards Muslims, and are therefore disinclined to believe good news. But as Bhalla wrote: 'If one looks jointly at poverty reduction and poverty levels, the preliminary conclusion has to be that the "Gujarat model" of development seems to have performed much better than most models on offer.'[18]

Zafar Sareshwala has been accused of being a Muslim who 'sold out' to Modi after earlier being a fierce critic. He now owns a flourishing BMW showroom. He says this of the conditions of Muslims under Modi:

Zakat is the easiest indicator to judge a Muslim's wealth profile because you pay zakat on your wealth. Zakat is what you pay to the needy. It is essentially used for helping meet some poor man's basic needs. Suppose this year I paid Rs 2,500 Zakat, you can immediately extrapolate that I am worth Rs 1,00,000. Next year if I pay Rs 5,000 Zakat, it means my wealth has increased from one lakh to two lakhs. Zakat has been continuously increasing in Gujarat year after year. In fact, you will find that 50 per cent of the Zakat of madrassas across the country comes from Gujarat and 50 per cent from the rest of India. If Modi had destroyed Muslims, their share of Zakat should have fallen. But in the last 10 years, the wealth of Muslims has increased.[19]

The New York Times subsequently issued a correction, conceding that it had got the figures for Muslim poverty in Gujarat from old data. The latest data, it conceded, showed significant improvement in poverty levels of Muslims in Gujarat.

Perhaps the greatest irony of the prejudice against Modi since 2002 is that it has actually helped him. It has provided Modi with a smokescreen for amending or evolving Hindutva in ways the VHP and its cronies would never have allowed otherwise.

So long as the media was vilifying him, despite his ongoing feuds with the VHP, Modi could count on the broad support of all the organizations under the Sangh Parivar umbrella. They assumed that he must have been doing at least some of their bidding if he was criticized so harshly by the liberal establishment. Each iteration of Modi's Hindu fanaticism in newspapers and on TV helped to blunt attacks from the forces of the Right against him, and there were many. Without his perpetual condemnation by the Left, Modi would never have been allowed by 'his own people' – and they were always much less his own people than is commonly believed – to transform the ideology of cultural nationalism so that it appealed to the broad electorate, Muslims included.

Paradoxically, without the condemnation of activists, NGOs and sections of the media – and without Sonia Gandhi calling him the 'merchant of death' and Nitish Kumar calling him 'Hitler' – Modi could never have been able to restore such Islamic monuments in Ahmedabad as the Seedhe Saiiyad ki Jaali, the Jhoolta Minara and the Sarkej Roza.[20] Nor would he have been able to organize festivals of Sufi music without a word of criticism from the VHP.

'In India, without the help of the media, it is very difficult for a politician to live; I am only a exceptional case,' Modi says today. 'Oh, media-bashing of me has been going on for the last thirteen years, but I adopted this strategy: let the media do its work, there shall be no confrontation. Let them enjoy, I will just do my work. And I did.'

Relentlessly being called communal allowed Modi to act in concrete secular ways without political costs in his own ideological backyard. When he became chief minister, the Sangh Parivar was campaigning to change the name of Ahmedabad to Karnavati in order to eclipse the city's Muslim heritage. It never happened.

Modi's considered approach has been to not contradict the slurs: 'I don't waste my time in confrontation. I never waste my time in debating,' he says impassively, sitting in his large, high-tech office, desk uncluttered with paper and files. He adds:

> Whatever people used to say, whatever allegations are there, I always keep it in my mind. And if genuine comments are there, I must improve myself. I was not arrogant; I am not against their criticism, I am not angry with their allegations. Whatever they say, I patiently read through the newspapers. As far as all that is concerned I always consider what they say as very important, even the negative. That is my approach. Then I think, how can I minimize my faults, how can I correct myself? All the allegations act as my fodder, all the criticism is my fodder, which improves me.

This is what Modi has been doing for over ten years now, ploughing his own furrow. And remarkable as it seems, neither the Congress nor the Sangh Parivar could spot it because they were too busy gazing on the double-faced Janus image of him that between them they created. Now, as prime ministerial candidate, Modi has gifted the RSS the prospect of one of its own in power.

The Right cannot now acknowledge Modi's softening of Hindutva, which they would otherwise have disapproved of, because they have made Modi their poster boy. Likewise, the Left cannot admit that Modi has become more 'inclusive' because he remains more than ever their hate figure. But ordinary voters can detect Modi has accomplished something in Gujarat – even if they are not quite sure what – and that he might have something to offer the nation.

India is not enamoured of the BJP but a large swathe of it is willing to trust Modi once. His tactic has always been to triangulate with ordinary, non-political people ('In a democracy, who is the final judge? The final judge is the voter,' he says) and in that manner he often sidesteps party politics, outflanking both the BJP and the Congress.

Modi frequently repeats that he was a 'non-political' chief minister. Hardly anybody takes the statement at face value. His critics cannot figure out what he means. Hence when he says, 'I always welcome criticism from the media,' he means it. Modi has calculated that on balance it boosts his popularity. 'Those who throw stones at me, I collect the stones and make a staircase, and I am going up and up. With the help of those stones I am rising and rising and rising.'

The tragedy which lies behind the failure of the decade-long vilification of Modi is that the Congress knew all along that it was not based on facts. It pursued him for ideological or electoral reasons, not humanitarian or moral ones.

Modi's critics say that he is a schemer and devious, coveting only ultimate control. Like Alexander Pope, they believe, Modi can hardly drink a cup of tea without a stratagem: 'His real goal was political power and he would choose any route provided he thought that the path would take him to the citadel,' says one critic.[21]

The key question remains: will Modi ever be prosecuted for his role in the 2002 riots?

He is surely guilty of dereliction of duty under Section 166 of the Indian Penal Code. The punishment for this? Simple

imprisonment for one year, or fine, or both – Non-cognizable
– Bailable – Trialable by Magistrate of the first class – Non-
compoundable.[22]

So that is all. Non-cognizable, non-compoundable, bailable.
The entire campaign is not designed to prosecute Modi, since
prosecution is not a realistic option, but to malign him so that he
poses no electoral threat to the established order in Delhi.

Modi's 'negligence' – as he did nothing actively illegal – is the
only possible charge that can ever be brought against him. A surfeit
of hard evidence testifies that Modi acted quickly and firmly in the
face of almost uncontrollable mass riot and performed better than
many other politicians in India before him.

Not only is there little chance that a charge will ever be brought
against Modi, but even if there is, it would probably be thrown
out. That is why, after twelve years, the Supreme Court–monitored
investigation has so far found nothing tangible against him – not
even dereliction of duty.

And yet reasonable doubts remain. Could Modi have done
more? Why has he not apologized for such a vicious communal
upheaval on his watch? Why has he not fully rehabilitated some
of the Muslim victims of the riots? Why has he not been tougher
in condemning the convicted rioters who served in his ministry or
party such as Maya Kodnani?

On 26 December 2013, a metropolitan magistrate's court in
Ahmedabad upheld the SIT's closure report exonerating Modi in
the Gulbarg Society case. The protest petition filed by Zakia Jafri
was rejected. Jafri said she will appeal the judgment in a higher
court but the adverse observations in Justice Ganatra's order against
Sanjeev Bhatt and others makes a reversal by the High Court or
Supreme Court extremely unlikely.

The Court has held that it is not established that Sanjeev Bhatt was present in the meeting called on 27.2.2002. It has also said that none of the officers who attended the said meeting have given any statement to SIT regarding any illegal instructions having been given by the CM in the said meeting. The Court has accepted in toto the findings of the SIT regarding this. [p. 106–107]

The court judgment also negated the oft-repeated charge that the Modi government was slow to respond to the riots.

SIT has come to the conclusion that from 27.02.2002, State Government was in constant touch with the Central Government to provide the help of the Army. Chief Minister had a talk with the Union Home minister on 28.02.2002. A written request was sent by the State Home secretary to the Central Defence Secretary. Due to the attack on Parliament, Army was at forward positions. 40 aircraft were used to air-lift the army personnel to Ahmedabad. First plane landed at Ahmedabad Airport at about 23.00 hrs on 28.02.2002 and the last plane landed at Ahmedabad Airport on 11.00 p.m. on 01.03.2002. From Ahmedabad some columns of Army were sent to affected Godhra, Vadodara and other districts. Logistic support of SDM and piloting vehicles were provided to conduct flag march in Ahmedabad city. The Court has observed that for this allegation, the SIT has made thorough investigation on this issue and hence it agrees with the findings of the SIT. [p. 223–229]

The charge of authoritarianism is often levelled at Modi. Was Gujarat run like a police state? The allegation of intrusive surveillance of a woman architect which took place in 2009 has been used by Modi's opponents to show that the Gujarat government snoops illegally on its citizens. There are three infirmities in this argument. One, it was the woman's family which asked the government for protection. Two, the woman was allegedly being stalked by an accused (and suspended) IAS officer Pradeep Sharma – from whom the woman's family had sought the government's protection. Three, the woman architect has not lodged a complaint against the surveillance even five years after the event.

Nonetheless, the fact that the Gujarat government was compelled to appoint a two-member commission of inquiry to probe the allegation of intrusive surveillance that occurred in 2009 demonstrates how vulnerable it has been rendered to public and media opinion by the constant battering it has received for over a decade. It alone is presumed guilty till it proves itself innocent.

Pursuing Modi was not about providing justice for Muslims. It was just politics as usual, and noxious politics at that. Modi was identified early on as an electoral threat, not only by the Congress but the entire political elite, because he proposed an alternative to the payola and patronage that was the system's stock-in-trade. More than anything, it was a case of the inside against an outsider. When the corrupt citadels of Lutyens's Delhi are threatened, those who live off its riches, as well as crumbs, close ranks.

'After 1947, it was expected that there would be a re-look at the colonial-era system and its laws,' wrote M.D. Nalapat. 'Instead, those who stepped into the shoes (and houses and offices) of the British soon discovered that colonial law and procedure was ideally suited towards their morphing into what many of them secretly wished they were, British colonials.'[23]

In this scenario the Congress is the new Raj and it starts to make sense that Sardar Patel and Mahatma Gandhi both said it should have been disbanded, or at least remodelled for new purposes, after Independence.[24] From the moment he showed up on their scanners, Modi represented a threat to this new Raj, including some in his own party. He was a man – a poor man, an OBC from a mofussil town – who meant business, and one who had to be stopped at all costs.

There was a bitter joke being told in 2013, shortly after one of the many breaches by Pakistan of the Line of Control. Five Indian soldiers had been massacred on the night of 5 August. During an earlier incursion on 8 January, two Indian soldiers had been murdered, one of them beheaded. The Indian public, incensed, was becoming impatient for retaliatory action. Defence Minister A.K. Antony subsequently read out a statement which contradicted the army's earlier one, and pleaded in the most abjectly pusillanimous terms that the murderers of the five Indian soldiers were '20 heavily armed terrorists along with persons dressed in Pakistani Army uniforms'. This implied that the Pakistan military and therefore the Pakistan government were innocent. It was an insult to the dead soldiers and failed to explain how a large contingent of irregulars could repeatedly pass through the heavily fortified Pakistan defences on its side of the LoC and go back again without difficulty.

Everybody on the subcontinent, including Antony, knew what complete nonsense this was, and after listening to the statement in the Lok Sabha, the anger of the Opposition NDA boiled over at yet another instance of state helplessness and cowardice. Hence the joke: Pakistan has two weapons: AK-47 and A.K. Antony.

To be fair, Antony was only doing what he was told, and he was not being told by Prime Minister Manmohan Singh, who long ago ceased to tell anybody to do anything. And anyway, the US needed India not to upset its terrorist-harbouring neighbour by retaliating while American troops remained in Afghanistan.

It was a low point; the point at which the spine of India's integrity and self-respect bent so far that it snapped. Antony's statement came as the rupee was gathering speed in its descent downhill, scattering foreign investors. The media was full of the latest developments in government-inspired scams of unbelievable audacity and reports of communal rioting in Muzaffarnagar.

India's defence and foreign policy had for many years been woefully weak-kneed, not only under the Congress but earlier too, when the BJP was in power.[25] Advani was home minister in Vajpayee's administration when terrorists, following the hijacking of Indian Airlines flight IC 814, were released. One of these, Masood Azhar, leader of Jaish-e-Mohammed, masterminded the December 2001 attack on Indian parliament. The ensuing border confrontation deprived Modi of the soldiers he would otherwise have had on hand to nip the Gujarat riots in the bud.

By contrast, Modi as prime minister would not have to peddle, or even speak of, 'hard Hindutva' in defence and foreign policy: his reputation precedes him. Speaking in Rewari, Haryana, in September 2013 at a rally comprising ex-servicemen among others, it was noted that his hawkish remarks directed at Pakistan were already beginning to be moderated owing to his new position as prime ministerial candidate.[26]

Modi is honouring President Theodore Roosevelt's injunction to 'speak softly and carry a big stick'. Modi's 'credibility' as a relative hawk has been backed up by a decade or more of demonstrable action fighting terrorism in Gujarat, where a low-profile but very successful operation was carried out against Pakistan-sponsored terrorists and the Indian Mujahideen. This occurred largely without alienating the law-abiding Muslim community. The polls indicate that in fact they approved of it.

In Gujarat, the police and intelligence services have uncovered many caches of weapons, explosives and fake Indian currency notes (FICN), and disrupted more than 100 mostly ISI-funded terror cells since 2007 and very many more prior to that.[27] Most of the actions taken against terrorists have been legitimate, but some of them were extrajudicial killings, or 'fake encounters'. Such 'fake encounters' are part of the police and intelligence culture in India, and in addition to the official investigations, arrests or killings of terrorists and gangsters (there is often a wide overlap), runs a parallel underground operation of police assassinations.

Between 2002 and 2007 in India there were 440 cases of alleged fake encounters, the majority in Uttar Pradesh with 231, then Rajasthan thirty-three, Maharashtra thirty-one, Delhi twenty-six, Andhra Pradesh twenty-two and Uttarakhand nineteen, according to the National Human Rights Commission of India.[28]

Statistics for 2007–09 are hard to find but from 2009–10 until February 2013 there were another 555 such killings across India.[29] Again, Uttar Pradesh topped the league with 138 killings, followed by Manipur with sixty-two, Assam fifty-two, West Bengal thirty-five and Jharkhand thirty.

In all there are records of more than 1,500 such police and intelligence-driven murders. Currently only eighteen are being investigated by the Central Bureau of Investigation (CBI). Of these, seventeen cases are from Gujarat, despite the majority of fake encounters occurring in Congress-controlled states.[30] Modi says that the investigations are politically motivated. He brackets these as Congress malevolence alongside the recent phenomenon of investors signing MoUs at Vibrant Gujarat events suddenly finding themselves targeted by tax inspectors for hostile investigations.[31]

But a crime is still a crime even if the police see it as performing a service to politicians rather than law and order. Delhi's unique focus on Gujarat began in 2004 after the shooting of four young people allegedly involved in a terror plot to kill Modi, according to Rajinder Kumar, then Gujarat station chief of the Subsidiary Intelligence Bureau (SIB).[32] One of them, a nineteen-year-old female student named Ishrat Jahan, was supposedly not, unlike her three companions, a member of the ISI-sponsored Lashkar-e-Taiba (although subsequent revelations indicated that she might well have been).

The police officer in charge, Deputy Inspector General D.G. Vanzara, was later jailed for his part in another fake encounter, that of Sohrabuddin Sheikh – a Lashkar-e-Taiba operative with links to the local Muslim mafia's extortion rackets, and in whose dwelling forty AK-47 assault rifles were discovered after his death in 2005.[33]

In its second charge sheet filed in February 2014, the CBI named four IB officers, including Special Director Rajinder Kumar, for murder in the Ishrat Jahan case. Kumar, now retired, has however challenged the charge sheet and publicly referred to the evidence against him and his IB colleagues as 'not worth the paper it is printed on'. While this remark has been widely published in the media, the CBI continues to pursue the case.

More significantly, Kumar added in his widely published comments that there was little doubt Ishrat Jahan and her three companions were terrorists. That of course is not the crux of the case in which the court has asked the investigating agency to probe whether or not the encounter in which the quartet was killed was genuine.

What seems to be an unfortunate consequence of the CBI's pointed investigation in Gujarat, however, is the damage it has done to anti-terrorist operations in India generally. The CBI has been intent in pursuing Rajinder Kumar. The IB says it simply passed on inputs for the Gujarat police to act on as part of normal intelligence work. Other local bureau chiefs and police, fearing a fate similar to Vanzara's and accusations similar to those levelled against Rajinder Kumar, are refusing to act on information from IB national headquarters unless in writing, which will of course not be forthcoming.

Without information to act on, state police forces have in certain instances ceased to act at all (perhaps in genuine as well as fake encounter cases) because they are not in receipt of the latest intelligence. This potentially leaves future terrorist plots undisrupted and arguably contributed to the sixteen Indian Mujahideen bombs that exploded at or around Modi's Hunkaar rally in Bihar on 17 October 2013. If the CBI is being politically directed, the security implications are grave.

Modi toughening India's stance on terror and Pakistan has not pleased everyone. 'That Washington has as much influence over Delhi since Manmohan Singh became PM in 2004 as London had over India's capital city during the British Raj is a perception widely shared within the country,' says Nalapat.[34]

However, the meeting between then US ambassador to India Nancy Powell and Modi on 13 February 2014 underscored two issues. First, that the US now recognizes the increasing possibility of Modi becoming India's prime minister at the end of May 2014. If a thaw has to take place in a difficult relationship, it cannot be left for too late. Second, the economic partnership with India remains paramount for the US: Modi's tough approach to Pakistan and on national security will be less of a concern to Washington in a post-2014 world following the NATO withdrawal of troops from Afghanistan in December 2014.

In the wake of the 2009 Lok Sabha election, author Tavleen Singh wrote a despairing article burying the BJP old guard and describing the party as entering 'what could be described as a post-Hindutva phase' where the young of India were no longer interested in the Ayodhya story. As a result, she wrote, 'Two roads stretch before the Bharatiya Janata Party. One will take it straight into history's dustbin. The other towards rebirth as a centre-right political party.' That rebirth, she thought, would have to be based around greater internal democracy and a lessening of ties with the RSS so that a talented politician freed from outmoded right-wing Hindu chauvinism could rise to lead the BJP.

'Wherever I travel I meet young people who are unhappy with the country's political leaders because they believe them all to be "corrupt and useless,"' Singh wrote.

They will vote for a political party that offers them better roads, cities, schools, hospitals and jobs. They will vote for a political party that offers them less corruption and better governance. The BJP could be that party if it chooses to move towards becoming a modern political party that can offer us in 2014 a grander idea of India than the shabby, rundown idea that the Congress has to offer.[35]

Despite economic and political turbulence India appears on the cusp of change for the better, still brimful of what V.S. Naipaul called 'the social antagonisms that give savour to life',[36] and all the more alive and vigorous for it.

India will never be a calm, cool, ordered nation like Switzerland or Sweden or Canada, and in temperament is more akin to the US – a boisterous, colourful, imaginative, innovative and irrepressible republic. India shares the diversity of the US, its religious and commercial enthusiasms, and most important of all its freedoms. India too has a wise constitution. Like Americans, India possesses a complex skein of beliefs, languages and histories, and these are still being woven into a pattern of identity sufficiently intricate to fully include all its inhabitants.

Economically, India is a caged tiger, prowling back and forth and snarling at its warders. It merely needs to be released from the vestiges of a feudal mentality – for which its poor and dependent cannot be blamed but the rich and privileged certainly can – and to remake its government so that it is for the people and by the people instead of for the politician and by the bureaucrat.

India's greatest strength lies in its population: youthful and energetic, optimistic, aspirational. Its fathomless and undeveloped internal markets and natural resources have hardly begun to be exploited; its agriculture is crying out for irrigation and power; Internet penetration is barely 25 per cent; its regulations may still be burdensome and inefficient – but all this spells opportunity, ready to be garnered by the right leadership.

Only about 3 per cent of Indians pay tax. I wasn't sure about this so I asked Modi. 'Yes, and many of them are government employees or employees of government PSUs and government companies,' he said. With such a tiny tax base, this means that if India grows only a little more prosperous, public revenues will increase exponentially as more of the population crosses the taxation threshold and begins to contribute for the first time. If only 10 per cent of the population pays tax, the funds available for infrastructure, if not usurped by politicians, will rise sharply. He points to other Asian countries where tax to GDP ratios are higher than India's.

Modi has long regarded China and Japan as pivots of India's future foreign and trade policy. He visited China in November 2011 to a red carpet welcome. Over the five-day trip, he met China's top political and business leadership. The reception he was accorded during his four-day visit to Japan a few months later, in July 2012, was equally telling: the two Asian giants had clearly decided where the centre of gravity of Indian politics had shifted.

A criticism of Modi's speeches is that while he attacks – rightly – Congress misgovernance, he does not provide an alternative vision, especially on the economy.

Modi, contrary to this view, has often articulated his own vision of an open, liberalized economy with a focus on infrastructure, job creation and fiscal discipline. It is one of the reasons global investment banks like Goldman Sachs and brokerages like CLSA have upgraded the 'India story' in the months leading up to the general election. 'It is simply,' says one banker in London, 'a reflection of support for Modi's business-friendly, decisive leadership.'

What then should be Modi's future economic agenda?

As author and editor Minhaz Merchant wrote in *The Times of*

India on the day, 13 September 2012, Modi was anointed the BJP's prime ministerial candidate:

> India's huge consumer market makes it a magnet for the world. Bad governance and retrospective legislation in recent years have led investors to lose faith in the India story. Credibility, like reputation, takes much to build, little to lose.

For centuries, India was exploited by foreigners. Indian resources were used for Western benefit. It is time to use Western money for Indian benefit. An open economy with firm, fair and fast law enforcement, a reliable tax regime and a sensible regulatory framework could attract well over $100 billion in FDI annually.

> For a new government led by Modi, the key issue is to re-liberate an economy swathed (once again) in red tape. Simultaneously, it must rescue our institutions from the damage they have suffered over the past nine years. Police, administrative and judicial reforms will give the economy the steel grid it needs to allow India to grow into a modern world-class nation.

The BJP's victories over the Congress in the December 2013 assembly elections in Rajasthan, Madhya Pradesh and Chhattisgarh echoed the mood of anger among voters. The scale of the Congress's rout, especially in Rajasthan and Madhya Pradesh, was a pointer to the outcome in the 2014 Lok Sabha election. Modi addressed dozens of rallies across the states, drawing large crowds, and with competent local leaders in place, proved to be a force multiplier.

Modi's campaign to build the Statue of Unity, in honour of Sardar Patel, is also likely to draw votes to the BJP from Gujarat and the rest of the country from a vast constituency of Indians who feel Patel did not get his due in a Congress dominated after Independence by Nehru.

World leaders have meanwhile begun to prepare for a Modi-led government at the Centre. British, European Union (EU) and Australian envoys have increased the frequency of their visits to his Gandhinagar office. The US too has announced it will grant Modi all diplomatic privileges should he be elected prime minister. Global investment analysts point to a 'Modi wave' reviving the Indian economy, boosting the stock market and firming up the rupee.

In India the threat to democracy is bureaucratic and dynastic; it comes from red tape and nepotism. The only dictatorship the country has endured since Independence was under Indira Gandhi. That today would be unthinkable, and constitutionally impossible.

Indians today are at ease with religion rather than paranoid about it. It has been subsumed into a cultural identity. Plurality and diversity coexist with India's age-old traditions.

Modi says he himself is not religious. He admires Swami Vivekananda and values spirituality, crediting his yoga with giving him stamina. He breathes Hindu culture and history and values its benefits in his own life and the life of the country. But he says he has no use for ritual or ritual observance.

'I do not believe in rituals. Those who believe in rituals, I am not against them. It is their strand of life and for them it may be required. In my strand of life, rituals are not required.' This easy-going attitude is what Modi of course would claim is the essence of Hinduism: a modern but very ancient faith that both predates and updates what is conventionally understood as belief. It contains narrative, philosophy and spirituality as well as worship. It is vast, tolerant and varied.

It is now the turn of the political system in India to catch up with its people; time for its rulers to stop acting like the British Raj and notice that India is now maturely content to be Indian.

Modi is regarded by the establishment as someone with rough edges, the OBC *chaiwala* who has no right to cross the threshold of 7 Race Course Road.

He calls it the Delhi Club. 'I will never be part of that,' he says. The Delhi Club – a metaphor for an overrated Indian political elite – is anyway a colonial relic, soon to be overtaken by a new, meritocratic India. That is Modi's constituency where what you do and how well you do it matter more than who you are and where you came from.

That is also a principle which a historic general election has set in stone for Prime Minister Narendra Modi.

11

A HISTORIC MANDATE

O N A HOT, HUMID Monday evening – 26 May 2014 – ten days after the election results to the sixteenth Lok Sabha had lifted the BJP to an unprecedented 282 seats in Parliament, Narendra Modi occupied centre stage in Rashtrapati Bhavan. A galaxy of political leaders, including all seven from the South Asian Association for Regional Cooperation (SAARC) and other eminences grises, watched in silence as Modi was sworn in as prime minister by President Pranab Mukherjee followed by forty-four cabinet ministers and ministers of state.

Modi had taken most by surprise by inviting the SAARC leaders to the inauguration ceremony. The next day, ceremony gave way to geopolitics as Modi met each of them separately. The meeting with Pakistani Prime Minister Nawaz Sharif was obviously the centrepiece. It went off well though Modi took the opportunity to tell Sharif, without mincing words, that terror and talks couldn't go together.

Pakistan army chief General Raheel Sharif and the brass of the Inter-services Intelligence (ISI) were against the Pakistani prime minister attending the Indian prime minister's swearing-in ceremony and wanted a high-powered delegation to go instead. They were against Nawaz Sharif moving too close to the Modi government too fast. But the Pakistani prime minister held firm. After several days of vacillation, spent in tense consultation with the Pakistani army and the ISI, Sharif accepted Modi's invitation. General Sharif finally met Nawaz Sharif's brother, Shahab Sharif, chief minister of Punjab, to iron out differences between the government and the army.

A businessman himself, Nawaz Sharif wanted to improve trade with India and saw the Modi invitation as a means to both break the ice with the new Indian prime minister and gauge his reputed image as a hardliner on Pakistan.

In a brief statement to the press after his meeting with Modi, Sharif remarkably, and dovishly, didn't mention Kashmir but said the two countries' foreign secretaries would soon meet to discuss various important issues. India's foreign secretary, Sujatha Singh, was more assertive. Her message encapsulated India's position: talks at the secretary level could carry on, but for a substantive dialogue, progress in the 26/11 Mumbai terror attacks and on dismantling Pakistan's infrastructure of terror should take place.

Sharif in his statement said:

> We agreed that our meeting in Delhi should be a historic opportunity for both our countries ... This provides us the opportunity of meeting the hopes and aspirations of our peoples that we will succeed in turning a new page in our relations.[1]

The cancellation of talks between the foreign secretaries, scheduled for 25 August, following meetings between the Pakistani high commissioner and Hurriyat separatist 'leaders', signalled to Islamabad that under the new government it wouldn't be business as usual.

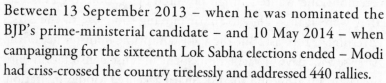

Between 13 September 2013 – when he was nominated the BJP's prime-ministerial candidate – and 10 May 2014 – when campaigning for the sixteenth Lok Sabha elections ended – Modi had criss-crossed the country tirelessly and addressed 440 rallies.

The pressure was intense. And Modi set a blistering pace. He woke before dawn, did nearly an hour's yoga and soon after left to board an aircraft for the day's rallies. Invariably, unless the rallies and campaign meetings extended over two days, he would fly back to Gandhinagar the same night, attend to administrative work as Gujarat chief minister and discuss poll strategies with senior colleagues over the phone before retiring after midnight.

As one report noted:

> His daily routine for the past couple of months: the alarm goes off at 4.30 a.m. The basic morning chores and an hour-long strict yoga routine prepare Modi for another day. No matter when he goes to sleep, he wakes up at 4.30 a.m. every day. Depending on the number of rallies, he could be going to bed as late as 1 a.m. at times. The police get busy by 6 a.m. to clear traffic for the chief minister's convoy. Modi catches up on the news and emails before heading to the airport. At Sardar Vallabhbhai Patel International Airport, three aircraft, a nine-seater Bombardier (CL600-2B), an eight-seater Beechcraft (Hawker 850XP) and a thirteen-seater Embraer (EMB 135 BJ), are waiting, engines running, to fly Modi to his day's rallies.[2]

Through the campaign, Modi traversed three lakh kilometres in what was India's most elaborate high-voltage, technologically savvy election blitzkrieg.

Fittingly, the last rally, as the blistering sun set on a summer evening, was at Ballia.

Modi wrote on his blog:

10 May, as the campaign drew to a close, marks the culmination of
a long campaign for the 2014 Lok Sabha election. I addressed my
final rally in Ballia, the land of the hero of 1857, Mangal Pandey, in
eastern UP. As I travelled across India, I could not help but think
– there is something in this soil that makes India special. History
is full of examples of how our land has shown the way to the world
and today once again, our destined role of a jagad guru calls us. Let
us rise to the occasion and create a strong, developed and inclusive
India that will show the way to the world.[3]

The technology behind the rallies to spread Modi's message beyond
the towns he could physically be present in was unique. London-
based Musion Systems created 3D holograms to beam Modi's rallies
live across multiple locations. Giovanni Palma, director of Musion,
said:

This was the largest deployment of our holographic technology and
reflected the ambition and belief of Narendra Modi and the BJP.
We delivered highly realistic images to over 1,500 rallies. [4]

The company's equipment for the campaign: over 30,000 square
metres of holographic projection foil, 200 Christie 20k and 14k
projectors, 400 satellite dishes, 5,500 metres of trusses, 1,300
lights, 500 audio speakers, 200 sound mixers and power amps, and
14,000 metres of speaker and power cables. To enable the campaign
team to monitor everything, Musion also built a receiving stage
at the headquarters, which received the same satellite feed as the
event stages. This helped Modi's team view exactly what was being
broadcast at any given time.

The 3D holograms enabled Modi to reach 5,800 locations. His
'Chai Pe Charcha' interactions were broadcast to 4,400 locations.

On 26 March 2014, as polling approached, Modi launched a series of Bharat Vijay rallies. In one month he addressed twelve rounds of 3D rallies covering 1,350 locations.

Speaking to BJP cadres on 1 June 2014, Modi said of the election campaign:

> In the United Kingdom, the election campaign of New Labour under Tony Blair [1997] was studied by political analysts. Similarly, Obama's first election campaign [2008] for presidentship was analysed and books written on it. The campaign had new dimensions, used new technology and methods. These were widely discussed.[5]

The extensive use of social media contributed to building the momentum in the months leading up to the Lok Sabha election. The party's 'war room', staffed by a phalanx of IT specialists and crack members of the Citizens for Accountable Governance (CAG), buzzed around the clock, feeding and disseminating information to an army of BJP workers, volunteers and campaigners.

Meanwhile, the BJP's IT team launched the campaign's India 272+ mission portal. The website sought ideas, recruited volunteers and increased engagement with potential voters. WhatsApp, increasingly popular in India and now owned by Facebook, was used extensively for spreading infographics to a wide audience.

A key decision of the campaign was, which constituency Modi would stand from. On 16 March, and with the first phase of the nine-phase voting schedule slated for 7 April, the BJP's Central Election Committee announced that Modi would contest from Varanasi. The choice of Varanasi had significant emotive and electoral appeal.

The choice in the end, though, was obvious. Modi's candidature from the ancient city would have a ripple effect across Uttar

Pradesh, Bihar and Jharkhand. The three states account for 134 MPs in the Lok Sabha. With the BJP eventually winning 105 of those seats, the decision to stand from Varanasi was clearly vindicated.

Amit Shah, in charge of Uttar Pradesh, had done a complete survey of the state. UP, he concluded, was ripe for the picking. Varanasi was scheduled to go to the polls in the ninth and final phase of the election on 12 May, giving Modi and his team time to strategize. In the event, he spent less time campaigning in the city than he would have liked. Denied permission by the local administration to address a rally in Varanasi in the last days of campaigning, Modi undertook a huge street 'rally'. Lakhs lined up on both sides of the streets as Modi's convoy wended its way through the city.

At a rally in Rohiniya, on the outskirts of Varanasi, Modi roared:

I don't know under whose pressure you [EC] are working. If Modi does give a speech, will the world sink? My silence has more power than speech. I was to speak at Benaras but those who have left the battlefield can't tolerate Modi any more. They can't even see Modi's face. I was to do more meetings, but those who are troubled with Modi conspired to stop me. The reason they gave was hard to digest. They said due to security reasons, I was not allowed to address the rally. How far is Varanasi from here? 12 km? If there is no threat to me here, how will there be threat to me in Varanasi?[6]

Mayank Gandhi is a member of the National Executive of the Aam Aadmi Party. He was its Lok Sabha candidate for Mumbai north-west. In an article written just before polling in Varanasi, he declared:

Varanasi was calling. It had become the centre of a battle of proportions that I had not envisaged. A battlefield of ideologies and, in a way, a battle between power on one hand and passion on the other.

The election there is attracting people from all parts of India and from Maharashtra, hundreds of volunteers left their daytime jobs to head to Varanasi and help in the campaign for Arvind Kejriwal. Trains tickets were sold out, and flights were expensive, but the pull was too strong. Some of us decided to spend a good bit of money and fly so we don't miss this once-in-a-lifetime opportunity.[7]

Kejriwal's Varanasi campaign was intense. Thousands of volunteers camped in the city for two months. Kejriwal himself abandoned campaigning for AAP candidates in other constituencies to focus on 'beating Modi' in Varanasi. In the end, he was routed. Modi's winning margin: 3.71 lakh votes. Varanasi proved to be Kejriwal's Waterloo.

The results began trickling in on 16 May 2014, around 8.30 a.m. The early trends were clear: the BJP was headed for a major victory – though how big a landslide it would be became apparent only later in the day. As one report described it:

By 9.30 a.m., just an hour and a half after counting began, the markets cheered the likely verdict. The Sensex crossed 25,000 points for the first time ever, with a massive burst of 1,000 points before falling into the red later and ending 0.9 per cent up at 24,021 points. The rupee breezed past 59 too, to hit 58.91 at the opening, for the first time since July 2013. By 10.30 a.m., PM-designate Narendra Modi was declared winner from Vadodara and was leading comfortably in Varanasi. He eventually won the Vadodara seat by 5,70,000 votes, missing the 2004 record of a 5,92,000 margin held by the CPM's Anil Basu from the Aarambagh constituency of West Bengal. Modi later addressed huge gatherings in Vadodara and also in Ahmedabad. Speaking in Hindi instead of Gujarati, the prime minister designate said the country would never get a better 'mazdoor' [labourer] than him.

Congratulations poured in for the BJP leader. Pakistani PM Nawaz Sharif called personally to invite him to Pakistan. Sri Lankan President Mahinda Rajapaksa, British Prime Minister David Cameron and Australian Prime Minister Tony Abbott also congratulated Modi. Congress president Sonia Gandhi conceded defeat and congratulated the new dispensation. She said the Congress may not have received the popular support it anticipated but would remain committed to its fundamental principles.[8]

Most exit polls had forecast between 230 and 240 seats for the BJP, and between 270 and 280 seats for the NDA. The scale of the BJP-led NDA victory – 282 and 336 seats respectively – was unprecedented. The results devastated the Congress. It was reduced to 44 MPs, losing an extraordinary 162 parliamentary seats from its 2009 tally of 206. The BJP comfortably surpassed its own target of India: over 272 seats.

It was the first majority government since Rajiv Gandhi's in 1984.

Almost the first thing Prime Minister Modi did on assuming office was meet seventy-seven senior bureaucrats across departments. He surprised many by addressing them by name and told them to be swift, transparent and result-oriented in their work.

Using his favourite tool for direct communication with people, Modi tweeted after the meeting:

> We talked about institutionalizing processes as they will last longer than any individual and give better results to the people ... I shared my views on the importance of teamwork and usage of technology, which has the potential to address peoples' grievances.

The 150-minute meeting empowered bureaucrats. Punctuality improved. Modi himself was at his desk every morning at 8.40.

Most ministers and secretaries were to soon get used to long hours, tight deadlines, crisp review meetings, and a focus on results. 'In this government,' says one observer, 'outcomes and output matter, not just theories and concepts. Secretaries are now prepared with power point presentations of key issues.' In August, the government amended the All India Service (Conduct) Rules, 1968, to include a nineteen-point guideline for bureaucrats. Among other rules, it mandates that they should maintain 'political neutrality', 'make recommendations on merit alone' and 'take decisions solely in public interest'.

Under the newly amended rules, officers must: [9]

- Declare any private interests relating to their public duties and take steps to resolve any conflicts in a way that protects public interest.

- Ensure that they do not place themselves under any financial or other obligations to any individual or organization which may influence the performance of their official duties.

- Not misuse their position as civil servants and not take decisions in order to derive financial or material benefits for themselves, their family or friends.

- Ensure courtesy and good behaviour with the public, display responsiveness to the public, particularly to the weaker sections.

- Take decisions solely in public interest and use or cause to use public resources efficiently, effectively and economically.

- Maintain high ethical standards, integrity and honesty, promote the principles of merit, fairness and impartiality in the discharge of duties.

- Maintain accountability and transparency.

- Make choices, take decisions and make recommendations on merit alone.

- Act with fairness and impartiality and not discriminate against anyone, particularly the poor and the underprivileged sections of society.

- Refrain from doing anything which is or may be contrary to any law, rules, regulations and established practices.

- Maintain discipline in the discharge of their duties and be liable to implement the lawful orders duly communicated to them.

- Perform and discharge their duties with the highest degree of professionalism and dedication to the best of their abilities.

- Be liable to maintain confidentiality in the performance of their official duties as required by any laws for the time being in force, particularly with regard to information, disclosure of which may prejudicially affect the sovereignty and integrity of India, the security of state, strategic, scientific or economic interests of the state, friendly relations with foreign countries or lead to incitement of an offence or illegal or unlawful gains to any person.

Most of these rules had been codified earlier, though not in such detail, and were followed more in the breach than the observance. Now they were mandatory.

Several days of consultation had preceded the formation and swearing-in of Modi's cabinet. While many portfolios suggested themselves – Rajnath Singh as home minister, for example – there were surprises as well. Sushma Swaraj got the External Affairs portfolio, while Arun Jaitley was given both Finance and Defence.

The 2014–15 Union Budget, presented by Jaitley on 10 July 2014, attracted criticism for not being 'visionary'. However, several innovative ideas were tucked away in the fine print of the Finance Bill. As the *Economist* wrote: 'Among the weeds of an overlong speech lurked some bold, potentially transformative ideas. Stock markets plunged as Mr Jaitley spoke, only to surge as his abstruse speech was decoded.' [10]

Economist Bibek Debroy, a long-time supporter of Modi's economic policies, wrote in *India Today*:

A Budget, especially the first one, is not the only instrument of policy and, indeed, as Finance Minister Arun Jaitley said, 45 days is too short a time for preparation, especially since decisions on both taxes such as Goods and Services Tax and expenditure require consultation with states. That said, the goal of the Budget should be clear: to simplify tax and expenditure, the core government functions. A Budget speech is sometimes used to signal broader reform intent in FDI, capital markets, banking and insurance. On this, one can't fault the liberalization measures proposed by the minister, barring the caveat that they are incremental.

This leaves predictability, which concerns rates and fiscal consolidation. GST rates are still up and direct tax ratios are presumably stable and predictable. Is the proposal to limit fiscal deficit-to-GDP ratio to 4.1 per cent in 2014–15 believable? I don't think so. I don't think the 13.4 per cent nominal GDP growth is achievable either. For with 5.5 per cent real growth, this requires the inflation, measured by the GDP deflator, to be under 7.5 per cent. Since that is unlikely, as with the last government, there will be questions about the quality of fiscal marksmanship. And achieving the target of a fiscal deficit-to-GDP ratio of 3.6 per cent in 2015–16 and 3 per cent the following year will be suspect. A more specific three-four-year road map would have made this more predictable. However, with a preparation period of a month-and-a-half, achieving the 'steep' goal proved too steep for the finance minister. Perhaps he will do better next year. [11]

The Budget seemed to reinforce Modi's preference for incremental reforms. But it was quickly obvious that speed lay at the heart of the Modi government's legislative and executive agenda. In its first full session of Parliament, ending 14 August 2014, the government introduced a slew of reformist legislation. These included a constitutional amendment to change the way judicial appointments are made. Executive orders simplified administrative procedures. Bills were tabled to enhance FDI in key sectors. The government was clearly not going to use an annual budget to announce reforms. Rather, it would be an ongoing process – which in itself represented a departure from the policy paralysis that afflicted the UPA 2 government.

～

As prime minister, Modi has kept his counsel, allowing his key ministers and spokespersons to articulate his vision. Critics said this was inadequate: many excellent schemes the government implemented at first went unreported and unnoticed.

Few, for example, noticed the decision to change the nomenclature – and direction – of the ministries:

- The Ministry of Environment & Forests to the Ministry of Environment, Forest and Climate Change.

- The Ministry of Shipping to the Ministry of Shipping and Ship-breaking.

- The Ministry of Water Resources to the Ministry of Water Resources, River Development & Ganga Rejuvenation.

- The Ministry of Sports and Youth Affairs to the Ministry of Skill Development, Entrepreneurship, Youth Affairs & Sports.

In an attempt to explain Modi's modus operandi, R. Jagannathan of Network 18 wrote:

> Modi's goal is not to offer sound bites to a hungry media, but to press ahead with his stated and unstated long-term goals. These are a Congress-mukt Bharat, and making BJP the natural party of governance. The other stated goals are to make India an easier place to do business in, and provide all Indians with the basics of livelihood [over ten years].
>
> Embedded in all this is Modi's unstated goal: he plans to be PM [voters willing] for at least a decade, if not more. He wants to be the man who changed India for the better – and hence his performance has to be better than all his predecessors put together. I suspect that the big economic moves will come during periods of low political activity – for example, after this December [when assembly elections will be out of the way] but before next June–July – after which we will have the Bihar elections.[12]

The PM's Independence Day speech and intense campaigning for the state assembly elections changed perceptions rapidly. Modi was now more visible, more engaged with the public. The PMO became the fulcrum of governance. Modi had been quick to appoint a veteran civil servant, Nripendra Misra, as his principal secretary. A former principal secretary to former UP Chief Minister Kalyan Singh, Misra combined swift, rigorous implementation of PMO directives with integrity. His vast array of contacts across political parties would come in handy in the next state assembly elections in UP where Misra spent much of his career. A former chairman of the Telecom Regulatory Authority of India (TRAI), Misra's appointment was made through an ordinance and later ratified in Parliament, overcoming the Congress' opposition in both houses.

Administrative skills were Modi's hallmark in Gujarat and he brought along with him to Delhi key personnel who had served him – some for a decade or more – there. Most were appointed to the PMO – Modi's eyes and ears as he eased himself into Delhi's unique political environment replete with the political and bureaucratic elite.

And yet, there was disquiet in some quarters that Modi was 'not doing enough' to change the country's direction. Modi was keenly aware of the criticism. His finance minister had shunned big-bang reforms in the 2014–15 Budget, disappointing many who had voted for the BJP and delighting those who had not.

The prime minister dealt with the criticism, first in a speech at the BJP's national executive on 9 August 2004, formally anointing Amit Shah as BJP president and, days later, at his maiden Independence Day address from the historic Red Fort. An extraordinary 144 of 153 accredited diplomatic missions were present. Crowds swelled at the venue from 5.30 a.m.

Modi spoke extempore, without a bullet-proof podium. The symbolism was strong. The sixty-five-minute address drew wide praise. It pledged an insurance-linked bank account for millions outside the financial mainstream, replaced the sixty-four-year-old Planning Commission with a compact, reformist think tank, stressed women's empowerment and sanitation, and told MPs to develop one model village in their constituencies every year with their local area development funds.

It was a virtuoso performance and impressed all but the most hardened critics. On 14 August 2014, according to an Instavani lightning poll conducted by Fourth Icon Technologies, Modi's approval rating was 82 per cent. After the speech, a 'high-speed' poll conducted on 15 August among 6,000 respondents showed that the PM's approval rating had spiked to 86 per cent.

Many had expected Modi to make his first overseas visit as prime minister to Japan or China – countries he had frequently visited as chief minister of Gujarat. However, following up on his 'neighbourhood diplomacy', Modi began his tenure with a short but politically important state visit to Bhutan.

Bhutan has been holding talks with China over a border dispute with its giant neighbour since the 1980s. More than twenty-five rounds have been completed. India and China are holding their own series of border negotiations. What Modi achieved in Bhutan was ensure that any discussion on resolving disputes in the long borders China, Bhutan and India share would not compromise India's security interests or territorial integrity.

Bhutan's king, Jigme Khesar Namgyel Wangchuck, and prime minister, Tshering Tobgay, gave the Indian prime minister a rousing welcome over the two days that Modi spent in the Himalayan kingdom. Raising a toast at the royal banquet in Thimphu, Modi said:

India is associated with the progress and happiness of Bhutan and will continue to do so. The two countries are made for each other. The colour of our passports may vary, but our heritage and values remain the same. Bhutan lays great emphasis on Gross National Happiness rather than Gross Domestic Product – and one of the parameters for measuring this could be the consideration that it has a neighbour like India.[13]

The other key issue during Modi's Bhutan visit was hydroelectric power. Both Bhutan and Nepal, which the PM visited weeks later, have vast hydroelectric power generation potential which dovetails with Modi's plan to provide 24x7 electricity across the country by 2022.

But the substance of the visit was border diplomacy. China has been coaxing Bhutan to establish full diplomatic ties. By getting Bhutan (and, later, Nepal, which too shares a border with China and India) on India's side, Modi was laying the groundwork for his own meeting with Chinese President Xi Jinping – first at the

BRICS summit in July and then during Xi's visit to India – on the vexed Sino-Indian border issue.

Commenting on Xi's growing clout, the *Economist* wrote:

> Since President Xi Jinping launched his anti-corruption campaign at the end of 2012, the question has been how high he would aim. On 20 July, an emphatic answer came with the news that Zhou Yongkang was under investigation by the Communist Party for 'serious violations of discipline', for which, read corruption.
>
> Mr Zhou was once one of the most powerful men in the land. Until two years ago, he was a member of the Politburo's ruling standing committee: in charge of the state's vast security apparatus, he controlled a budget bigger than the army's. It had long been an unwritten rule of China's power politics that men of Mr Zhou's stature were untouchable. By flouting the rule, Mr Xi has left no doubt about the authority he believes he now wields. He appears to be the most powerful Chinese leader since the late Deng Xiaoping.[14]

In his first multilateral meeting, the prime minister flew to the Brazilian city of Fortazela in July for the BRICS summit. The meeting allowed Modi to showcase his global vision for India. He led the debate on the formation of the BRICS New Development Bank (NDB). The Indian prime minister suggested the bank's name and insisted that the five countries should have equal shareholding in its initial capital of $50 billion (Rs 3 lakh crore). Shanghai would be the NDB's headquarters while an Indian would head the bank for the first six years.

As one senior journalist wrote in the *Times of India*:

> The bank will in time draw in more emerging economies such as the group of nations dubbed MIST [Mexico, Indonesia, South Korea and Turkey]. The NDB will enable intra-BRICS payments in local

currencies, providing a cushion against volatility. Geopolitically, India's voice will carry more weight. China has invited India to take part, for the first time, in the powerful Asia-Pacific Economic Cooperation [APEC] trade forum, which includes the US, at its summit in November. Chinese president Xi Jinping has said he will back India for full membership of the Shanghai Cooperation Organization [SCO], a Eurasian political, economic and military grouping.[15]

Britain's *Financial Times* published a strong piece:

The BRICS plan is good for the world, although you would not know it from the sniffy reaction in the West. There have been two default positions. One is to scoff at the very idea of five such disparate nations organizing anything coherent or staying the course. The other is to worry that the world order reflected in the two US-led institutions set up at the Bretton Woods conference of 1944 is about to crumble. It is indeed a minor miracle that five countries whose initials happen to form a catchy acronym have so quickly gone from Brics to a bricks-and-mortar bank. This is a reprimand to Western-led institutions that have failed to adapt. If the postwar order really is being upended, the right response is 'hear, hear'. The Bretton Woods institutions reflect the realities of a receding age. The world has changed, mostly for the better, as poor countries close the gap on rich ones. The BRICS bank encapsulates this. It is a glimpse of the future.[16]

Modi's bilateral meetings in Brazil with Chinese President Xi Jinping and Russian President Vladimir Putin were especially significant. Ostracized by the West over Ukraine, Putin needs India more than ever. Modi was quick to understand this. He had met Putin in Moscow in 2001 and developed a working relationship.

Beyond the rhetoric in Fortazela, though, lay cold, hard realpolitik. As India fine-tunes its relationship with Washington, it will keep both China and Russia on its side. The BRICS Bank is just one instrument to help achieve a balance in the global power equation. It will help India become strong not only in finance and banking, but also enable it to become a geopolitical pivot in a new world order.

The BRICS meetings set the stage for the prime minister's summits with China and Russia later in the year. Xi Jinping is regarded by analysts in Beijing as the most powerful Chinese leader since Deng Xiaoping. In Modi he sees a strong leader who can counter Washington's trans-Pacific influence. The US – as successive visits by Secretary of State John Kerry and Defence Secretary Charles 'Chuck' Hagel and Modi's summit with Barack Obama in Washington underscored – regards India as a long-term strategic partner to balance China's hegemonic ambitions across Asia.

As a democracy with strong demographics, the next twenty-five years present India a window of opportunity to get its economic and foreign policies in synchrony. Modi clearly knows this. Strengthening ties with the SAARC neighbours will allow him to craft a broader foreign policy doctrine with the US and China.

Secretary of State John Kerry, on the defensive after External Affairs Minister Sushma Swaraj said that the US's snooping on the BJP 'was unacceptable between friends', was compelled to reply that the US 'fully respects and understands the feelings expressed by the minister and that the US would continue to work with India wherever they saw a threat to their shared interests'.[17]

Hagel's visit to India came less than a week after that of Kerry and Commerce Secretary Penny Pritzker, again underscoring the importance the Obama administration attaches to establishing a close working relationship with the Modi government.

Modi was always seen to be close to Japanese Prime Minister Shinzo Abe. It was not surprising, therefore, that his first major foreign bilateral summit was with Japan. This was Modi's third meeting with Abe. As strong nationalist leaders, the two have a natural affinity towards each other. Japan is a significant investor in Gujarat and will be one of the key financial and technological stakeholders in the proposed Mumbai–Ahmedabad bullet train project.

The Japan International Cooperation Agency (JICA) decided in 2013 to provide a loan of Rs 11,400 crore for funding various infrastructure projects in India, including the Delhi–Mumbai Industrial Corridor (DMIC). JICA said the loan would be used for construction of a dedicated freight corridor for the development of DMIC, a metro project in Chennai, and a piped water project in West Bengal.

To be repaid over a forty-year period (with a ten-year grace period), the loan carries an annual interest of only 0.20 per cent. With similar soft loans, Japan promises to be the partner-of-choice for the government's other ambitious infrastructure projects, including bullet trains and smart cities. Modi's summit with Abe in Tokyo on 1 September has further strengthened bilateral ties – not only in economic terms but, keeping China's geopolitical ambitions in mind, strategic terms as well. The conversation included a nuclear power deal in which Japan will supply reactor technology to India.

Within weeks of his successful summit with Abe in Japan and shortly after completing four months in office, Modi led a high-powered delegation to the United Nations General Assembly in New York where, like his predecessor, he spoke in Hindi. But the centrepiece of his visit to the United Sates was a summit meeting with President Barack Obama in Washington on 30 September.

The India–US relationship has been in deep-freeze for several years. The Nuclear Liability Bill, the diplomatic incident involving Devyani Khobragade, Modi's firm stand on the WTO's Trade Facilitation Agreement (TFA) and New Delhi's tough stance over US spying on the BJP demonstrated new steel in India's approach to Washington.

Despite differences over trade and security, the US has reacted positively to Modi's crisp, business-like position on both bilateral and multilateral issues. Washington respects power and it welcomes a decisive leader who speaks his mind. The clear message emerging from the US administration: India is America's indispensable ally in both Asia and – as its economy and military prowess expand – globally.

Amit Shah is a man of few words. He led the BJP's campaign in Uttar Pradesh with a combination of grassroots worker support, booth-level engagement, technology and ideological fervour. The result: an unprecedented statewide sweep. The BJP won seventy-one out of eighty seats in UP. Its ally, Apna Dal, won two. The Bahujan Samaj Party (BSP) was wiped out. The Congress won just their two pocket burroughs of Rae Bareli and Amethi. The Samajwadi Party (SP) was reduced to five seats – all relatives of Mulayam Singh Yadav. There was little doubt that winning at least twenty more seats in UP than most opinion polls had forecast enabled the BJP to cross the 272-seat mark.

Following state assembly elections in Maharashtra and Haryana, Shah's organizational skills and electoral acumen have been fully tested. As president of the BJP, Shah's job was twofold. First, win state elections across the country; second, enhance party–government coordination.

Shah generated much interest. 'He is extraordinarily hard working, with remarkable skills for political strategizing,' Gujarat BJP treasurer and veteran leader Surendra Patel told a business daily. According to the same report:

Shah was a student of biochemistry. He started out by dabbling in the stock market before trying his hand at the family business of PVC pipe-making. Born into a well-established business family in

1964, Shah was drawn to the RSS as a boy and his association with Modi goes back to the 1980s.[18]

The assembly elections in four key states under Shah's presidency are important in two ways. First, they will test how strong Modi's electoral appeal is six months after the BJP's stunning victory in the 2014 Lok Sabha election. Second, they will determine the future composition of the Rajya Sabha, where the NDA lacks numbers. Big victories in MLA-heavy states can change that equation significantly.

A few months are obviously not enough to judge the performance of a government. But questions abound. Can Prime Minister Modi deliver on his promise of *Sabka Saath, Sabka Vikas*? How will he manage legislative business in the Rajya Sabha where the BJP has barely a quarter of the seats? Will his foreign and economic policies be a mere continuation of those of the UPA as critics have said, or will calibrated changes herald a confident new India?

In Parliament, the NDA's 336 MPs dominate proceedings. With forty-four MPs, the Congress was allotted just two front row seats, occupied by party president Sonia Gandhi and the Congress designated leader of the Opposition in the Lok Sabha, Mallikarjun Kharge. Rahul Gandhi sits in the second row with senior leaders Kamal Nath and Veerappa Moily while Jyotiraditya Scindia occupies the third row.

In a situation where the Congress has been reduced to a minuscule number in the Lok Sabha, bitterness is inevitable. By accepting Attorney-General Mukul Rohatgi's advice that the Congress did 'not merit' being designated leader of the Opposition (LoP), Speaker Sumitra Mahajan raised the hackles of the Congress. Party Vice-President Rahul Gandhi alleged bias in the Speaker's verdict but there was little the Congress could do.

Despite its reduced numbers, however, the Congress has managed to stall several bills due to the BJP's vulnerability in the Rajya Sabha. A joint session of both houses would give the NDA just over 400 seats in a combined Lok Sabha and Rajya Sabha strength of 795 seats. It is an option the BJP could exercise if the Congress and its allies, despite their truncated numbers in the Lok Sabha, inordinately block important legislation in future parliamentary sessions.

Modi has great faith in the Gujarat model: 24x7 power, good infrastructure, water in abundance, clean cities, e-governance and a result-driven administration. Sloth in the bureaucracy has been replaced by punctuality. By disbanding groups of ministers (GoMs) as well as empowered groups of ministers (EGoMs), the PM had sent a clear message at the very start of his prime ministership: that no indecision would be accepted. The EGoMs formed by the UPA government were often used to stymie decision-making, leading to policy inertia. In the Modi government, ministers sort out inter-departmental queries promptly. Bureaucrats have specific timelines. Delivery and results are key.

Once timelines and budgets are set by the PMO, strict adherence to both is monitored. This is a government that works quietly but efficiently. Media interaction has been kept to a minimum. There is, though, clearly a need for Modi to communicate directly with people more often – for communication was his greatest strength during the 2014 Lok Sabha election campaign. This could be achieved, perhaps, in a structured way, as President Obama has done through his weekly radio address to the nation. Prime Minister Modi could do so through Doordarshan, fortnightly or monthly, to ensure government policies are explained to the public with clarity and transparency.

As the government settles in for the long haul, this is an important step to bring the government closer to the people who gave the prime minister his historic mandate.

NOTES AND REFERENCES

Prologue

1.   Modi's protection was further upgraded after the bomb blasts at his Patna rally on 27 October 2013. 'Narendra Modi now has three layers of protection: one group to take on any attackers, a second to provide cover and a third to get him to safety.' ('Govt throws rings of protection around BJP PM candidate Narendra Modi', *The Times of India*, 4 November 2013)

(http://timesofindia.indiatimes.com/india/Govt-throws-rings-of-protection-around-PM-candidate-Narendra-Modi/articleshow/25206558.cms)

2.   Amitabh Srivastava, 'Narendra Modi No. 1 target of IM, says Bhatkal', *India Today,* 3 September 2013

(http://indiatoday.intoday.in/story/yasin-bhatkal-says-narendra-modi-is-no-1-target-of-indian-mujahideen/1/305242.html)

3.   *The Indian Express*, 'Both Prime Minister and rupee have turned mute, says Narendra Modi', (Press Trust Of India), 24 August 2013

(http://www.indianexpress.com/news/both-prime-minister-and-rupee-have-turned-mute-says-narendra-modi/1159560/00)

1: The Early Years

1. A 'kund, called Nagdharo, with a lake, pool, locks, and feeding channel, built during the Solanki period, is a specimen of high quality engineering. It is believed that the Hatkeshwar temple and Sharmishtha Lake, now on the outskirts of Vadnagar, once stood in the center of town, testifying to just how vast Vadnagar was at one point.'

(http://www.gujarattourism.com/showpage.aspx?contentid=277& webpartid=773)

2. M.V. Kamath and Kalindi Randeri, *Narendra Modi: The Architect of a Modern State*, New Delhi, Rupa & Co., 2009, p. 12

3. Aakar Patel, 'Separating fact from fluff about Narendra Modi', *Live Mint & The Wall Street Journal*, 27 April 2013: 'Modi is a Ghanchi, from the trading caste of oil-pressers and grain sellers called Teli in north India. Ghanchis are categorized as Other Backward Class ... Ghanchis are "savarna" (upper caste) in Gujarat. If even this Manu Smriti category becomes low-caste, then 90 per cent of India is low-caste.'

(http://www.livemint.com/Leisure/PGoQ9lXh0 mliPwWrMXbVhI/Separating-fact-from-fluff-about-Narendra-Modi. html)

4. Sandhya Jain, 'The nationalists do not have to be defensive', *The Daily Pioneer*, 24 September 2013. Modi may modify this stance during the general election campaign: '... at the veterans rally at Rewari, Haryana, on September 15 ... Mr. Modi wisely used this platform to inform the nation about his background, unfulfilled dreams, and aspirations ... Describing with elan how poverty frustrated a desire to study at the Sainik school in Jamnagar district ... he skilfully nixed the demeaning factoids put out by some admirers about his caste and class origins.'

(http://www.dailypioneer.com/cloumnists/edit/the-nationalists-do-not-have-to-be-defensive.html for how he can use it to good effect)

5. Kamath and Randeri, op. cit., p. 16

6.   Kamath and Randeri, ibid., p. 15

7.   Kamath and Randeri, ibid., p. 13

8.   M.D. Nalapat, 'The prophet of enlightened liberalism', *Organiser*, 10 November 2013: 'Rather than spending time on the surface of faith, Vivekananda entered its core, and discovered that as he progressed deeper and deeper in his intellectual quest, the different faiths got subsumed into a common insight related to the universality and omniscience of the Divine.'

(http://organiser.org//Encyc/2013/1/19/The-prophet-of-enlightened-liberalism.aspx?NB=&lang=3&m1=&m2=&p1=&p2=&p3=&p4=)

9.   Pravin Sheth, *Images of Transformation: Gujarat and Narendra Modi*, Ahmedabad, Team Spirit (India) Pvt. Ltd, 2007, p. 27: 'Again, the internal relations and transactions among the cities and villages of Gujarat are comparatively stronger than other states. This is primarily due to interlinked economic activities and transportation.'

10.   The term 'Left' is used in its British sense of referring to a broad spectrum of political opinion from soft socialism to communism, whereas in India it appears to apply more strictly to parties at the communist and Naxalite end. In this book the Congress party is referred to as of the Left because of its socialistic policies and statist outlook.

11.   V.S. Naipaul, *An Area of Darkness*, London, André Deutsch, 1964, p. 258

2: On the Road

1.   Kamath and Randeri, op. cit., p. 17

2.   Nilanjan Mukhopadhyay, *Narendra Modi: The Man, The Times*, New Delhi, Tranquebar Press, 2013, p. 30

3.   Kamath and Randeri, op. cit., p. 21

4.   Narendra Modi, *Jyotipunj*, Ahmedabad, Pravin Prakashan, 2008

5.   27°47'27"N 91°42'40"E

6.   Naipaul, op. cit., p. 248

7.   See also Hiranmay Karlekar, 'Spare a thought for our brave jawans', *The Daily Pioneer*, 24 October 2013

(http://www.dailypioneer.com/columnists/oped/spare-a-thought-for-our-brave-jawans.html

8.   Tavleen Singh recalls that before the Chinese attack 'that scoundrel Menon' had given over munitions factories to producing coffee percolators (*Durbar*, Gurgaon, Hachette India, 2012, p. 10)

9.   See note 4, Chapter 1: In that speech Modi confirmed for the first time that it was lack of money which prevented him from attending the Sainak school.

10.   David Blair, 'Prisoners of their own ignorance', *The Daily Telegraph*, 6 October 2013

(http://www.telegraph.co.uk/news/worldnews/asia/pakistan/10359567/Prisoners-of-their-own-ignorance.html)

11.   Kingshuk Nag, *The NaMo Story: A Political Life*, Roli Books, 2013, p. 38

12.   Refer to Article 14 and Article 51 (A) of the Indian Constitution

13.   Kamath and Randeri, op. cit., p. 18

14.   Ibid., p. 19

15.   Ibid., p. 18

16.   Rupak Banerjee, 'Modi wanted to be Ramakrishna monk', *The Times of India*, 10 April 2013

(http://articles.timesofindia.indiatimes.com/2013-04-10/kolkata/38432940_1_belur-math-ramakrishna-mission-rkm)

17.   Kamath and Randeri, op. cit., p. 19

18.   Ibid., p. 19

19.   Banerjee, 'Modi wanted to be Ramakrishna monk', op. cit.

20.   Kamath and Randeri, op. cit., p. 20

21.   Syed Firdaus Ashraf, 'My son loves everyone: Modi's mother', *Rediff.com*, 7 December 2002

(http://www.rediff.com/election/2002/dec/07guj2.htm)

22.   Kamath and Randeri, op. cit., p. 21

3: Political Awakening

1. Kamath and Randeri, op. cit., p. 49

2. Achyut Yagnik and Suchitra Sheth, *Ahmedabad: From Royal city to Megacity*, New Delhi, Penguin Books India, 2011 (section: 'Riots and the Political Economy of Urban Land')

3. Kamath and Randeri, op. cit., p. 50

4. The best account of the plight of refugees in 1970s Calcutta remains Geoffrey Moorhouse, *Calcutta: The City Revealed*, New Delhi, Penguin, 1994 (4th Edition)

5. Kamath and Randeri, op. cit., p. 22

6. Mukhopadhyay, op. cit., p. 111

7. Ibid., p. 111

8. Kamath and Randeri, op. cit., p. 23

9. Ibid. Pravin Sheth also mentions Modi's political science studies (at MA level) at various points in his book because he was for a time his university tutor.

10. Mukhopadhyay, op. cit., p. 112

11. Shubham Ghosh, 'A cornered Mrs Gandhi roared back', *OneIndia News*, Thursday, 27 June 2013

(http://news.oneindia.in/feature/2013/1975-emergecncy-cornered-mrs-gandhi-roared-back-1245655.html)

12. Tavleen Singh, *Durbar*, Gurgaon, Hachette India, 2012, pp. 26–27

13. Ibid., p. 25

14. Patrick French, *India: a Portrait*, London, Penguin Books, 2012, p. 45

15. Kamath and Randeri, op. cit., p. 23

16. Kishore Trivedi, 'Navnirman Movement (1974): When student power rattled the unhealthy status quo!' www.narendramodi.in: *Citizen Journalism*, 15 June 2012

(http://www.narendramodi.in/navnirman-movement-1974-when-student-power-rattled-the-unhealthy-status-quo/)

17. Shubham Ghosh, 'What happened after Emergency was imposed', *OneIndia News*, 26 June 2013: 'Efforts were also made to defame the RSS by claiming weapons were found in its office while documentaries were used to demonise the Opposition parties, including Jayaprakash Narayan.'

(http://news.oneindia.in/feature/2013/what-happened-after-emergency-was-imposed-1245682.html)

18. Kamath and Randeri, op. cit., p. 31

19. Chhayank Mehta, 'Emergency, Gujarat and Narendra Modi', www.narendramodi.in: *Citizen Journalism*, 26 June 2012

(http://www.narendramodi.in/emergency-gujarat-and-narendra-modi/)

20. Kamath and Randeri, op. cit., p. 30

21. Ibid., p. 31

22. Mukhopadhyay, op. cit., p. 123

23. At the same time, Balasaheb Deoras, leader of the RSS, had gone so far as to write a letter to Indira Gandhi seeking rapprochement and implicitly accepting the state of Emergency. It may have been his attempt to get out of, or stay out of prison. See Tavleen Singh, op. cit., p. 57

24. 'The inexplicable torture that the police had conducted on one of the brothers of one of the Opposition leaders George Fernandes is still fresh in the memory of many who had followed those times closely.' Shubham Ghosh, op. cit., 26 June 2013

25. Mukhopadhyay, op. cit., p. 123

26. Singh, op. cit., p. 57

27. *The Economist* of 4 December 1976 hailed the RSS as 'the only non-left revolutionary force in the world', and said 'its platform at the moment has only one plank: to bring democracy back to India'.

28. Singh, op. cit., p. 58

4: Learning the Ropes

1. Kamath and Randeri, op. cit., p. 38

2. Mukhopadhyay, op. cit., p. 125

3. Ibid., p. 126

4. Ibid.

5. Barun S. Mitra, '"Our" socialist agenda: the time to oust it has come', *Live Mint & The Wall Street Journal*, 16 January 2008

(http://www.livemint.com/Opinion/85pBNYJBwJc3PTSkEU433L /8216Our8217-socialist-agenda-the-time-to-oust-it-has.html)

6. Mukhopadhyay, op. cit., pp. 132–33

7. M.J. Akbar, 'Why some political parties lost the plot', *The Times of India*, 15 November 2009

(http://blogs.timesofindia.indiatimes.com/TheSiegeWithin/entry/ why-some-political-parties-lost)

8. V.S. Naipaul, *A Wounded Civilisation*, London, Macmillan 2010, p. 160

9. Mukhopadhyay, op. cit., p. 135

10. Ibid.

11. See Japan K. Pathak, 'When do voters of Gujarat change the government they elected?', *DeshGujarat*, 10 December 2012, for an excellent discussion of the disaster that was the Anamat andolan (partial imposition of Rane Commission recommendations under Solanki).

(http://deshgujarat.com/2012/12/10/when-do-voters-of-gujarat- change-the-incumbent-government/)

12. Kamath and Randeri, op. cit., p. 41

13. Ornit Shani, *Communalism, Caste and Hindu Nationalism: The Violence in Gujarat*, Cambridge, CUP, 2007, pp. 57–58

14. Pathak, op. cit., 10 December 2012

15. For the sheer difficulty in accurately identifying minorities and underprivileged castes and classes, see A. Ramaiah, 'Identifying Other Backward Classes', *Economic and Political Weekly*, 6 June 1992, pp. 1203–07 (http://web.archive.org/web/20051230030051/http://www. tiss.edu/downloads/ppapers/pp1.pdf)

16. Gail Omvedt, *Reinventing Revolution: New Social Movements and the Socialist Tradition in India*, East Gate, New York, 1993, p. 69

(http://books.google.co.uk/books?id=Wlxb0uacnRcC&printsec=fr
ontcover&source=gbs_ge_summary_r&cad=0#v=onepage&q&f=false)

17. Mukhopadhyay, without evidence, implies Modi instigated the
riots: 'It cannot be construed that Modi was the puppeteer of the anti-
reservation stir of 1985, but given the penchant of the man to be in the
thick of things, it is difficult to envisage that he was disconnected with
such a major upheaval.' (ibid., p. 146).

18. Kamath and Randeri, op. cit., p. 41

19. Pathak, op. cit., 10 December 2012

20. Mukhopadhyay, op. cit., p. 146

21. Aseema Sinha, *The Regional Roots of Developmental Politics in
India: A Divided Leviathan*, Bloomington, Indiana University Press,
1995, p. 177

22. IN THE SUPREME COURT OF INDIA (Original Civil
Jurisdiction) WRIT PETITION (CIVIL) NO. 98 OF 2002 .pdf,
pp. 10, 18

23. S. Gurumurthy, 'Boss, read the true history before speaking', *The
New Indian Express*, 6 April 2013

(http://newindianexpress.com/opinion/article1532597.ece)

5: The Yatra to Power

1. Sheth, op. cit., p. 1

2. Kamath and Randeri, op. cit., p. 42

3. Ibid., p. 45

4. Yagnik and Sheth, op. cit., (section: 'Riots and the Political
Economy of Urban Land')

5. Mukhopadhyay, op. cit., p. 147

6. Prashant Dayal, 'Latif was state BJP's first whipping boy', *The
Times of India*, 12 June 2008

(http://articles.timesofindia.indiatimes.com/2008-06-12/
ahmedabad/27783531_1_bjp-ticket-bjp-leader-assembly-elections)

7. Nag, op. cit., p. 51

8. Mukhopadhyay, op. cit., pp. 138/148

9. Singh (op. cit., p. 249) uses the word 'fundamentalist' in relation to the Muslim clerics agitating over the Shah Bano case.

10. Singh, ibid., p. 250

11. 'The Shah Bano Legacy', *The Hindu*, 10 August 2003 (http://www.hindu.com/2003/08/10/stories/2003081000221500.htm)

12. Sarvepalli Gopal (ed.), *Anatomy of a Confrontation: Ayodhya and the Rise of Communal Politics in India*, New Delhi, Penguin Books (India), 1991, p. 15

(http://books.google.co.uk/books?id=47AARF595dUC&printsec=frontcover&source=gbs_ge_summary_r&cad=0#v=onepage&q&f=false)

13. From the second of four lectures delivered by Upadhyaya in Bombay during 22–25 April 1965 (See 'A Complete Deendayal Reader', http://deendayalupadhyaya.org/leacture2.html)

14. Spoken at the fourteen annual session of the BJP in Calicut, December 1967, when Deendayal was elected president

(http://en.wikipedia.org/wiki/Deendayal_Upadhyaya)

15. Mukhopadhyay, op. cit., p. 153

16. Nag, op. cit., p. 53

17. Naipaul, op. cit., 2010, p. 158

18. Modi has wisely begun to refer to his background in election rally speeches: high stakes demand big sacrifices, and he now appears willing to expose his past for the sake of leading the country.

19. See Priya Sahgal, '1990 – L.K. Advani's rath yatra: Chariot of fire', *India Today*, 24 December 2009

(http://indiatoday.intoday.in/story/1990-L.K.+Advani per cent27s+rath+yatra:+Chariot+of+fire/1/76389.html)

20. Rajesh Kumar Pandey, 'Advani remembers Massanjore', *The Times of India*, 18 January 2005

(http://articles.timesofindia.indiatimes.com/2005-01-18/patna/27833455_1_lal-krishna-advani-dumka-guest-house)

21. Neera Chandhoke, 'The tragedy of Ayodhya', *Frontline*, Volume 17, Issue 13, 24 June – 7 July 2000

(http://www.frontline.in/static/html/fl1713/17130170.htm)

22. Kamath and Randeri, op. cit., p. 55

23. Ibid., pp. 57–58

24. Ibid., p. 60

25. See for instance Mukhopadhyay, op. cit., p. 193

26. Ibid.

27. Shekhar Gupta, 'Tearing down Narasimha Rao', *The Indian Express*, 7 September 2011

(http://www.indianexpress.com/news/tearing-down-narasimha-rao/547260/0)

28. Christophe Jaffrelot, *The Hindu Nationalist Movement in India*, p. 314, quoted in Baldev Raj Nayar, 'The Limits Of Economic Nationalism: Economic Policy Reforms Under The BJP-Led Government', McGill University 2000, p. 5 [.pdf]

6: Rising to Responsibility

1. Kamath and Randeri, op. cit., p. 60

2. Mukhopadhyay, op. cit., p. 194

3. Ibid., p. 195

4. Nag, op. cit., p. 61

5. Kamath and Randeri, op. cit., p. 62

6. Nag, op. cit., p. 61

7. Ibid., p. 63

8. Ibid., p. 62

9. 'Shishya's coup: How Modi, Advani fell apart', *The Times of India*, 10 June 2013

(http://articles.timesofindia.indiatimes.com/2013-06-10/india/39872207_1_sitabdiara-l-k-advani-advani-and-modi)

10. Kamath and Randeri, op. cit., p. 216

11. Kamath and Randeri, ibid., p. 69

12. Ibid., p. 69; for Chandigarh Municipal Corporation victory see ibid., p. 71 and Mukhopadhyay, op. cit., p. 217; for Himachal victory see Nag, op. cit., p. 74; for Punjab assembly in 1997 – ninety-three out of 117 against fourteen for Congress, see Mukhopadhyay, op. cit., p. 218.

13. Baldev Raj Nayar, 'The Limits Of Economic Nationalism: Economic Policy Reforms Under The BJP-Led Government', McGill University, 2000, p. 3 [.pdf]

(http://kellogg.nd.edu/faculty/research/pdfs/Nayar.pdf)

14. Kamath and Randeri, op. cit., pp. 66-68

15. Nag, op. cit., p. 66

16. Ibid., p. 77

17. Mukhopadhyay, op. cit., p. 224

18. Kamath and Randeri, op. cit., p. 69

19. Swapan Dasgupta, 'Is Keshubhai up to it?', *India Today*, 12 February 2001

(http://indiatoday.intoday.in/story/gujarat-earthquake-gujarat-cm-keshubhai-patel-hardpressed-to-explain-sluggish-response/1/233050.html)

20. Kamath and Randeri, op. cit., p. 71

21. Mukhopadhyay, op. cit., p. 230

22. Dasgupta, op. cit., 12 February 2001

23. Nag, op. cit., p. 80

24. Kamath and Randeri, op. cit., p. 80

25. Dionne Bunsha, 'An ambitious pracharak', *Frontline*, Volume 19 – Issue 26, 21 December 2002 – 3 January 2003

(http://www.frontline.in/static/html/fl1926/stories/200 30103007400800.htm)

26. Sandhya Jain, 'The nationalists do not have to be defensive', *The Daily Pioneer*, 24 September 2013

(http://www.dailypioneer.com/columnists/edit/the-nationalists-do-not-have-to-be-defensive.html)

27. Nag, op. cit., p. 78

28. The best – most complete – version is in Kamath and Randeri, op. cit., pp. 81–82

29. Information for foreign readers: many Sikhs and Hindu Punjabis moved to Delhi after Partition when they were forced out of their homeland in what became Pakistan. They took over neighbourhoods vacated by migrating Muslims.

30. Obituary: 'The Last Assignment', *India Today*, 15 October 2001 (http://archives.digitaltoday.in/indiatoday/20011015/obituary.html)

31. Manas Dasgupta, 'Modi sworn in Gujarat CM amidst fanfare', *The Hindu*, 8 October 2001 (http://www.thehindujobs.com/thehindu/2001/10/08/stories/02080001.htm)

32. Kamath and Randeri, op. cit., p. 83

7: The Riots

1. Report by the Commission of Inquiry Consisting of Mr Justice G.T. Nanavati and Mr Justice Akshay H. Mehta [*The Nanavati Inquiry*], p. 95

2. Ibid., p. 87

3. Justice Tewatia Committee report [*The Tewatia Report*], p. 23: '7. Head of a passenger of S-6 coach was cut when he tried to get out of the window. The head was later thrown back into the coach to burn.'
(http://soc.culture.indian.marathi.narkive.com/JcK2YZNy/full-text-godhra-carnage-justice-tewatia-report)

4. *The Nanavati Inquiry*, op. cit., p. 88

5. *The Tewatia Report*, op. cit., p. 20

6. Ibid., p. 19: 'Crying and shouting Shakuntla took out her bangles and offered them to the two policemen with rifles. The policemen fired a few shots in the air. That did not deter the mob.'

7. V. Venkatesan, 'A victory and many pointers', *Frontline*, Volume 19, Issue 5, 2–15 March 2002
(http://www.frontline.in/static/html/fl1905/19050240.htm)

8.   Mukhopadhyay, op. cit., p. 259, confirms this; Modi also confirmed the approximate time to me.

9.   Chief minister's press release, Godhra, 27 February 2002 (quoted in Kishwar, *Modinama*, p. 33)

10.   Kamath and Randeri, op. cit., p. 101

11.   Kishwar, op. cit., p. 34: '62 Companies of State Reserve Police Force and Central Para Military Forces companies deployed on February 27; Out of 62, 58 were of SRPF and 4 were of CPMF.'

12.   Kishwar, ibid., p. 85

13.   *The Tewatia Report*, op. cit., p. 17; Kishwar, op. cit., p. 86

14.   Manas Gupta, 'No evidence of Modi promoting enmity: SIT', *The Hindu*, 9 May 2012: 'The SIT was also of the opinion that the bodies were brought to Ahmedabad in the dead of night and disposed of quietly the next day without being paraded before the riotous mob as was alleged by the Chief Minister's critics.'

(http://www.thehindu.com/news/national/no-evidence-of-modi-promoting-enmity-sit/article3398456.ece)

15.   Present were Ashok Narayan, additional chief secretary (Home); P. K. Mishra, principal secretary to the chief minister; K. Chakravarthi, director general of police; P. C. Pande, chief of police for Ahmedabad City; Anil Mukim, additional personal secretary to the chief minister; M. K. Nityanandam, secretary (Home) and Prakash S. Shah, additional secretary (Law and Order). (See Kishwar, op. cit., p. 78)

16.   Exhibit : 2671 before the special court, designated for conducting the speedy trial of riot cases, situated at old high court building, Navrangpura, Ahmedabad. [*Naroda Patiya Common Judgement*], p. 15

17.   'Report in Compliance to the Order DTD 12.09.2011 of the Hon'ble Supreme Court of India in the Complaint DTD 08.06.2006 of Smt. Jakia Nasim Ahesan Jafri [*SIT Final Closure Report*]: "On the day of bandh, i.e. 28.02.2002, a huge mob comprising about 20,000 Hindus gathered unlawfully, armed with deadly arm [sic] weapons, in furtherance of their common intention and indulged in attack on the properties, shops and houses of Muslims."'

18. *Naroda Patiya Common Judgement*, op. cit., p. 281 onwards

19. Ibid., p. 655

20. Kishwar, op. cit., p. 17, quotes the Special Investigation Team (SIT) report that 5,000 people were saved from Noorani mosque by Ahmedabad Police; 240 were saved at Sardarpura in Mehsana district; 450 were saved in Pore and Nardipur villages; 200 persons were saved in Sanjoli village; 1,500 were saved in Fatehpura village in Vadodra district; 3,000 people were saved in Kawant village.

21. Manmath Deshpande, 'A flawed judgement, bad in law', *The Organiser*, 16 September 2012: '*India Today* (April 22, 2002) reported that the police saved 2,500 Muslims in Sanjeli, 5000 in Bodeli and at least 10,000 in Viramgam areas of Gujarat. Hindus were also saved from violent Muslim mobs in areas like Bharuch, Jamalpur area of Ahmedabad, etc.'

(http://www.organiser.org/Encyc/2012/9/11/-b-A-flawed-judgement,-bad-in-law--b-.aspx?NB=&lang=4&m1=&m2=&p1=&p2=&p3=&p4=&PageType=N)

22. Dhananjay Mahapatra, 'NGOs, Teesta spiced up Gujarat riot incidents: SIT', *The Times of India*, 14 April 2009: 'The SIT said it had been alleged in the Gulbarg Society case that Pandey, instead of taking measures to protect people facing the wrath of rioters, was helping the mob. The truth was that he was helping with hospitalisation of riot victims and making arrangements for police bandobast, Gujarat counsel, senior advocate Mukul Rohtagi, said quoting from the SIT report.'

(http://timesofindia.indiatimes.com/india/NGOs-Teesta-spiced-up-Gujarat-riot-incidents-SIT/articleshow/4396986.cms?; also see http://ibnlive.in.com/news/guj-riots-exdgp-p-c-pandey-gets-clean-chit/90211-3.html)

23. At least, that much was claimed, although the post-mortem examination established that Jafri had been shot three times but neither hacked nor burned. See Chandan Mitra, 'A Sting Without Venom', *Outlook India*, 12 November 2007

(http://www.outlookindia.com/article.aspx?235985)

24. Kishwar, ibid., p. 26

25. Ibid., pp. 15, 26

26. For the list of convicted Congressmen see Manmath Deshpande, 'Congress leaders involved in terror', *The Organiser*, 13 March 2011; 'Four get life imprisonment', *The Times of India*, 16 October, 2003

(http://organiser.org/archives/historic/dynamic/modulesc39f.ht ml?name=Content&pa=showpage&pid=388&page=7; http://www. gujaratriots.com/index.php/2012/10/myth-21-no-one-was-brought-to-justice-for-the-riots/)

27. Nag, op. cit., p. 17

28. Kishwar, op. cit., p. 24

29. Ibid., p. 24

30. Patrick French, op. cit., p. 82

31. See Kamath and Randeri, op. cit., p. 44, for statistics in Gujarat

32. Tavleen Singh, op. cit., p. 291

33. Kamath and Randeri, op. cit., p. 104. See also Rajesh Ramachandran, 'Cong silent on cadres linked to Guj riots', *The Times of India*, 9 August 2003

34. The video is at http://www.youtube.com/watch?v= 4CiuBBKJ30Q

35. Kamath and Randeri, op. cit., p. 111

36. Documents quoted in Kishwar, ibid., pp. 95–96

37. The video is at https://www.youtube.com/watch?v= CSkEZ9hcIdM

38. *SIT Final Closure Report on Gulbarg*, op. cit., pp. 250–54: 'the so-called utterances by Chief Minister Narendra Modi are not sufficient to make out a case against him.' (p. 253)

39. Kamath and Randeri, op. cit., p. 111

40. *SIT Final Closure Report on Gulbarg*, p. 251

41. Kishwar, op. cit., p. 38

42. Uday Mahurkar, 'Modasa, a strong base of SIMI', *India Today*, 30 September 2008

[http://indiatoday.intoday.in/story/Modasa,+a+strong+base+of+ SIMI/1/16438.html)

43. See Kamath and Randeri, op. cit., p. 116

44. Gujarat High Court Order – Special CA No: 3773 of 2002, (3 May 2002), quoted in Kishwar, op. cit., p. 23

45. Kamath and Randeri, op. cit., pp. 107-8

46. Uday Mahurkar, 'The Modi effect: Gujarat', *India Today*, 29 April 2002

(http://indiatoday.intoday.in/story/despite-gujarat-riots-narendra-modi-rides-the-crest-of-enhanced-stature-and-popularity/1/220199.html)

47. *The Tewatia Report*, op. cit., pp. 14-15

48. For ISI involvement see Kamath and Randeri, op. cit., p. 143

49. *The Tewatia Report*, op. cit., p. 34

50. Rediff.com, 27 November 2002: 'The careful study of a bulky register of a guesthouse in Godhra has added an entirely new dimension to the investigation into the Godhra carnage. The new findings led to the arrest of Ali Mohammad and Ghulam Nabi Dingoo of Anantnag district in Jammu and Kashmir in the last week of October.' See also *The Economic Times*, 'Godhra killing was Pak sponsored: Probe panel', 27 April 2002

(http://www.rediff.com/news/2002/nov/27spec.htm; http://articles.economictimes.indiatimes.com/2002-04-27/news/27342369_1_godhra-haji-bilal-rioting-mobs)

51. Kamath and Randeri, op. cit., p. 143.

52. Sheth, op. cit., p. 32

53. Mukhopadhyay, op. cit., p. 244

54. Kamath and Randeri, op. cit., p. 99

55. *The Tewatia Report*, op. cit., pp. 36–37

56. *The Nanavati Inquiry*, op. cit., p. 50

57. See for example, Nag, op. cit., p. 90. He does not mention any of the other inquiries or reports.

58. *The Tewatia Report*, op. cit., pp. 31–32

59. Ibid., p. 33

60. Kishwar, op. cit., p. 13

61. Mukhopadhyay, op. cit., p. 256

62. Kamath and Randeri, op. cit., p. 138

63. Quoted in ibid., p. 138

64. That is Modi's version. An article in Rediff.com, 12 April 2002, stated it somewhat differently: 'The Bharatiya Janata Party on Friday night at its executive meeting in Goa asked Gujarat Chief Minister Narendra Modi to dissolve the state assembly and seek verdict of the people.' However, it is almost inconceivable that the BJP would voluntarily have contested Gujarat at that time. Most of the Rediff.com despatches from Goa were being sent by Sheela Bhatt, then a critic of Modi, who may have been expressing a wish not a fact.

(http://www.rediff.com/news/2002/apr/12train1.htm)

65. On 26 July 2008, within a span of 70 minutes, a series of 21 bombs set by SIMI and the Indian Mujahideen exploded in Ahmedabad. They resulted in 56 deaths and over 200 people injured. Again, there as no rioting or revenge-taking against Muslims even though the death toll was almost identical to Godhra in 2002. Something really had changed in Gujarat.

8: Fighting for Gujarat

1. 'The efforts put in by the State Government in this behalf, as indicated above, are required to be appreciated' (Gujarat High Court Order - Special CA No: 3773 of 2002, (3 May 2002), quoted in Kishwar, op. cit., p.26. See also p. 188, *SIT Final Closure Report on Gulbarg*, ibid., which states: '121 relief camps were organised by NGOs or various institutions which were closed by 30-06-2002 except 10 camps of Ahmedabad district.' Pages 182–197 contain much detail about the relief effort.

2. Mukhopadhyay, op. cit., p. 275

3. Sheila Bhatt, 'The Rediff Interview/KPS Gill', Rediff.com, 20 May 2002

(http://www.rediff.com/news/2002/may/20inter.htm)

4. Kamath and Randeri, op. cit., p. 144

5. Transcript of Modi speech, 'Some journalists asked me recently, "Has James Michael Lyngdoh come from Italy?"', *Outlook India*, 30 September 2002

(http://www.outlookindia.com/printarticle.aspx?217399)

6. Onkar Singh, 'Violence in Gujarat hits the hotel industry hard', Rediff.com, 6 March 2002

(http://www.rediff.com/news/2002/mar/06train2.htm)

7. Kamath and Randeri, op. cit., p. 112

8. Ibid., p. 113

9. Mukhopadhyay, op. cit., pp. 347–48

10. V.K. Chakravarti, 'Far from business as usual', *The Hindu*, Magazine, 5 May 2002

(http://www.hindu.com/thehindu/mag/2002/05/05/stories/2002050500020400.htm)

11. Kamath and Randeri, op. cit., p. 113

12. 'EC shapes Gujarat plea amid Lyngdoh-Modi duel', *The Times of India*, 24 August, 2002

(http://articles.timesofindia.indiatimes.com/2002-08-24/india/27326499_1_lyngdoh-modi-commissioner-j-m-lyngdoh-james-michael-lyngdoh)

13. Ashok Malik, 'Modi kept calling him James Michael, RSS sent Lyngdoh a letter: you have made us proud', *The Indian Express*, 4 July 2002

(http://archive.is/PMN3m)

14. 'Gujarat Assembly dissolved, early poll sought', *The Economic Times*, 19 July 2002

(http://articles.economictimes.indiatimes.com/2002-07-19/news/27337221_1_gujarat-cabinet-polls-gujarat-assembly)

15. Mukund Padmanabhan, 'Lyngdoh's truth', *The Hindu*, 21 September 2004

(http://www.hindu.com/br/2004/09/21/stories/2004092100221300.htm)

16. Mukhopadhyay, op. cit., p. 299

17. Kamath and Randeri, op. cit., p. 149

18. 'SC upholds EC order on Gujarat', *Times of India*, 28 October 2002; J. Venkatesan, 'Supreme Court upholds EC decision on Gujarat polls', *The Hindu*, 3 September 2002

(http://articles.timesofindia.indiatimes.com/2002-10-28/india/27317593_1_constitution-bench-gujarat-polls-assembly; http://hindu.com/2002/09/03/stories/2002090305670100.htm)

19. *The Hindu*, ibid., 21 September 2004

20. 'Modi Flags Off Rathyatra', *The Financial Express*, 12 July 2002

(http://www.financialexpress.com/news/modi-flags-off-rathyatra-/51933)

21. Dionne Bunsha, 'Narendra Modi's long haul', *Frontline*, Volume 19, Issue 19, 14–27 September 2002. Sheela Bhatt, 'VHP general secretary Dr Jaideep Patel shot at in Naroda', Rediff.com, 3 December 2002

(http://www.frontline.in/fl1919/19190300.htm; http://www.rediff.com/election/2002/dec/03guj2.htm)

22. 'Modi defers his "Gujarat Gaurav Yatra" again', Rediff.com, 2 September 2002

(http://www.rediff.com/news/2002/sep/01guj.htm)

23. 'Confidential no.j/2/BJP/Yatra/525/02 office of additional director general of police (INT)Gujarat State, Gandhinagar. Date : 12/9/2002', p. 3 [.pdf]

24. 'Dictator' because after his coup d'état of 13 October 1999 against Nawaz Sharif, Musharraf would not graduate to elected president until 10 October 2002 – still several days away.

25. 'Gujarat Chief Minister Narendra Modi hospitalised', Rediff.com, 22 November 2002

(http://www.rediff.com/election/2002/nov/22guj.htm)

26. 'Modi's Gaurav Yatra May Become Vaghela's Victory Parade', *The Financial Express*, 16 September 2002

(http://www.financialexpress.com/news/modi-s-gaurav-yatra-may-become-vaghela-s-victory-parade/57268/0)

27. 'Survey predicts close finish in Gujarat polls', Rediff.com, 6 December 2002

(http://www.rediff.com/election/2002/dec/06guj4.htm)

28. Kamath and Randeri, op. cit., p. 160

29. Mukhopadhyay, op. cit., pp. 292, 336

30. Debraj Mookerjee, 'Gujarat and the secular overkill', *The Daily Pioneer*, 28 December 2002

(http://www.hvk.org/2002/1202/292.html)

31. Sheela Bhatt, '"I see an emotional frenzy in the BJP's favour"', Rediff.com, 12 December 2002

(http://www.rediff.com/election/2002/dec/12guj.htm)

32. Swapan Dasgupta, 'Master of the National Game', *India Today*, 31 December 2012

(http://indiatoday.intoday.in/story/narendra-modi-is-a-player-of-national-politics-feels-swapan-dasgupta/1/238905.html)

33. 'BJP will get comfortable mandate: Advani', Rediff.com, 12 December 2002

(http://www.rediff.com/election/2002/dec/12guj4.htm)

34. Swapan Dasgupta, 'Modi Mania ... the Formula', *Digital India*, 30 December 2002

(http://archives.digitaltoday.in/indiatoday/20021230/cover.html)

35. Kamath and Randeri, op. cit., p. 171

36. Uday Mahurkar, 'Gujarat: Shankersinh Vaghela appointment as PCC chief forces BJP to change its poll tactics', *India Today*, 29 July 2002

(http://m.indiatoday.in/story/gujarat-shankersinh-vaghela-appointment-as-pcc-chief-forces-bjp-to-change-its-poll-tactics/1/219168.html)

37. Mukhopadhyay, op. cit., p. 304

38. Kishwar, op. cit., p. 26

39. Nag, op. cit., p. 13

40. Sheth, op. cit., p. 226; Ajay Umat, 'Once Hindutva twins, Narendra Modi and PravinTogadia no longer conjoined', *The Times of India*, 9 February 2013

(http://articles.timesofindia.indiatimes.com/2013-02-09/india/37007205_1_ashwin-patel-hedgewar-bhavan-maninagar). See also Sheth, ibid., pp. 158, 210–11

41. Kishwar, op. cit., p. 26

42. Sheth, op. cit., p. 211

43. Shekhar Gupta, 'National Interest: Modi versus his party', *The Indian Express*, 15 June 2013

(http://www.indianexpress.com/news/national-interest-modi-versus-his-party/1129321/0)

44. Gareth Price, 'How the 2004 Lok Sabha election was lost', *Chatham House Briefing Note*, July 2004, pp. 2–3 [.pdf]

(http://www.chathamhouse.org/sites/default/files/public/Research/Asia/bngp0704.pdf)

45. M.D. Nalapat, 'Like him or hate him, Modi is here to stay', *The Sunday Guardian*, 14 July 2013

(http://www.sunday-guardian.com/analysis/like-him-or-hate-him-modi-is-here-to-stay)

46. Mukhopadhyay, op. cit., p. 305

47. Pritish Nandy, 'Modi offers a new Camelot', *The Times of India*, 20 June 2013

(http://blogs.timesofindia.indiatimes.com/extraordinaryissue/entry/modi- offers-a-new-camelot)

48. Shekhar Gupta, 'Arvind Panagariya: I am a little worried. Now there is 10-20 per cent chance that we might see 1991 again', *The Indian Express*, 30 July 2013

(http://www.indianexpress.com/news/i-am-a-little-worried.-now-there-is-1020-per-cent-chance-that-we-might-see-1991-again/1148384/0)

49. Saba Naqvi, 'Manna for Modi', *Outlook India*, 4 September 2006
(http://www.outlookindia.com/article.aspx?232370)

50. Mukhopadhyay, op. cit., p. 246

51. 'The first requirement of any progressive country is internal and external security.' (Quoted in French, op. cit., p. 25)

52. Kamath and Randeri, op. cit., p. 211

53. Sheth, op. cit., p. 158

54. In Atul Kumar Thakur (ed.), *India Since 1947: Looking Back at a Modern Nation*, New Delhi, Niyogi Books, 2013

55. Nag, op. cit., p. 165

56. Exact figures for the number of MoUs signed at various Vibrant Gujarat events vary according to the source consulted, although they are roughly in alignment. I am mostly using the figures that Kingshuk Nag quotes because you can be sure they are conservative ones and that there will be absolutely no exaggeration of Modi's success.

57. According to Wikipedia the number of MoUs was 675.

58. Ashok Gulati, Tushaar Shah Ganga Shreedhar, 'Agriculture performance in Gujarat since 2000', International Water Management Institute, International Food Policy Research Institute, May 2009, p. 2 [.pdf]

(http://www.gujaratcmfellowship.org/document/Agriculture/ Agriculture per cent20Performance per cent20in per cent20Gujarat per cent20since per cent202000_IWMI per cent20& per cent20IFPRI per cent20Report-_May per cent202009.pdf)

59. Kamath and Randeri, op. cit., p. 233

60. For an amusing account of this see Kishwar, op. cit., p. 26

61. Vidya Subrahmaniam, 'Modi versus the rest in Gujarat', *The Hindu*, 15 December 2007

(http://www.hindu.com/2007/12/15/stories/2007121556241300. htm)

62. Yogendra Yadav, 'Modi's moment of truth', *The Indian Express*, 11 December 2007

(http://www.indianexpress.com/news/modi-s-moment-of-truth/248518/)

63. 'Gujarat Elections 2007, beyond Modi', IBNlive Chat

(http://ibnlive.in.com/news/ibnlive-chat-gujarat-elections-2007-beyond-modi/53948-3-2.html)

64. Swapan Dasgupta, 'The Modi phenomenon', Indian Seminar. com, 2008

(http://www.india-seminar.com/2008/581/581_swapan_dasgupta. htm)

65. 'Satta bazaar trashes Modi, swings in favour of Cong', IBNlive, 21 December 2007

(http://ibnlive.in.com/news/satta-bazaar-trashes-modi-swings-in-favour-of-cong/54737-3.html)

66. Kamath and Randeri, op. cit., p. 252

67. Kishwar, op. cit., pp. 63, 65

68. Kamath and Randeri, op. cit., p. 254

69. Ibid., p. 259

70. Sanjeev Nayyar, 'Why the BJP lost Elections-2009', Rediff.com, 9 June 2009

(http://election.rediff.com/slide-show/2009/jun/05/slide-show-1-why-the-bjp-lost-elections-2009.htm#8)

71. Ibid.

9: Development and Governance

1. 'Indian bureaucracy rated worst in Asia, says a Political & Economic Risk Consultancy report' *The Economic Times*, 11 January 2012

(http://articles.economictimes.indiatimes.com/2012-01-11/news/30616306_1_report-malaysia-indian-bureaucracy)

2. Hernando de Soto, *The Mystery Of Capital*, New York: Basic Books, 2000

3. See World Economic Forum, 'The Global Competitiveness Report 2010–2011', p. 182 pas [.pdf]

4. The World Bank, 'Doing Business: Measuring Business Regulations', available online at http://www.doingbusiness.org/reports/global-reports/doing-business-2012

5. Prem Shankar Jha, 'Use Argument, Not Stones: Why civil society must not let key democratic reforms drown in cynicism', *Outlook India*, 14 February 2011

(http://www.outlookindia.com/article.aspx?270317)

6. For good statistics and links on Gujrat development and budget, etc, see Prof. Mukul G. Asher, 'Gujarat's budget reflects sound development strategy', *East Asia Forum*, 3 April 2012

(http://www.eastasiaforum.org/2012/04/03/gujarat-s-budget-reflects-sound-development-strategy/)

7. For a discussion of dynasty v. development, see Minhaz Merchant, 'Left, right and centre: redrawing India's ideological map', *The Times of India*, 8 April 2013

(http://blogs.timesofindia.indiatimes.com/headon/entry/left-right-and-centre-redrawing-india-s-ideological-map)

8. 'Human Rights activist Shabnam Hashmi slams Narendra Modi's "Gujarat model" as myth', *The Indian Express*, 10 August 2013

(http://www.indianexpress.com/news/human-rights-activist-shabnam-hashmi-slams-narendra-modis-gujarat-model-as-myth/1153706/)

9. Sandeep Singh, *Third Curve: Sage of Women and Child Development – Gujarat*, forthcoming

10. Kamath and Randeri, op. cit., p. 205; Mukhopadhyay, op. cit., p. 358

11. Dionne Bunsha, 'Dissent in the Parivar', *Frontline*, Volume 21, Issue 04, 14–27 February 2004

(http://www.frontline.in/static/html/fl2104/stories/20040227002404200.htm)

12. Nag, op. cit., p. 12

13. 'Agriculture performance in Gujarat since 2000', op. cit., p. 10

14. Tushaar Shah and Shilp Verma, 'Real-time Co-management of Electricity and Groundwater: An Assessment of Gujarat's Pioneering "Jyotigram" Scheme', International Water Management Institute

(http://publications.iwmi.org/pdf/H041811.pdf)

15. Central Statistics Office, National Statistical Organization, Ministry of Statistics and Programme Implementation, Government Of India, 'Energy Statistics 2013, See esp. table on p.15

(http://mospi.nic.in/mospi_new/upload/Energy_Statistics_2013.pdf.)

16. 'Gujarat Congress, Narendra Modi government engage in "power" packed duel', *The Economic Times*, 3 September, 2013

(http://articles.economictimes.indiatimes.com/2013-09-03/news/41726944_1_power-generation-capacity-power-policy-gujarat-congress)

17. Central Electricity Authority, Ministry of Power, Government of India, January 2013: 'Installed Capacity (in MW) Of Power Utilities In The States/UTs Located In Northern Region Including Allocated Shares In Joint & Central Sector Utilities'

(http://www.cea.nic.in/reports/monthly/inst_capacity/jan13.pdf)

18. R.K. Gupta, 'The role of water technology in development: a case study of Gujarat State, India', paper delivered at UN Water International Conference (Zaragoza, Spain, 3–5 October 2011), Water in the Green Economy in Practice: Towards Rio +20

(http://www.un.org/waterforlifedecade/green_economy_2011/pdf/session_5_technology_cases_india.pdf)

19. 'Secret of Gujarat's Agrarian Miracle after 2000', Shah et al., *Economic and Political Weekly*, 26 December 2009, p. 48 pas

(http://www.gujaratcmfellowship.org/document/Agriculture/Secret per cent20of per cent20Gujarat per cent20Agrarian per cent20Miracle_EPW_26Dec09.pdf)

20. Sheth, op. cit., p. 183

21. Ibid., p. 71

22. Friends of River Narmada, 'The Greater Common Good', April 1999

(http://www.narmada.org/gcg/gcg.html)

23. News Bharati, 'Focus on Agriculture: Reason of Modi's success', 14 October 2012

(http://en.newsbharati.com/Encyc/2012/10/14/Focus-on-Agriculture-Reason-of-Modi-s-success.aspx)

24. Abhishek Kapoor, 'Krushi Mahotsav: a mix of fun and learning for Gujarat farmers', *The Indian Express*, 23 May 2008

(http://www.indianexpress.com/news/krushi-mahotsav-a-mix-of-fun-and-learning-for-gujarat-farmers/313402/)

25. Guillaume P. Gruere and Yan Sun, 'Measuring the Contribution of Bt Cotton Adoption to India's Cotton Yields Leap', IFPRI Discussion Paper 01170, April 2012

(http://www.ifpri.org/sites/default/files/publications/ifpridp01170. pdf; also see http://www.thehindubusinessline.com/features/a-decade-of-agricultural-revolution/article4365650.ece)

26. Virendra Pandit, 'A decade of agricultural revolution', *The Hindu Business Line*, 31 January 2013

(http://www.thehindubusinessline.com/features/a-decade-of-agricultural-revolution/article4365650.ece)

27. Swaminathan Anklesaria Aiyar, 'Agriculture: Secret of Modi's success', *The Economic Times*, 22 July 2009

(http://articles.economictimes.indiatimes.com/2009-07-22/news/27665876_1_check-dams-gujarat-india-chak)

28. News Bharati, 14 October 2012, op. cit

29. Kamath and Randeri, op. cit., p. 264; Sheth, op. cit., p. 205

30. Ibid., p. 213

31. Mukhopadhyay, ibid., p. 350

32. Kamath and Randeri, op. cit., p. 268

33. The texts of the letters can be found here: http://www.cricketvoice.com/cricketforum2/index.php?topic=17589.0

34. Amrendra Jha, 'From plague ugly to khub-Surat', *The Times of India*, 31 July 2005

(http://articles.timesofindia.indiatimes.com/2005-07-31/ahmedabad/27866029_1_city-light-area-ghod-dod-road-diamonds)

35. Surat Municipal Corporation, 'Project Overview Surat 2009'

(http://jnnurm.nic.in/wp-content/uploads/2011/01/Brochures_Published_surat.pdf)

36. Sandeep Singh, op. cit., p. 30

37. Narendra Modi, speech addressing the twenty-ninth Annual Session of the FICCI Ladies Organization (FLO) in New Delhi on Monday, 8 April 2013

(http://gujaratindia.com/media/news.htm? enc=KIN4q/jNm90+toii5qZl5EPC7kzGIsfoo/Golnrswj78NpfESrq E09hRQNO1zOWHO6+qGP23QYeg9ISv QHM1Jwg

TKh5mjWzFyUYcGIYJgcu Xj5kKoHarSdss7d6/Rs/
yV4LAgACYdAjfa3YCD/32nw==)

38. The United Nations uses slightly different criteria to India so sometimes there are variations for the same place and year; also, the measurements were changed in 2010. The figures here use the Indian version, which renders lower figures than the UN's.

39. Bibek Debroy, 'Gujarat's data on social indicators shows positive impact of policies', *The Economic Times*, 6 August 2013

(http://blogs.economictimes.indiatimes.com/policypuzzles/entry/gujarat-s-data-on-social-indicators-shows-positive-impact-of-policies)

40. Figures taken from Bibek Debroy, 'Gujarat's data on social indicators shows positive impact of policies', ibid. (See also http://en.wikipedia.org/wiki/List_of_Indian_states_and_territories_by_Human_Development_Index)

41. All available online at http://planningcommission.nic.in/data/datatable/index.php?data=datatab

42. Bibek Debroy, *Gujarat: Governance for Growth and Development*, New Delhi: Academic Foundation, 2012

43. Bibek Debroy, 'Gujarat's data on social indicators shows positive impact of policies', op. cit

44. Narendra Modi, speech, 8 April 2013, op. cit

45. Arvind Panagariya, 'The Gujarat miracle: No denying the economic advances the state has made under Narendra Modi', *The Economic Times*, 22 September 2012

(http://articles.economictimes.indiatimes.com/2012-09-22/news/34022206_1_poverty-ratio-narendra-modi-gujarat)

46. Minhaz Merchant, 'Gujarat *vs* Bihar: settling the development debate', *The Times of India*, 2 August 2013

47. R. Jagannathan, 'Is the Gujarat growth story for real? Apparently, yes', *FirstPost.Economy*, 8 October 2012

(http://www.firstpost.com/economy/is-the-gujarat-growth-story-for-real-apparently-yes-483390.html)

48. Sheth, op. cit., p. 221

49. Panagariya, 'The Gujarat miracle', op. cit

50. Sheth, op. cit., p. 191

51. 'Modi's wealth grew by almost Rs 90 lakh in the last 5 years', *India Today*, 12 November 2012

(http://indiatoday.intoday.in/story/modi-wealth-grew-by-almost-rs-90-lakh-in-last-5-years/1/235503.html; for Mayawati wealth see http://www.rediff.com/news/slide-show/slide-show-1-mayawati-s-wealth-jumps-to-rs-111-cr-in-2-years/20120314.htm)

52. Sheth, op. cit., pp. 166–67

53. Ibid.

54. Ibid.

55. Ibid.

56. 'Economic freedom in 20 Indian states, Gujarat is No.1', *Rediff. com*, (*Rediff Business*), 12 November 2012

(http://www.rediff.com/business/slide-show/slide-show-1-economic-freedom-in-20-indian-states/20121112.htm#1)

57. 'Economic Freedom Rankings for the States of India, 2012', Cato Institute, p. 30 [.pdf]

(http://www.cato.org/economic-freedom-india/Economic-Freedom-States-of-India-2012.pdf)

10: And Now, Prime Minister Modi

1. Saba Naqvi, 'Manna for Modi', op. cit

(http://www.outlookindia.com/article.aspx?232370)

2. Ram Jethmalani, 'India gets a leader, finally', *The Sunday Guardian*, 21 September 2013

(http://www.sunday-guardian.com/analysis/india-gets-a-leader-finally)

3. M.D. Nalapat, 'Why the BJP Lost a Sure Election', The Jewish Institute for National Security Affairs , 29 May 2009

(http://www.jinsa.org/publications/research-articles/central-south-asia/why-bjp-lost-sure-election#.Uf-64lMlPrM)

4.   Surjit S. Bhalla, 'Rotting food, rotten arguments, *The Indian Express*, 4 September 2013

(http://www.indianexpress.com/news/rotting-food-rotten-arguments/1164123/0)

5.   M.D. Nalapat, 'Modimatics: target 220, minimum 175', *The Sunday Guardian*, 20 July 2013

(http://www.sunday-guardian.com/investigation/modimatics-target-220-minimum-175)

6.   M.J. Akbar, 'Why is Syed Shahabuddin writing to Modi?' *The Times of India*, 2 December 2012

(http://blogs.timesofindia.indiatimes.com/TheSiegeWithin/entry/why-is-syed-shahabuddin-writing-to-modi)

7.   V.S. Naipaul, *Beyond Belief,* London, Little, Brown and Co., 2001, p. 380

8.   'Narendra Modi can't be blamed for post-Godhra riots: KPS Gill', *The Economic Times*, 31 October 2013

(http://articles.economictimes.indiatimes.com/2013-10-31/news/43561650_1_narendra-modi-security-advisor-post-godhra-riots)

9.   Vijaita Singh, 'KPS Gill, former security adviser to Modi, gives him clean chit on riots', *The Indian Express*, 1 November 2013

(http://www.indianexpress.com/news/kps-gill-former-security-adviser-to-modi-gives-him-clean-chit-on-riots/1189776/0)

10. M.J. Akbar, 'Dial "M" for trouble', *The Times of India*, 18 November 2012

(http://blogs.timesofindia.indiatimes.com/TheSiegeWithin/entry/dial-m-for-trouble)

11. Editorial, 'Cat is out of the bag', *The Daily Pioneer*, 30 October 2013

(http://www.dailypioneer.com/columnists/edit/cat-is-out-of-the-bag.html)

12. 'Muslims in Gujarat Poorer: NYT', *India Facts*, 28 October 2013: 'It is emphatically clear from the data that the poverty level of Gujarat's Muslims, which stood at 39.4 per cent in 1999-2000 and 37.6 per cent

in 2009-10 has declined to a mere 11.4 per cent in 2011-12. The poverty level of Muslims nationally stands at 25.5 per cent.'

(http://www.indiafacts.co.in/muslims-in-gujarat-poorer-nyt/#sthash. wiqEJ6rq.dpuf)

13. Sukhadeo Thorat and Amaresh Dube, 'Has Growth Been Socially Inclusive during 1993-94 – 2009-10?', *Economic and Political Weekly*, 10 March 2012, p. 45

(http://www.environmentportal.in/files/file/Socially per cent20Inclusive.pdf)

14. Professor Arvind Panagariya and Vishal More, 'Poverty by Social, Religious & Economic Groups in India and Its Largest States, 1993-94 to 2011-12', School of International and Public Affairs (SIPA) and the Institute for Social and Economic Research and Policy (ISERP), Working Paper No. 2013-02 (Program on Indian Economic Policies, Columbia University)

(http://indianeconomy.columbia.edu/sites/default/files/working_ papers/working_paper_2013-02-final.pdf)

15. Arvind Panagariya, 'Narendra Modi's real report card', *Business Standard*, 29 October 2013

(http://www.business-standard.com/article/opinion/arvind-panagariya-narendra-modi-s-real-report-card-113102801007_1.html)

16. Surjit S. Bhalla, 'The Modi Metric', *The Indian Express*, 13 December 2012

(http://www.indianexpress.com/news/the-modi-metric/1044536/0)

17. See Bhalchandra Mungekar, 'Gujarat: Myth and reality', *The Times of India*, 12 June 2012

(http://articles.timesofindia.indiatimes.com/2012-06-12/edit-page/32176123_1_gujarat-narendra-modi-industrial-growth)

18. Surjit S. Bhalla, 'Lessons from the Gujarat model', *The Financial Express*, 26 October 2013

(http://www.financialexpress.com/news/lessons-from-the-gujarat-model/1187332/0)

19. Kishwar, op. cit., p. 39

20. Ibid., p. 64

21. Mukhopadhyay, op. cit., p. 300

22. Ibid., p. 301

23. M.D. Nalapat, 'Political class should follow the Mahatma, not Nehru', *The Sunday Guardian*, 29 Dec 2012

(http://www.sunday-guardian.com/analysis/political-class-should-follow-the-mahatma-not-nehru)

24. 'Mahatma Gandhi and Sardar Patel are said to have held the view that the INC was formed only for achieving independence and should have been disbanded in 1947'. Jesudasan, Ignatius, *A Gandhian Theology of Liberation*, Gujarat Sahitya Prakash: Ananda India, 1987, p. 225

25. M.D. Nalapat, 'Why the BJP Lost a Sure Election', op. cit

26. Shekhar Iyer, 'Modi less the hawk, more the PM candidate at Rewari rally', *Hindustan Times*, 15 September 2013

(http://www.hindustantimes.com/India-news/NewDelhi/Modi-less-the-hawk-more-the-PM-candidate-at-Rewari-rally/Article1-1122520.aspx)

27. 'Terrorism-related Incidents in Gujarat since 2007', South Asian Terrorism Portal

(http://www.satp.org/satporgtp/countries/india/database/gujarat_Incidents.htm)

28. S. Gurumurthy, 'Sohrabuddin: Interrogating the media', *The New Indian Express*, 16 May 2012

(http://newindianexpress.com/opinion/article482874.ece)

29. Sandeep Joshi, '555 fake encounter cases registered across India in last four years', *The Hindu*, 15 July 2013

(http://www.thehindu.com/todays-paper/555-fake-encounter-cases-registered-across-india-in-last-four-years/article4916004.ece)

30. 'NHRC stats show there were more fake encounters in Congress-ruled states than in Narendra Modi's Gujarat', *India Today*, 4 July 2013

(http://indiatoday.intoday.in/story/fake-encounters-congress-ruled-states-narendra-modi-gujarat/1/286891.html)

31. 'Vibrant Gujarat MoUs under I-T scanner, Rediff.com, (*Rediff Business*), 16 March 2011; 'Narendra Modi: Infosys served I-T notice for praising Gujarat', *The Times of India*, 24 May 2013

(http://www.rediff.com/business/slide-show/slide-show-1-vibrant-gujarat-mous-under-i-t-scanner/20110316.htm http://articles.timesofindia.indiatimes.com/2013-05-24/software-services/39501043_1_policy-paralysis-social-media-kris-gopalakrishnan)

32. Aman Sharma, 'Our officer Rajendra Kumar had no play in fake encounter: IB chief Asif Ibrahim to MHA', *The Economic Times*, 15 June 2013

(http://articles.economictimes.indiatimes.com/2013-06-15/news/39993113_1_ib-chief-fake-encounter-ishrat-jahan)

33. Ashish Khetan and Harinder Baweja, 'Death By Firing Squad', *Tehelka*, 12 May 2007

(http://archive.tehelka.com/story_main30.asp?filename=Ne120507Death_by_CS.asp)

34. Madhav Nalapat, 'Defence Minister Antony & "Indian way"', *Pakistan Observer*, 9 August 2013. (http://pakobserver.net/201308/09/detailnews.asp?id=215108)

35. Tavleen Singh, 'Between Hindutva and modernity', *The Indian Express*, 20 December 2009

(http://www.indianexpress.com/news/between-hindutva-and-modernity/556702/)

36. V.S. Naipaul, *An Area of Darkness*, ibid., p. 33

11. A Historic Mandate

1. Nawaz Sharif's statement, 'India PM Narendra Modi Presses Pakistan's Sharif on Militants', BBC News, 27 May 2014

2. 'An Average 2,500 km of Travel, 14-15 Hours of Work', *Business Standard*, 12 May 2014

3. 'Satisfying: The Story of 2014 Campaign', Narendramodi.in, 10 May 2014

4. 'How London Techies Helped Modi Create Campaign Buzz', *Hindustan Times*, 25 May 2014

5. 'Modi Thanks Partymen for Pulling Off a Blair and Obama-like Campaign', *The Economic Times*, 2 June 2014

6. 'My Silence Has More Power Than My Speech, Says Modi in Varanasi', Indiatoday.in, 8 May 2014

7. 'Campaigning for Arvind Kejriwal in Varanasi', Ndtv.com, 8 May 2014

8. 'Election Results 2014: Historic Win for NDA with 336 seats, 282 for BJP', Firstpost.com, 17 May 2014

9. 'Thou Shalt Not: Modi Govt. Issues List of 19 Dos and Don'ts for Bureaucrats', *The Indian Express*, 8 August 2014

10. 'Going for Growth', *The Economist*, 25 July 2014

11. 'Arun Jaitley Has To Do Much Better Next Year', *India Today*, 21 July 2014

12. R. Jagannathan, 'The 99:1 Media Strategy: Modi is Speaking to the Right Audience', Firstpost.com, 31 July 2014

13. 'Prime Minister Shri Narendra Modi's Visit to Bhutan', Narendramodi.in, 16 July 2014

14. 'No Ordinary Zhou', *The Economist*, 2 August 2014

15. 'BRICS, Sport, Racism and the Shift in the Relevance of Global Power', *The Times of India*, 17 July 2014

16. 'The BRICS Bank is a Glimpse of the Future', *Financial Times*, 30 July 2014

17. 'When John Kerry Met PM Narendra Modi', *India Today*, 1 August 2014

18. 'Up and Rising: Meet the New Shah of the Saffron Party', *The Economic Times*, 17 May 2014

INDEX